In this timely book Jonathan Valdez explores the role of ideology in the maintenance and subsequent collapse of Soviet influence in Eastern Europe. He begins by examining how to define ideology, proposing that it should not be viewed as any specific body of thought but as the interpretation of a body of thought for a political purpose. Valdez then looks at how Marxism-Leninism was used to legitimize Soviet influence. He shows how it was interpreted to rationalize policy actions, to communicate Soviet intent and policy desires to East European elites, and to explain change in socialist systems.

Valdez argues that the use of the fundamental principles of Marxism-Leninism to perform various functions ultimately brought about a change in the basic assumptions of the theory itself. This resulted in the abandonment of the previous insistence on a universal model of socialism and of the idea that the international interests of the socialist bloc must take precedence over individual national interest. Soviet influence in Eastern Europe rested on little else than these ideological principles and consequently stood little chance of surviving their re-interpretation. Finally Valdez assesses the re-interpretation of the fundamental principles of the Soviet–East European relations by reformist scholars in the Soviet Union, and the response by conservative members of the party apparatus.

By focusing upon both the political debates between the Soviet Union and Eastern Europe and the political uses of ideology within that relationship, Jonathan Valdez makes an important and innovative contribution to the study of Soviet external relations. *Internationalism and the ideology of Soviet influence* will be widely read by students and specialists of Soviet and East European studies, international relations and political science.

T0370788

INTERNATIONALISM AND THE IDEOLOGY OF SOVIET INFLUENCE IN EASTERN EUROPE

Soviet and East European Studies

INTERNATIONALISM AND THE IDEOLOGY OF SOVIET INFLUENCE IN EASTERN EUROPE

JONATHAN C. VALDEZ

University of California, Los Angeles

CAMBRIDGE
UNIVERSITY PRESS

CAMBRIDGE UNIVERSITY PRESS
Cambridge, New York, Melbourne, Madrid, Cape Town, Singapore,
São Paulo, Delhi, Dubai, Tokyo

Cambridge University Press
The Edinburgh Building, Cambridge CB2 8RU, UK

Published in the United States of America by Cambridge University Press, New York

www.cambridge.org
Information on this title: www.cambridge.org/9780521121323

First published 1993
This digitally printed version 2009

A catalogue record for this publication is available from the British Library

Library of Congress Cataloguing in Publication data
Valdez, Jonathan C.
A euphemistic reality: the ideology of Soviet influence in
Eastern Europe / Jonathan C. Valdez.
        p.   cm. – (Soviet and East European studies: 89)
Includes bibliographical references and index.
ISBN 0–521–41438–5
1. Europe, Eastern – Politics and government – 1945–1989.
2. Soviet Union – Foreign relations – Europe, Eastern.
3. Europe, Eastern – Foreign relations – Soviet Union.
4. Ideology.   5. Communism – Europe, Eastern.
I. Title. II. Series.
DJK50.V35   1993
327.47–dc20   92–11480 CIP

ISBN 978-0-521-41438-8 Hardback
ISBN 978-0-521-12132-3 Paperback

To my mother, for the greatest gift of all.

Contents

Acknowledgments

Thanks are due to many: to Patty for inspiration, to Mary Jo, Ray, Angela, Janel, and the staff of the Library of Congress, where much of the research was done. I am grateful to Linda Racioppi of Michigan State University for reading and commenting on parts of the manuscript, and many thanks go to Karen Dawisha of the University of Maryland for going above and beyond the call of duty to read some chapters twice – once as advisor and again as friend. Finally, field research and interviews with many of the participants in these debates were carried out during six months of research at the Moscow Higher Party School between January and July of 1991, under the auspices of the American Council of Teachers of Russian. All interpretations, ideological or otherwise, are of course the responsibility of the author.

The US Board of Geographic names transliteration system is used for all but those names and terms which have commonly accepted spellings in the West. *Gorbachev* and *perestroika*, for example, should literally be *Gorbachëv* and *perestroyka*, but will be rendered in their more familiar form except where transliterated from the original Russian.

Introduction

Analysis of the collapse of Soviet-style socialism in Eastern Europe in 1989 will continue for years. Superficial explanations are easy to come by – the simple yearning of the East Europeans for political and economic freedom, the moral bankruptcy of "communism." But it would seem that such explanations beg a deeper understanding of the reasons behind the events of the fall of 1989. This book is an examination of one aspect of the collapse of socialism – Soviet political and ideological debates which prepared the groundwork for promoting and accepting change in Eastern Europe and in Soviet policy toward the region, rather than frustrating it.

The advent to power of Mikhail Gorbachev in 1985 accentuated trends in Soviet policy which had already begun to develop earlier in the decade, such as a reluctance to use military force in the resolution of crises and a disinclination to continue subsidizing Eastern Europe, for instance with cheap energy. His advocacy of market-oriented reforms and proposals for troop withdrawals from Eastern Europe suggested that the Soviet Union no longer looked upon either itself or Eastern Europe in the same fashion as before.

Changes in the ideological sphere more often than not preceded these developments. Albeit subtle, there were definite indications that among Soviet elites there was sentiment for rethinking the prevailing patterns and norms of the Soviet–East European relationship. By the late 1980s, attempts to explain recurring crises in Eastern Europe developed into a questioning of the nature of socialism as an international system and within the Soviet Union. The collapse of Soviet-style socialism in Eastern Europe in the fall of 1989 may be seen as the culmination of these trends.

In this book I investigate the role of ideology in the maintenance and collapse of Soviet influence in Eastern Europe. I focus on two aspects of ideology: (1) The definition of Soviet objectives through domestic

1

ideological debate; and (2) the political uses of ideological concepts in the attainment of those objectives.

In the 1980s, through ideological debate over the concepts of "socialist internationalism" and "antagonistic contradictions" in socialist societies Soviet interests in Eastern Europe were redefined and scaled down in ways that made it less likely that the Soviets would feel compelled to intervene militarily to guarantee them. By the end of 1989, "socialism" had been redefined so broadly that it was possible to see social-democracy as an acceptable and legitimate variant, at least in Eastern Europe. Not only were models of socialism other than the Soviet deemed acceptable, but the non-universality of previously binding "general laws of socialist development" was also asserted. Finally and most importantly, the Soviet Union officially rejected the class-based "internationalism" which for over seventy years had formed the basis of its foreign policy, and which had become an especially contentious issue in relations with Eastern Europe. These were basic changes in the fundamental tenets of Marxism-Leninism and facilitated the collapse of pro-Soviet regimes in the fall of 1989 by fundamentally refuting much of its legitimacy.

Ideological debates in the two decades following the invasion of Czechoslovakia can be seen broadly as a continuous debate over how to respond to crises in socialist states. I argue that ideological debates in the early 1980s can be seen as attempts on the part of reform-minded elites to change the fundamental principles of Marxist-Leninist theory in such a way as to accommodate the possibility of change at home and abroad. Reality, and the responses to a changing international environment, can drive change as well as theory itself, and I do not mean to imply that ideological debates provide the sole explanation for the collapse of Soviet-style governments in Eastern Europe in the fall of 1989. They are simply one element of that change. Through such debates the ideological basis of the East European regimes was called into question, facilitating open challenges for power from indigenous social groups.

In examining the role of ideology in maintaining Soviet influence in the region between 1968 and 1989, I focus on how Soviet views of their relationship with Eastern Europe developed in ideological discourse both within the Soviet Union and between it and its allies. Focusing on this period gives us the opportunity to determine how crises in Czechoslovakia and Poland affected Soviet perceptions of their objectives in Eastern Europe, and to see what adjustments were made in the ideology on which political mechanisms were based.

Economic developments during this period include the oil shock of the mid-1970s, when the price of Soviet oil deliveries to Eastern Europe lagged far behind the world price, in effect constituting a subsidy of these regimes (see Bunce, 1985; Marer, in Terry, 1984a). It was also during the latter part of this period that the Soviet economy began to stagnate and decline, thus making economic attempts at influencing East Europe behavior less attractive. The international response to the Soviet invasion of Afghanistan, meanwhile, demonstrated to many Soviets that the usefulness of military force as an instrument of policy had declined.[1] Finally, the Soviet disinclination to intervene directly in Poland most likely decreased the value of the threat of intervention in the eyes of many East Europeans. It is irrelevant whether it was a disinclination to intervene or a determination that to do so was unnecessary. With the example of three previous interventions and many more threats, the expectation among East Europeans was that the Soviets were more than willing to intervene directly, and the fact that they did not could only be interpreted as an unwillingness to do so.

The problem of ideology

As with the relationship between ideology and policy, the importance of Soviet theoretical debates has often been questioned. More often than not, debate was seen as a cover for power struggles within the elite (See Ra'anan, 1983). Alternately, it has been suggested (Dzirkals, 1982) that such debates were strictly controlled and monitored during the Brezhnev era, and thus less accurately reflected policy differences, or were even purposely orchestrated in order to allow the leadership to evaluate the merits of different policy options. The same study, however, also pointed out that "in times of relaxation or leadership turmoil, the media reveal more about the Soviet system" (Dzirkals, 1982: xii). Such was certainly the case in the early to mid-1980s, when leadership turnover and the approaching succession to Brezhnev loosened the restrictions on what could and could not be said.

At the same time, personal conversations with many of these scholars and the fact of the debates themselves suggest that even in the 1970s the press was not as tightly controlled as is commonly assumed. A book which criticized the orthodox understanding of many basic ideological principles, for example, was published by Butenko and company in 1975, a year many would see as the nadir of ideological openness. We should also not forget that Aleksandr Yakovlev, the "architect" of *perestroika* in the 1980s, was ousted from his position as first deputy head of the Central Committee Propaganda Department (responsible for control over the media) and in effect exiled as Ambassador to Canada in 1973 for his outspoken criticism of conservative "Slavophiles" in the Soviet establishment. This indicates that even in the 1970s fundamental differences of opinion could find expression in ideological debate in what was assumed to be a tightly controlled press. In any case, it is certainly true that ideological debate became more open with the death in January 1982 of Mikhail Suslov, the long-serving party secretary for ideology and propaganda.

I examine the roles of ideology in promoting and defining Soviet objectives *vis-à-vis* Eastern Europe through an exhaustive and thorough analysis of primary Soviet sources. Such sources include official and competing viewpoints as expressed in periodicals and newspapers, official accounts of multilateral meetings between communist party representatives, and other statements by the leadership. The documents and articles to which I refer directly are not, of course, the only ones which were examined. An approach such as that utilized in this study entails sifting through literally hundreds of articles in order to determine which are most notable, and in Chapter 1 I present some guidelines on how to read ideological texts.

One helpful way to view ideology is to see it as either a negative or positive phenomenon.[2] The original Marxian conception of ideology was negative in that it saw ideology as a false consciousness arising from material conditions. It was involuntarily so; because of their relationship to the means of production, ideologists did not know they were concealing the contradictions of a society by their actions (Larrain, 1979: 13). Later, more modern interpretations of the negative concept of ideology focused on voluntarist aspects; that is, ideology as a conscious manipulation or deception (for example, see Stojanovic, 1988: 82). Vladimir Lenin gave the Marxian negative concept of ideology as "false consciousness" a positive meaning, in which ideology serves to explain the world and to express the worldview of a certain class (Schapiro, in Cranston and Mair, 1980).

In addition to viewing ideological debates as the use of fundamental principles to perform different functions, they may therefore also be viewed *prima facie* as struggles to assert the primacy of a positive or negative concept of ideology. In other words, those who asserted that antagonistic contradictions were possible in Soviet-style socialism were implicitly promoting a positive concept of ideology in which

Marxism-Leninism could be used to explain and understand social phenomena. Their opponents were adherents of a negative conception of ideology in that they attempted to conceal society's contradictions in the interests of promoting and defending an existing social system.

In this book I utilize a concept of ideology which identifies it within the context of the political theory on which it is based and how it is used. It takes into account the fact that the fundamental principles of a political theory may be used to perform several different ideological functions simultaneously. I argue that theoretical change can be explained in part by inconsistencies between the fundamental principles of a political theory and the functions they perform as ideology in a political system.

In one sense, this approach to ideology is implicitly deconstructivist. A full explication of deconstructivism is beyond the scope of this study, but certain features may be utilized in order to better illustrate how fundamental theoretical principles change. As one Western analyst has pointed out:

> The most compelling way ... in which political language undermines itself is through its inversions of the value hierarchies implicit in the actions and in other language with which it is associated: To wage war is to foster peace. Capital punishment is a means to curb violence. (Edelman, 1988: 115)

After 1968, the invasion of Czechoslovakia was paradoxically described as a means of guaranteeing its sovereignty.

It is not only inversions of "value hierarchies" which erode the meaning of political language, but also the very language itself. Deconstruction of political language also takes place "through the use of adverbial or adjectival qualifiers that purport at one level of meaning to intensify an affirmation while they negate it at another level" (Edelman, 1988: 116). This author's concern was political language in the United States, but he could just as well have been describing, for example, "People's Democracy," the ideological construct developed to describe the socialist states of Eastern Europe after the Second World War (see Chapter 2).

I do not mean to imply here that every use of fundamental theoretical principles to perform a political function necessarily contradicts those principles and works to undermine them. By definition, fundamental principles are contradicted when they are used to rationalize or justify actions taken for other than ideological reasons. This is not necessarily the case, however, when ideology is used for elite communication.

1   Ideology and the ideologists

The vexing question of the relationship between ideology and policy faced specialists on the Soviet Union throughout its history, and simply how to define ideology has long been a fundamental problem for scholars of any political system. Those who studied the Soviet Union were confronted by a state which claimed to be based on and guided by a "scientific" ideology, but which displayed many aspects of typical great-power behavior and often acted in a manner which seemed to bear little relation to its oficially proclaimed ideology. Yet, the amount of energy which the Soviets themselves devoted to ideological discourse and the fact that Soviet leaders seemed to view the world through a specific prism suggested that an important link existed at some level.

Before embarking on a study of ideology and its role in promoting and defining Soviet interests in Eastern Europe, we must come to some understanding of what is meant by the term "ideology." Whether due to the pejorative connotations the term has taken on[1] or simply to its slipperiness, it is a concept which does not lend itself to simple definition. European political scientists have been more willing to study ideology than their counterparts in the United States, due perhaps to the latter's traditionally dim view of what were seen as ideological political systems. Notable exceptions to this were studies done in the field of Sovietology but, even here, treatments of ideology were more often marked by their disagreement over how to understand it than by anything else.

Ideologies, fundamental and operative

One helpful approach is to break ideology down into component parts. The notion of fundamental and operative ideologies has been utilized by many who study communist political systems (Moore,

1950; Brzezinski and Huntington, 1965; Schurmann, 1968; Taras, 1984) and informs this study as well. Other terms for fundamental ideology include the "ideology of ends" (Moore); "pure" ideology (Schurmann); or the "doctrinal" component (Brzezinski and Huntington). It represents the goals of a movement or political party, the *raison d'être*. Operative ideology may also be thought of as the "ideology of means" or "practical" ideology, or the methods political actors utilize to achieve the goals embodied in the fundamental ideology (again, Moore, 1950, and Schurmann, 1968). Brzezinski and Huntington labelled this the "action program," noting its dynamism (Brzezinski and Huntington, 1965: 21). Another scholar has pointed out that "the Chinese themselves overtly recognize these two forms, calling the former 'theory' and the latter 'thought'" (Holmes, 1986: 98). In his seminal work, *Ideology and Politics*, Martin Seliger argued that every ideology contains both a fundamental and operative dimension (Seliger, 1976: Part III). The first is where "traditional principles are upheld," while in the latter, "the actual policy decisions of a political party are defended" (Seliger, 1976: 16). Ideological change, in this view, is produced by tensions between what is *desirable* and what is *possible*; in other words, between the fundamental and operative ideologies.

Some approaches to ideology suggest that an ideology may serve a number of functions at once, but few examine how the fulfillment of functions (or failure to fulfill them) may influence the development of the fundamental principles. I utilize the notion of fundamental and operative dimensions of an ideology in a slightly different fashion to illustrate more clearly how contradictions between them may drive changes in the former. In this view, functions are fulfilled through interpretations of the fundamental principles of a political theory. A fundamental principle of Leninism such as the "vanguard party," for instance, could be interpreted in a number of ways; either to legitimate single-party rule, or to call for the creation of such parties as a generally applicable revolutionary tactic, for example. Another use of the term could be to designate another party as a "vanguard" as a way to bestow ideological approval.

Theoretical change takes place within the realm of fundamental principles; such change is produced by tensions between the fundamental principles and the functions the ideology is called upon to perform in its operative dimensions.

At the same time, it is important to recognize that not only may fundamental principles be used in ways which contradict them, but also political functions themselves may interact or conflict. For example, use of a concept to justify a policy action may make its use to perform other functions problematic.

Finally, we should remember that the fundamental principles themselves may contradict one another as well. Political philosophies are not necessarily coherent systems of thought, and they tend to contain contradictory elements. It is only when the demands of environment necessitate application of one or another fundamental principle that these contradictions are exposed and may facilitate change. The ultimate usefulness of studying change in fundamental principles lies in the fact that the political philosophy from which they derive is a guide to action. Changes in the basic philosophy on which an ideology is based will dictate changes in political objectives.

"Fundamental principles" can be thought of as those basic suppositions on which an ideology is based. As Seliger has written, "in most cases [ideology] depends for its principles on the specific content of political philosophies" (Seliger, 1976: 120). In other words, a political philosophy or theory forms the basis of an ideology and provides the terms in which ideological argumentation proceeds. In this respect, Marxism-Leninism is more properly thought of as a political theory than as an ideology. Similarly, the notion of the "party line" is often thought of as dogmatic ideology in the West, but should more properly be seen as operative ideology.

Fundamental principles also are often labelled as "dogma" or are said to be "axiomatic," and hence unchangeable. In the short-term such principles could be perceived as dogmatic, but the history of Marxism–Leninism is more accurately seen as a continual process of adjustment. The hallmark of the Gorbachev era was the reversal of more previously sacrosanct dogmas than had been the case under earlier leaders.

Prior to the Gorbachev era, the fundamental principles on which Soviet ideology was based including the following:

dialectical and historical materialism: the view that all reality is determined and can be explained by material processes; also, that contradictions are a source of societal change;

a class-based approach to domestic and international affairs: from this stemmed the concept of "internationalism";

ideological concepts endorsed in the past: peaceful paths to socialism, separate paths of socialist development, peaceful coexistence, developed socialism, among others; and

international norms, such as elements of international law and commonly accepted standards of behavior such as non-intervention in internal affairs, state sovereignty.

It should be kept in mind that the third category is rather broad and flexible. The exigencies of political succession in the Soviet Union invariably entail rejection of many of the previous leadership's ideological concepts, while others are retained. These concepts are necessarily more prone to change than the fundamental tenets of Marxism–Leninism. While in practice the Brezhnev leadership may have ignored or downplayed many of Khrushchev's revisions, the fact that they were announced from the highest rostrum of the Soviet Communist Party meant they were enshrined as fundamental principles and available for use by other political actors.

At the same time, the continued existence of the state, both domestically and in terms of the international system, meant that the Soviets were forced to acknowledge certain international norms such as state sovereignty, independence and the inviolability of borders as fundamental principles of conduct, despite attempts to develop the theoretical concept of "international relations of a new type." This concept was often used to suggest that relations between socialist countries were somehow qualitatively different from those between capitalists and socialists, or between capitalist states.

Fundamental principles can be interpreted so as to fulfill any number of roles; the use of fundamental principles to perform funcions constitutes an ideology. The fundamental principles themselves (the political philosophy or theory) do not constitute an ideology; rather, only when they are put to use do they become an ideology. One author implicitly shared this view when making a distinction between political theory and ideology: "Only if a theory is *used* by a group to guide it and defend its actions does it become an ideology" (Holmes, 1988: 97, original emphasis). In the next section, I investigate how political actors may use fundamental principles.

The functions of ideology

A series of articles published in *Soviet Studies* in the mid-1960s represented one of the most thorough (if unsystematic) attempts to come to grips with the relationship between Soviet ideology and Soviet behavior.[2] The debate was unsystematic in that it did not seek to apply any one framework to the concept of ideology; rather, contributors to the debate engaged in a constructive and lively polemic with each other. The main articles still deserve attention as some of the most insightful treatments of the role of ideology in the Soviet system.

The almost simultaneous publication of articles by Alfred G. Meyer in *Soviet Studies* and Daniel Bell in *Slavic Review* extended the debate begun in the late 1950s over the "end of ideology" to the field of Soviet studies. Neither suggested that studying ideology would no longer be valid in Sovietology, but each argued in his own way that ideology had lost much of its value.

Meyer saw ideology as a "body of doctrine which the Communist Party teaches all Soviet citizens"; in other words, a major vehicle of socialization (although he does not use the term). He noted two functions of ideology, beginning with "the exceedingly trite observation that ideology is the language of politics in the USSR." Within this, ideology was seen as a "frame of reference ... [or] set of concepts for perceiving the world and its problems" (Meyer, 1966: 276). In this respect, it served a positive function.

Also within the broad rubric of ideology as political language, Meyer stated "even more tritely" (!) that ideology was the code of elite communication (Meyer, 1966: 278). Here, he noted especially its importance in "downward communication." This, however, should not blind us to the importance of ideology as a means of horizontal communication between elites in different political systems, or even within systems.

A further function Meyer saw was that of ideology as a "legitimizing device" (Meyer, 1966: 279). This role of ideology as a means of legitimizing the system was also stressed by Bell; indeed, in the view of some Sovietologists, it was *the* most important role played by ideology. Bell pointed out that this took on added importance when a group claims "justification by some transcendent morality (for instance, history)" (Bell, 1965: *fn.*, 595). More importantly, he noted the use of ideologies as "justifications which represent some specific set of interests" (Bell, 1965: 593).

The debate which followed these two articles was in fact rather inconclusive. That a definitive explanation could be decided upon in a field as politically and emotionally charged as Sovietology was perhaps too much to ask. The best contribution was a thought-provoking article by David Joravsky, in which he stated his view of ideology as "unacknowledged dogma that serves social functions. The main purpose of scholarly analysis is to discover the functions" (Joravsky, 1966: 4). Joravsky's own analysis led him to conclude that an ideology's main purpose "is to rationalize a group's readiness to act, or to refuse to act" (Joravsky, 1966: 15). This implied a conception of ideology as false consciousness, in that the act of rationalization is one which hides other motives.

The notion that ideology can serve the interests of a ruling elite, within which various groups co-exist and struggle for power, has dominated the literature for some time. In many cases, however, this was seen against the backdrop of a concept of ideology as false consciousness; ideas are used not because of any inherent belief in them but as mere instruments in political struggle. In the present study the emphasis is on what Stephen White calls "the politics of ideology-making," or the process by which interests are articulated and defined within the context of ideological discourse (White, in White and Pravda, 1988: 16). It is appropriate to see ideology as the language and medium in which Soviet bureaucracies defined their interests and those of the state.

In his oft-quoted work on the ideology of the Brezhnev period, Donald Kelley's term for this was "theory as political weapon" (Kelley, 1986: 9). Discussing the Soviet concept of developed socialism, Kelley stated that it "may in part be regarded as a sophisticated theory of conflict management, articulating the institutional and behavioral mechanisms through which [political] conflict is to be channeled" and setting "the parameters of political conflict that will keep the level of competition within acceptable boundaries." (Kelley, 1986: 10). His most important contribution, however, was his conception of theory as "political formula." As Kelley used the term, theory as political formula reflected "not only the specification of the nature of the present society and the tasks confronting Soviet leaders but also the embodiment of a particular style of leadership" (p. 13). The development of such a political formula, in Kelley's view, was an important component of a Soviet leader's attempt to build his authority.

I see the importance of unofficial ideologists in the Soviet Union in the creation and elaboration of *many* such formulas from which political leaders could choose in the attempt to characterize their political program. Ideological discourse at the unofficial level can be seen as the creation of a "menu" of political formulas, from which aspiring and accomplished party leaders could choose in order to encapsulate their political programs.

One example of how a Soviet leader could choose from the ideological menu to promote his political program was Gorbachev's 1987 declaration that capitalism and militarism were not deterministically linked. This view had been developed in the pages of the party theoretical journal *Kommunist* before Gorbachev's speech by Yevgeniy Primakov, then director of the Institute of the World Economy and International Relations and later an advisor to the Soviet President. In almost the same language that Gorbachev was to use in his speech marking the seventieth anniversary of the October Revolution, Primakov, too, claimed that the experiences of some capitalist countries had shown that militarism was not essential for the growth and survival of capitalism (compare Gorbachev, 1987c, and Primakov, 1987).

Another example testifies to the idea that even Stalin, the "great genius" of the revolution, chose from the menu of ideological interpretations created by his ideologists. Burlatskiy (1990: 127) relates how A. M. Rumyantsev attended a meeting of economists called by Stalin in the late 1940s to discuss the economic problems of socialism. The topic of the meeting was whether or not the law of value was still valid under socialism. Rumyantsev offered a compromise, saying that the law remained in effect but that it operated "in a transformed form;" economic laws still had to be taken into account, but politics remained dominant. This compromise appealed to Stalin, who appropriated it for his 1952 work, "The Economic Problems of Socialism in the USSR". Rumyantsev, meanwhile, was made head of the Central Committee Science Department, and began a career in the upper reaches of the Soviet ideological establishment.

Another Western author's view was that despite the fact that "the historical record indicates that changes in official ideology most often follow rather than precede policy changes," the theoretical basis for policy remained "an important part of an authority-building strategy" (Thompson, 1989: 2). It may be appropriate to suggest that while *official* ideology changed rather slowly and often only after noticeable changes in policy, shifts in ideology at the *unofficial* level were commonly evident to the discriminating observer.

A recent well-researched work on the Soviet theory of international relations also proposed that Soviet ideology performs various functions (Light, 1988: 327–30). In her treatment of the functions of ideology, Light focused on the functions of legitimation, justification and worldview. Another function to which she referred was that of ideology as a cohesive device. Finally, she pointed out that ideology may function to elaborate and debate party policy: "In relation to politics . . . its purpose is to identify issues, resolve differences and raise support, particularly from Party members, but arguably in a one-party state, also from the populace as a whole" (Light, 1988: 330).

Finally, in addition to his excellent work (Lynch, 1989) on the development of Soviet international relations theory, Allen Lynch has done a penetrating analysis of the roles of ideology in Soviet foreign policy (Lynch, 1990). He defined ideology as "both a set of conscious assumptions and purposes, derived from a given philosophical tradition, with corresponding authoritative 'texts' (formal and informal), as well as part of the set of the total historical, social, and personal background of the given political leaders and citizens" (p. 2). He listed several functions that such an ideology could perform in the political system, including the provision of categories in which to perceive the world; the legitimation of the one-party system; the "disciplinary" purpose of defining "the acceptable language of political discourse;" and lastly, the justification of policies "which may have been taken for reasons independent of ideological considerations and to affect foreign perceptions of Soviet policies" (pp. 2–3). Lynch makes an excellent case for the point of view that whatever successor states emerge will continue to be influenced in important ways by the inherited legacy of thinking in ideological categories.

What is ideology?

Thus, Sovietologists readily acknowledge that an ideology may perform a number of functions. The most common conceptions of ideology are as (1) a means of communication; (2) a device to legitimate party rule; (3) the expression of the worldview of Soviet elites; or (4) the rationalization of policy.

A worldview is also a guide to action, although nothing so all-encompassing as a "blueprint." As a rationalization, ideology may be characterized as a false consciousness which serves to conceal either the true motives of the Soviet leadership, or, more simply, struggles for power within the system. Few, however, have explored how the fulfillment of functions may change the fundamental assumptions of the theory on which ideology is based.

The notion that a political philosophy can in general be seen as the "social reality" of a group (Mills, 1962: 12) is attractive; I build on this by suggesting that ideology is the *assertion* of a reality by which an individual or social group lives and acts. One way in which individuals or groups assert "their" reality is by interpreting the fundamental principles of a political theory. In other political systems, it may take the form of the interpretation of facts in order to promote a political agenda. The body of thought itself from which the fundamental principles are drawn is not ideology; it only becomes ideology when interpreted and put to political use.

In the Soviet case the task of definition was made more simple by the existence of an almost canonical body of thought in Marxism-Leninism, and by the fact that "every public official in the USSR is *ex officio* an ideologist" (Meyer, 1966: 278). Thus, public statements by the leadership and even by lesser officials should be seen as ideology, inasmuch as they contributed to the process of ideological interpretation and served a political purpose. I include as well contributions by unofficial theorists in scholarly journals, newspapers, and party publications as elements of ideological argumentation.

Thus, ideology may be defined in the Soviet context as the interpretations given by political actors to the canons of Marxism-Leninism, which served the political purposes of explanation, rationalization, communication, and legitimation. These are the functions which remained most germane to the exercise of political power in the Soviet Union over the past seventy years.

Changes in the fundamental principles on which an ideology is based can be explained in part by contradictions or tensions between those principles and the functions they are called upon to perform, and by the ways in which the functions themselves work at cross-purposes. In addition, the theory itself may contain fundamental principles which contradict one another.

For example, rationalizing an action which is inconsistent with the fundamental principles of the ideology may eventually cause them to change. The rationalization comes to be ritualistically repeated in an act of symbolic communication, which changes the meaning of these concepts in the minds of listeners and speakers. For example, when the Warsaw Pact invasion of Czechoslovakia was characterized as a manifestation of socialist internationalism, this was an example of the use of fundamental ideological principles to rationalize an act inconsistent with certain principles. Socialist internationalism, as we shall see in the next chapters, included not only the defense of socialism and the applicability of general laws of socialist development, but also non-interference in internal affairs and the validity of different forms of socialist development. The interpretation of socialist internationalism which made the collective defense of socialism a duty, in fact, was stressed mainly after 1968.

Similarly, an inability to successfully explain the world and account for change can be an impetus for adjustment in fundamental principles. In other words, failure to successfully fulfill the roles required of fundamental principles may be a source of change. Most Soviet theorists were singularly unable to utilize the prevailing interpretations of dialectical materialism to explain periodic crises in Eastern Europe satisfactorily. Those who could had great difficulty persuading their colleagues to accept their arguments.

There is an important distinction to be made between the functions of rationalization and legitimation. Legitimation is a broader notion than rationalization, and is systemic in that it refers to the social and political system as a whole. In other words, I use the term "legitimation" to describe attempts on the part of a regime to establish its authority among the populace. Rationalization is a narrower concept in that it refers to specific policy actions, and may also be referred to as justification.

By legitimation I mean not only legitimating the political system, but also the process of defining the ways in which legitimacy is to be measured. This will become crucial when we turn our attention to the debate which took place in the early 1980s over the possibility of antagonistic contradictions in socialism. Here we shall see that legitimation concerned not so much an attempt to convince people that the system was in fact legitimate, but attempts to broaden or narrow the range of acceptable political phenomena within socialism.

I should also stress that when looking at the function of ideology as communication, I focus primarily on *inter-elite* communication. Downward communication, from political leaders to subordinates or non-elites, is undoubtedly important, but more within a system (*intra-elite*) than between systems. East European leaders may once have justifiably been considered the subordinates of Soviet leaders, but the Soviet–East European relationship developed in such a way after 1968 as to make it more appropriate to consider this horizontal communication. Like-minded elites may communicate by professing adherence to the same interpretations of fundamental principles or utilizing the same concepts, which is one element in building informal political alliances. The communicative function of ideology is also often an attempt to control the political agenda by monopolizing the language in which political argumentation proceeds.

The function of communication appears to be a form of political communication peculiar to Soviet-style systems, although it has elements of what is commonly thought of as "diplomatic language." Those who use ideology and those who use diplomatic language both speak in code; each is a language, in which certain words and phrases have accepted meanings. Ideology differs from diplomatic language, however, in that the elements of ideological language are much more fluid and subject to interpretation. It is that process, of course, which is under examination in this study: the redefinition of certain elements of the ideological language on which the rationale of Soviet power at home and abroad was based.

When ideology is used as a communicative device, we should recognize that in many cases it is a simplification of more complex ideas. Something similar was proposed by the anthropologist Clifford Geertz (1973), who saw ideology largely as "figurative language" or metaphor. In Geertz' view, an ideological symbol "may in fact draw its power from its capacity to grasp, formulate, and communicate social realities that elude the tempered language of science." (Geertz, 1973: 210). What he meant is that an ideological concept, for instance socialist internationalism, is a metaphor which may convey many meanings at once.

It seems appropriate to see the function of rationalization as the embodiment of the negative concept of ideology, as mentioned in the Introduction. That is, by rationalizing policy actions inconsistent with the fundamental principles of the basic theory, the contradictions of that political system are concealed. Similarly, ideology as explanation or worldview is the embodiment of the positive conception.

It is worth pointing out the subjective nature of judging the positions of participants in these debates, however. Conservative Soviet ideologues did not see themselves primarily as defenders of the privileges and interests of the ruling elite. From their point of view, they were promoting proper (positive) interpretations of Marxism-Leninism, opposing those who promoted what they saw as a false consciousness. But, after all, that is exactly the point of the negative conception of ideology; when ideologists conceal the contradictions of the social system, they are unaware of their role.

As mentioned earlier, I see ideology as a necessary component of any political system. The proper methodological question is not whether ideology matters, but rather under what conditions, in what roles, and for which social groups it becomes important. Ideological debate in the Soviet Union gained the importance it did because of the lack of a civil society. In other words, there was no other realm in which to pursue change, political or otherwise. All non-dissident political activity took place within the confines of the CPSU, and in such an atmosphere ideology took an added importance. Ideology is unlikely to regain its former importance in the Soviet Union's successor states if only because in a more market-oriented society, there will be other spheres in which people may direct their energy. In the old Soviet Union, the importance of ideology waxed and waned; it became more important in the early 1980s because of a perceived need to search for new policies in the face of economic decline.

Reading ideology

It is useful to devise a series of questions to ask about a text, in order to determine its significance, which ideological functions it performs, and how. What follows is a series of questions which can provide a useful starting point when evaluating ideology.

First, what kind of text is being considered? A speech given at a party gathering carried more weight than an article in a scientific journal, for example. A roundtable article, on the other hand, could provide a useful encapsulation of the existing points of view on a topic, but remained unofficial.

Second, where did it appear? A speech at a Party Central Committee plenum, conference, or congress would normally carry progressively more weight. The mass media were an important channel of communication, and we may distinguish certain levels of importance here as well. *Pravda*, as the organ of the Central Committee, was certainly the flagship Soviet newspaper, followed by the Government newspaper *Izvestiya*. The newspapers of various ministries – Defense and Culture, for example – occupied a second tier of importance, depending on the issue. Similarly, as far as journals were concerned, a similar division held, with the party theoretical organ *Kommunist* being the most definitive, followed by the journals of the scientific institutes of the Academy of Science.

Third, we should note the timing of the article or speech. Articles or speeches appearing in the run-up to a party meeting such as a congress or plenum could be important opportunities to promote one or another point of view. Similarly, articles on the "meaning" of such a party meeting could be a means of disseminating decisions to lower echelons. Holidays or anniversaries were usually important opportunities for members of the leadership to state their views; we should also keep in mind "hidden" anniversaries, such as the birthday of a discredited leader (Stalin being a prime example) or the date of an odious event (for instance the invasion of Czechoslovakia or Hungary), which could be used to pursue a political agenda.

The fourth aspect to consider is the political significance of the author of the text. Did he or she hold an official position? That is, were they a full-time party or government official, such as a member of the Politburo, the Secretariat, the Central Committee apparatus, or the Foreign Ministry? Or did he or she hold an unofficial position? In other words, were they a person of known stature who is a full-time worker in a subsidiary field such as academia or journalism? Was the article written under a well-known pseudonym? The pseudonyms of some Central Committee officials were common knowledge at home and abroad, affording both a measure of anonymity and authority to the author. Lastly, was it an unsigned editorial in one of the more authoritative party organs such as *Kommunist* or *Pravda*? These were usually harbingers of a collective opinion of the leadership on a divisive issue.

With these initial assessments in mind, we can then proceed to analyze the substance of the message.

Was the article critical of an individual or institution by name? Or, in the time-honored fashion of coded language, did the author only name "certain comrades" or condemn certain schools of thought? Was the article or author itself later subjected to criticism?

Next, the theoretical basis of the article is also critical. Which of the canons of Marxist-Leninist thought did the author interpret? If the author made use of abundant quotations from Lenin, for example, from which period were they taken? The Lenin of War Communism (1918–20), or the Lenin of the New Economic Policy (1921–4)? Was the proffered interpretation novel or dogmatic?

Finally, how can we tell what functions the text serves? Was it specifically aimed at a foreign audience, either by place of publication or explicitly? For example, did the article appear only in foreign-language, Soviet-controlled publications? What solutions did the author propose? To which problems?

Such questions certainly can facilitate the task of sifting through scores of articles in order to find those which offer a fresh perspective. Even the most reform-minded authors had to bow to the demands of their institute's scientific plan, and often published unexceptional articles merely to "meet the plan."

Ideological debates

The issues

With the approach to ideology in place, let us now turn to the structure and content of this study. Chapter 2 lays out the ideological basis of the Soviet–East European relationship as it developed between the end of the Second World War and the invasion of Czechoslovakia, focusing on the response of Soviet theorists to the establishment of the "People's Democracies" in Eastern Europe. I also examine other aspects of the ideological basis of Soviet foreign policy, notably the rise of socialist internationalism to describe Soviet–East European relations, and early views on the possibility of contradictions in socialism.

In Chapters 3, 4, and 5, I examine two ideological debates and their significance for the development of Soviet policy toward Eastern Europe between 1969 and 1989: The first debate concerned the proper interpretation of "socialist internationalism," while the second dealt with the nature of contradictions in socialist societies.

The debate over the concept of socialist internationalism was in many ways an extension of the debate sparked by the Prague Spring and subsequent Warsaw Pact invasion of Czechoslovakia. Two chapters are devoted to this topic.

In Chapter 3, I examine how the Soviet interpretation of socialist internationalism was challenged from without by the West European communist parties, and from within by reform-minded Soviets who remained active despite the "stagnation" of the Brezhnev era. I examine how the concept was defined in the multilateral forums of international communist party conferences and in Warsaw Pact meetings from 1969 to 1980. Specifically, I analyze the communiqués and political declarations of Warsaw Pact Political Consultative Committee (PCC) meetings, in order to determine the extent to which the Soviets were successful in gaining East European acceptance of their interpretation of the meaning of socialist internationalism. More often than not, they failed.[3] I also examine attempts during the 1970s by reform-minded Soviets to support a greater role for what they called "common democratic" principles in the application of socialist internationalism.

In Chapter 4, I investigate attempts to re-interpret socialist internationalism in the Soviet Union before the election of Gorbachev to the post of general secretary, and its subsequent demise during his tenure. An essential aspect of this debate was the question of whether or not a single (Soviet) model of socialism or set of "objective laws" or regularities (zakonomernosti), ought to be applied to Eastern Europe. Soviets and East Europeans alike, since the time of Stalin, have insisted that "specific national conditions" must be taken into account in the construction of socialism; at the same time, the Soviets similarly insisted on the applicability of their experience for other socialist states and for the East European regimes in particular. This is related to the question of legitimacy, since universal applicability of the Soviet experience was used in attempts to validate the Soviet system.

More broadly, the question of socialist internationalism is also one of how the Soviets viewed their role and interests in Eastern Europe. For example, when the Soviets ceased insisting on the applicability of the Soviet model, this implied that they no longer needed to maintain control to the extent they once did. In addition, debates over internationalism often focused on the correlation of national and international interests in the socialist community. How were the differing interests of socialist states to be reconciled?

I also examine the debate carried out in the mid-1980s as to the role of small states in international affairs. This debate, while at first seemingly unconnected to the question of political influence, in fact was directly relevant both in terms of defining Soviet objectives and of East European adherence to a Soviet-defined political line. Since this debate was of a more limited nature than those mentioned previously, it is included in the debate over socialist internationalism.

The Hungarians and East Germans were strong proponents of the idea that small states in the center of Europe had an obligation and a right to maintain the process of détente despite downturns in the superpower relationship, something the Soviets strenuously denied. The emphatic insistence on this point of two East European states and a similarly vehement Soviet rejection of it brought up the question of adherence to a Soviet-defined political line: would the East European regimes be allowed to carve out their own niche in international life independent of Soviet objectives, interests and policy?

In Chapter 5, I examine a second important debate, on the nature of contradictions in Soviet-style socialism, and its growth into an effort to define a new concept of socialism. "Contradiction" is the Marxist term for the non-coincidence of interests of different groups within a single social entity. In capitalist societies the basic contradiction is said to be between the proletariat and the bourgeoisie, whose interests are irreconcilable because of their different positions in relation to the means of production. This is an "antagonistic" contradiction, and as such had been held to be typical only of capitalist systems. Such contradictions as did exist in socialism were traditionally characterized – again, under Stalin – as "non-antagonistic," and hence not capable of driving change in the system. The pre-Gorbachev Soviet view of the non-antagonistic nature of socialist contradictions was based on a dogmatic interpretation of Lenin's dictum that "antagonism and contradiction are not one and the same. The first disappears, the second remains under socialism" (Lenin, 1931: 357). The standard Soviet explanation was that the Communist Party of the Soviet Union (CPSU) or other "vanguard" parties reliably united and expressed the interests of all social groups.

When some Soviet scholars began in the early 1980s to re-interpret this basic element of Marxism-Leninism, they were vehemently attacked. Officially accepting the possibility of such contradictions would legitimize the representation of different social interests by groups not sanctioned by the state. In other words, the claims of independent organizations such as Solidarity in Poland to represent working-class interests against those of other classes could in principle be true. At the very least, this debate had serious implications for how the Soviets defined socialism and, therefore, their interests in Eastern Europe. The implication for Soviet objectives in Eastern Europe is that a broader definition of socialism reduced the need to maintain control, and hence the possibility that military force would be used to that end.

As with the principle of internationalism, this too was intimately related to the legitimating function of ideology. If the Soviets insisted on a strict definition of socialism, legitimacy as a function of the successful construction of socialism in Eastern Europe became that much harder to attain. Defining socialism more broadly, for example by relaxing insistence on a single "model" or set of "objective laws" which should apply in its building, would make it easier to view a variety of social systems as legitimate. This was one way in which these two debates were connected, and it illustrates as well the influence of domestic debates on the conduct of Soviet policy toward Eastern Europe.

In addition, the debate over contradictions was part of a broader concern in Soviet theoretical circles with the notion of "interests" (see Hill, 1980). Another way in which these two debates were related, then, was the question as to whether contradictions could arise not only *within* socialist states, but *between* them. As in the debate over internationalism, the question of the proper relationship between national and international interests within the socialist community was raised here as well.

In the final chapter, in addition to a general summing up, I investigate how the debates over socialist internationalism and contradictions influenced the theoretical exercise within the Soviet Union in 1988–9 aimed at defining a new "concept of socialism." This was not so much a debate as a broad search among Soviet theoreticians for what exactly was implied in the notion of socialism, and as such it had important implications for how the Soviets defined socialism both at home and abroad.

The participants[4]

Many of those who challenged the orthodox positions in these ideological debates came from the institutes of the USSR Academy of Sciences. Although not a formal "alliance," there was a definite congruence of views between scholars from the Institute of the Economics of the World Socialist System and the Institute of Philosophy, for example. What is more, these views were in many ways the intellectual precursors of Gorbachev, which lends credence to the view of some Western scholars that Gorbachev was originally a creature of the *intelligentsia*. It also suggested that the revision of ideological tenets more often than not took place within the intellectual community and percolated up to, as well as down from, the leadership.

These debates on internationalism and contradictions took place in the 1970s to mid-1980s largely between a group of scholars from the Institute of the Economics of the World Socialist System (IEWSS),[5] on the one hand, and members of the conservative party *apparat* on the other. The IEWSS was the major Soviet institute dedicated to the study of world socialism, and as such was a critical source of ideas about policy toward the region.[6]

This made the participation and leading role of IEWSS scholars in these debates all the more significant. Anatoliy Butenko wrote most forcefully in favor of the view that socialist "non-antagonistic" contradictions could become antagonistic; Yevgeniy Ambartsumov also took this view in the journal *Voprosy Istorii* (Questions of History) in 1984. Yuriy Novopashin, meanwhile, by 1985 had become one of the most vociferous critics of the concept of socialist internationalism as the basis of bloc relations. Ambartsumov and Novopashin were both heads of sections at the IEWSS in Butenko's Department of Political and Ideological Problems. The long-time director of the IEWSS (since 1969) was another outspoken reformer, Oleg Bogomolov, who later would become an advisor to Russian President Boris Yel'tsin. (Ambartsumov also became active in the Democratic Russia movement and was elected a People's Deputy to the Russian Congress of People's Deputies.)

Butenko and Novopashin both published in the journal of the Institute of Philosophy, *Voprosy Filosofii*, whose chief editor was Vadim Semënov. He took positions similar to those of Butenko in his own articles in the journal and in a book on dialectics published in 1987.

Significantly, Butenko was one of two readers for Semënov's book, representing another connection of those involved in these debates.

On the other side of the debate were those who defended what had for years been the official position. Notable participants of this persuasion included Richard Kosolapov, editor-in-chief of the CPSU theoretical journal *Kommunist*, whose views we examine in detail when analyzing the debate over contradictions in socialism. A direct participant in the debate over socialist internationalism was Oleg Borisovich Rakhmanin, first deputy chief of the CPSU Central Committee (CC) department responsible for relations with socialist countries (the Liaison Department).[7] Rakhmanin wrote pseudonymously in at least two publications: under the name "O. Vladimirov" in *Pravda* (June 1985), and as "O. B. Borisov" (or, in one case, "O. V. Borisov") in the journal *Voprosy Istorii KPSS* (*Questions of History of the CPSU*).[8]

Links between those on the conservative side of the debate were indicated by the fact that the harshest criticism of Ambartsumov's position was written by a member of the *Kommunist* editorial board, and published in this journal – of which Kosolapov was the editor. *Kommunist* also published an article by a member of Rakhmanin's Central Committee Liaison Department which strongly supported the East German reform experience (thereby tacitly endorsing the East German rejection of Gorbachev's reforms) (Martynov, 1986). Finally, both Kosolapov and Rakhmanin published important articles in the party newspaper *Pravda*, suggesting that their positions had strong backing within the Central Committee apparatus.

All of this is important by way of background information for the debates which were a more or less permanent feature of Soviet political life, but which intensified especially in the early 1980s. It is difficult to point precisely to a clear beginning of the debate over socialist internationalism; it is perhaps more accurate to note simply that views which challenged the orthodox position have been in circulation essentially since 1917 (if not since the split between the Bolsheviks and Mensheviks in 1902). The history of Marxism-Leninism is one of continual polemics between the defenders and challengers of orthodoxy. It was only in response to certain conditions, however, that the adherents of orthodox views felt it necessary to answer such challenges.

The coalescence of informal alliances around the re-interpretation of theoretical concepts was an important feature of Soviet political life, and study of them is one of the main features of this work. In the following chapters we shall examine these theoretical debates and their influence on the conduct of Soviet policy toward Eastern Europe.

2 The ideological basis

This chapter examines the major Soviet statements in which the ideological basis of the Soviet relationship with Eastern Europe was developed prior to 1968. It is important to lay out this basis for a number of reasons. First, in order to examine later ideological change, we need to know the starting point. It was during this period that concepts such as socialist internationalism and the non-antagonistic nature of socialist contradictions were confirmed as fundamental principles. In addition, an examination of the process of ideology-making in the post-war period will provide important insights into both the nature of the Soviet–East European relationship and the process by which the boundaries of ideological debate were defined.

Finally, this period is crucial because, in many ways, the continuing process of change in the former Soviet Union even today is an attempt to grapple with the legacy of Stalinism. Soviet hegemony in Eastern Europe was but one element of that legacy; another, more subtle, was the continued dominance of Stalinist ideological tenets within the Soviet Union.

Broadly, I see the "ideological basis" of a relationship as the principles which govern it, defined within the framework of a specific set of ideas having its own referents and rules of discourse. In the case of Soviet–East European relations, this developed on a number of different levels. There were what appear to have been genuine attempts to use Marxist categories to explain the nature of the People's Democracies. At the same time, the development of Soviet theoretical concepts describing Eastern Europe was also driven by domestic political factors and should be seen in important respects as a product of these. Finally, there were clear attempts to assert Soviet leadership of the bloc by relegating the People's Democracies to a lower level in terms of the historical process.

As to the ideological tenets which were developed to explain the character of the Soviet–East European relationship in this period, two crucial concepts emerged and were accompanied by changing descriptions of the bloc itself. First was the theory of *People's Democracy*, which was developed between 1947 to 1951 to explain the nature of the East European regimes. During this time, the Soviet Union, China and Eastern Europe were described as the socialist "camp," with the attendant imagery of a militant and vigilant bloc.

During the Khrushchev period the rules of conduct in the Soviet Union's relations with the East European countries began to change, although the assessment and description of them as People's Democracies remained the same. With the death of Stalin and Khrushchev's initial attempts at détente, the "camp" became the "world socialist system," suggesting a less militant line. With China's defection from this system, however, another term was needed to distinguish and legitimate the new order. In addition, despite the invasion of Hungary (or perhaps because of it), the Soviets seemed to recognize that coercion alone would not guarantee fealty in Eastern Europe. The notion of the "socialist commonwealth" served as the new ideological construct in the activation of the Warsaw Treaty Organization (WTO) and Council for Mutual Economic Assistance (CMEA) as instruments of bloc management in the early 1960s.

By this time, the East European countries could no longer be described as "People's Democracies;" this was said to be a transitional stage between capitalism and socialism, yet, by the early to mid-1960s, most of the East European countries had declared themselves "socialist" in new constitutions. Similarly, relations traditionally were said to have been based on proletarian internationalism, but now a new term came to be used for inter-state relations: *socialist* internationalism. An in-depth examination of this concept as it developed in the 1970s and early 1980s forms the basis of Chapters 3 and 4. In the present chapter I examine Soviet views on internationalism prior to the invasion of Czechoslovakia, and offer a brief treatment of the development of the concept of contradictions during the same period.

Contradictions and Soviet society

The victory of the Bolshevik revolution and the establishment of the Soviet state led to the question of its future development and the transition to communism. In a 1920 comment on Nikolay Bukharin's *The Economy of the Transitional Period* (that being War Communism), Lenin had expressed the view that "antagonism and contradiction are not one and the same. The first disappears, the second remains under socialism" (Lenin, 1931: 357).[1] Despite this distinction, many Soviet theorists continued to identify the two throughout the 1920s and 1930s (see Karambovich, 1989: 5). This led to a rejection of the possibility of contradictions in socialism, which was only reinforced in 1938 by Stalin's assertion (in the Communist Party of the Soviet Union History *Short Course*) that under socialism, a full correspondence of production relations and productive forces prevailed. Stalin's reasoning was that "the social character of the process of production is reinforced by the social ownership of the means of production" (Stalin, 1940: 38). This statement effectively killed any suggestion that the political super-structure of the Soviet state would ever be in need of reform as the economic base developed.

The logic of the argument against the existence of contradictions was straightforward. Marxism-Leninism held that all class societies were subject to contradictions between the exploiters and exploited, and between a non-correspondence of productive forces and pro-duction relations. Stalin's statement foreclosed the possibility of the latter in the Soviet Union, while the lack of a capitalist class sup-posedly removed one side of the first type of contradiction. While not classless (two classes existed, the workers and peasants, plus a "layer" of intelligentsia), Soviet society was said to be free from the antagon-isms which plagued capitalist societies due to the lack of an exploita-tive bourgeoisie.

Abortive discussions on the possibility of contradictions took place before the Second World War, as well as after. In 1940, articles on the possibility of contradictions in socialist societies appeared in *Pod znamenem marksizma* (Under the banner of Marxism) and *Problemy Ekonomiki* (Nazarov, 1975: 64; Karambovich, 1989: 9). The Stalinist ideological tenet on the correspondence of production relations to productive forces, however, held firm. In the famous discussions after the war on G. F. Aleksandrov's book on West European philosophy, the idea that the dialectic applied to Soviet society in the form of contradictions was broached once more (Karambovich, 1989: 13–14). Thus, like so many other ideological concepts, the idea circulated at lower levels for some time before its official acceptance. The issue was raised again in mid-1955 with the publication of an article "for discuss-ion" in *Voprosy Filosofii* (Stepanyan, 1955). A noted philosopher, Tsolak Stepanyan, threw his weight behind the position that contradictions could arise in the Soviet Union, but the notion that this contradiction could become antagonistic was still denied.

This discussion died down in the late 1950s and early 1960s, and the possibility of contradictions was still more or less denied. It was only in 1967 that party ideologist Mikhail Suslov finally and officially approved the possibility of contradictions. In a booklet published to mark the fiftieth anniversary of the October revolution, Suslov stated that socialism in fact did away with antagonistic contradictions.

> However, this in no way means that thereby contradictions in general in the development of society are abolished. Notions that contradictions in the conditions of socialism disappear or are only a "sickness," an "ailment," or a "shortcoming" diverge with the basic theses of Marxist-Leninist theory, with the real practice of socialist construction. (Suslov, 1967: 27)

Suslov's interpretation was quickly accepted as the definitive view, and allowed for a profusion of scholarly works which attempted to cast the study of contradictions in its proper light. The appropriate dialectical law which applied was said to be that of the "unity and struggle of opposites," in which unity was stressed much more than struggle, justifying the notion that communist parties were the unifying factor in socialist societies. The crux of the argument thirty years later would be that contradictions in socialism were non-antagonistic, but could become antagonistic under the right circumstances despite the unifying role of the Communist party. Meanwhile, the Soviet bloc was developing from a camp to a system, and then a commonwealth, in which each of its members had varying and sometimes conflicting interests.

Lenin, internationalism, and the Comintern

There is a long history of ideological wrangling over the concept of internationalism. One of Lenin's clearest statements on internationalism was contained in his 1918 pamphlet, *The Proletarian Revolution and the Renegade Kautsky*. He attacked Kautsky, a German Social Democrat who had voted for war credits at the beginning of the First World War, and later criticized the establishment of the dictatorship of the proletariat in Russia. Lenin's pamphlet established the measure of internationalism in a communist's attitude to the world revolution and a willingness to sacrifice national interests to the broader interests of the world communist movement (Lenin, 1967: 93). Stalin's subsequent identification of the Soviet Union in 1927 as the "base" of the world communist movement thus redefined the true measure of internationalism in a revolutionary's attitude toward the Soviet Union (Stalin, 1954: 53–4). He declared bluntly: "An internationalist is one who is ready to defend the USSR without reservation, without wavering, unconditionally; for the USSR is the base of the world revolutionary movement, and this revolutionary movement cannot be defended unless the USSR is defended" (Stalin, 1954: 53–4). This statement was made during the 1927 war scare, which Stalin used to consolidate his power and deal the *coup de grace* to the Left Opposition (Cohen, 1980: 264–8).

Even before Stalin's redefinition of the true measure of internationalism, there had been a certain amount of tension between the interests of other communist parties and those of the CPSU. Throughout the 1920s and 1930s, communist parties which were reliant in some measure on Soviet support were often forced to sacrifice their own interests for those of the Soviet Union. The argument was that as the center of the world communist movement and the world's first socialist state, the interests of the Soviet Union and the movement were identical.

In practical terms, this meant the prerogative of the Soviet Union to define both sets of interests and determine when a communist party had overstepped the bounds to threaten either. The institutional mechanism for enforcing obedience was the Communist International (the Comintern), headquartered in Moscow until its dissolution in 1943. Given the illegality of most communist parties, the Soviet Union was an important base of operations and safe haven; the tradeoff was acceptance of the infamous "21 conditions" for Comintern membership, which effectively subordinated the communist parties to the Soviet-dominated Executive Committee of the Communist International (ECCI) (see Carr, 1982: 4–5).

The most restrictive conditions called for the tailoring of propaganda and agitation "in accordance with the decisions of the Comintern," and the removal of "reformist elements" from member parties. Point 15 called for member parties to give wholehearted support to the Soviet Union in the struggle against "counterrevolutionary forces" (Novopashin, 1989: 4). An additional restraint on the independent activity of communist parties was the difficulty of obtaining funds and collecting membership dues in their home countries. Therefore, most became dependent during the 1930s on Soviet funds (Carr, 1982).

Some examples of disastrous subordination of local communist parties to Comintern decisions include the decision to expose to the Kuomintang the inner-party structure of the Chinese Communist

Party (in the name of the "united front from below") which resulted in the 1927 Shanghai massacre; the vehement condemnation (in the name of ultra-leftism) of social-democracy and the consequent blindness to the rise of fascism in Germany, prohibiting an electoral alliance between the Communists and Social Democrats in the early 1930s; and the dissolution (in the name of the fight against ultra-leftist Trotskyism) of the Polish Communist Party by Comintern decree in 1937.

More examples could be cited, but the point here is that even before the establishment of Soviet-style socialism in Eastern Europe after the Second World War, many precedents existed for the assertion of the leading role of the Soviet Union and the CPSU within the world communist movement.

People's Democracy, 1947–1953

Despite the later importance of Eastern Europe to the Soviet Union, the nature of the regimes established in Eastern Europe after the Second World War was accorded surprisingly little attention by Soviet scholars. This was, in part, undoubtedly due to the fact that neither Stalin nor the other major Soviet leaders offered their assessment of events in the region. Nor was any clue offered as to how to characterize the regimes which were taking shape there, at least until 1947. Neither Stalin nor Molotov, for example, made any reference to the contemporary situation in Eastern Europe in their Supreme Soviet election speeches of February 1946 (Stalin, 1946; Molotov, 1946).

It is unlikely that the Soviets intended to impose full-fledged Stalinism on Eastern Europe after the Second World War, whether as a means of guaranteeing their security through pliant regimes or to advance the cause of communism. The notion that the gradual tightening of Soviet control over Eastern Europe in the late 1940s was part of an overall design gained popularity only after the fact of Soviet domination. If we keep in mind that full "Sovietization" of Eastern Europe did not take place until after 1947 (Brzezinski, 1967: Chapters 4–7), then the absence of any serious theoretical attempt until then to deal with Eastern Europe can be taken as a sign that the Soviets themselves were unsure what types of states would emerge.

Soviet domination of Eastern Europe in an immediate sense stemmed from the defeat of Germany and its allies, extending Soviet military power into the heart of Europe. From 1944 to 1946, Soviet control was extended only gradually, suggesting a reluctance to

unduly challenge the West. This period witnessed coalition govern-
ments throughout most of the region (except for Yugoslavia and
Albania), in which communists occupied such key positions as Prime
Minister, Minister of Defense or Interior (Brzezinski, 1967: Chapter 1).

In late 1946 and early 1947, with no response from the West, East
European communists with Soviet backing became more bold in
taking state power. The Bulgarian, Polish and Romanian parties all
came to occupy dominant positions within national or patriotic fronts
by early 1947. August of that year saw the electoral success of the
Communist-dominated Front in Hungary after pressure on the Small-
Holders Party.

The following month, representatives of the Soviet, Italian, French,
and East European communist parties (with the exception of Albania)
met in Poland to establish a new multilateral organization, the Communist Information Bureau, or Cominform. The choice of locale
seemed well calculated to displease the Polish leader Gomułka, who
was known to harbor reservations about any organization smacking of
central control over non-Soviet communists (Ulam, 1974: 460).

The Cominform was set up ostensibly to promote the exchange of
views and experience between communist parties. In practice this
meant more emphasis on following Soviet guidance; an early manifestation of the principle of internationalism in inter-socialist relations.
The East European states were displaying dangerous signs of independence, ranging from willingness to join the Marshall plan in mid-1947
(Poland and Czechoslovakia) to excessive zeal in following the Soviet
development model (Yugoslavia).

Such independence extended to early Soviet theoretical attempts to
explain the nature of the East European states. An exhaustive survey
of articles published in Soviet journals after the war reveals that only a
half-dozen articles or so were published in 1945–6 on Eastern Europe.
None of these dealt to any significant extent with how to characterize
the new states. It was only in early 1947 that three articles appeared
which grappled with the question of the nature of the systems taking
shape in the region (Leont'yev, 1947; Traynin, 1947; Varga, 1947). All
three proposed different understandings, consistent with what
remained an uncertain situation in many respects. All stressed the
impossibility of labelling these systems either socialist or capitalist,
given the mixture of public and private forms of ownership, and the
existence of coalition governments. Some Western authors have
pointed out the similarity of the East European economies at this time
to the Soviet New Economic Policy of the 1920s (D'Agostino, 1988: 166),

and the question of whether or not to characterize them in this fashion in fact became an important issue for Soviet writers in the early 1950s.

It was even impossible at this juncture to settle on what to call them. One author preferred "democracies of a new type" (Varga, 1947); another pointed out their supposed similarity to the National Front in Spain from 1936 to 1938 and held that they were therefore not democracies of a new type, but rather of a "special type" (Traynin, 1947). Varga's article was adapted from a chapter of his book on *Changes in the Economy of Capitalism as a Result of the Second World War*, which soon earned him criticism for its unorthodox assessment of capitalism (see below). Varga seemed to be suggesting not only that capitalism could stabilize itself, but that the East European societies could develop along different lines than either the Soviet or Western economies.

These articles, however, were less significant than the assertion made by the Bulgarian leader Georgi Dimitrov at the end of 1948 that both People's Democracy and Soviet power were "two forms of the dictatorship of the proletariat." The Bulgarian leader stated that one of the "basic regularities" of the transition to socialism was that it could not take place without such a dictatorship for the "suppression of capitalist elements and the organization of the socialist economy." Dimitrov declared that People's Democracy was a form of the "power of the working class in union with the laborers of the city and village, headed by the working class," and that it was therefore necessary "to study and widely utilize the experience of socialist construction in the Soviet Union" (Dimitrov, 1948b). Until this time, no official word had been given as to whether or not the People's Democracies would follow the Soviet experience more closely, and the concept of People's Democracy was still generally associated with the idea that the East European states would enjoy limited domestic autonomy. Some theoretical articles had maintained that the Soviet experience was relevant for Eastern Europe (see, for example, Mirov, 1947; Fedoseyev, 1948), but none had openly identified them as dictatorships of the proletariat as existed in the Soviet Union.

There is some indication that despite his long association with the Comintern and exile in the Soviet Union, Dimitrov was opposed to the imposition of the "dictatorship of the proletariat" in the People's Democracies (Carillo, 1978: 154). It was in fact only in his closing speech to the Bulgarian party congress that Dimitrov characterized People's Democracy as a "form" of the dictatorship of the proletariat; in his opening speech, he described it only as *fulfilling* its functions, the standard characterization at the time (Dimitrov, 1948a). It is significant that Mikhail Suslov, then chairman of the Cominform as well as Soviet secretary for ideology and inter-party affairs (Petroff, 1988: 62) was in attendance at the Bulgarian Congress ("Otkrytiye 5-go s"yezda," 1948). It is probable that Suslov was performing one of his first acts in a role that was to become increasingly familiar over the next forty years – that of ideological control over the world communist movement. In a speech which foreshadowed later Soviet interpretations of socialist internationalism, Suslov described the Bulgarian Workers Party (Communists) as "an experienced organizer and leader, which combines the struggle for the interests of its fatherland with fidelity to the principles of proletarian internationalism" ("Otkrytiye 5-go s"yezda," 1948).

Of course, it was the break with Yugoslavia which was most responsible for the impetus to tighten Soviet control over the rest of Eastern Europe and the necessity of justifying it in ideological terms. Here, too, Suslov played a cardinal role. He was present at the Cominform meeting which saw the ouster of Yugoslavia, and was in fact rumored to have authored the resolution (Nicolaevsky, 1965: 260). In the other East European countries, 1948 saw the forced merger of the socialist parties into the communist (Brzezinski, 1967: 85), much as 1947 had witnessed the stifling of opposition on the right. The fact that Yugoslavia was in some ways more Soviet than the Soviet Union (Brzezinski, 1967: 19–20) suggested that the break was not caused by any lack of zeal on the part of Tito. It has been well-documented (see, for example, Ulam, 1952) that the issue was generally one of Yugoslav unwillingness to submit to Soviet control. In this respect, the close identification of People's Democracy with the Soviet experience was certainly a justification for increasing Soviet control through the mechanism of the dictatorship of the proletariat.

It is only after Dimitrov's pronouncement of the doctrine in December 1948 that purges and show trials of the type seen in the Soviet Union before the war began in Eastern Europe (Brzezinski, 1967: 93–7). Of course, there was political violence before the declaration of People's Democracy as a form of the dictatorship of the proletariat, but it was largely directed at non-communist opponents. Declaration of People's Democracy as a form of the dictatorship of the proletariat signalled that Stalin's "teaching" on the "intensification of the class struggle" would also apply to Eastern Europe, and that the role of the East European communist parties in leading that dictatorship would grow as well.

At the same time, the identification of People's Democracy with the Soviet Union raised the uncomfortable question of what was unique in the latter's experience which justified its leading role in the international communist movement. For, despite the adulation and deference shown by many foreign communists to Stalin and the Soviet party, Tito's example had shown that one could be both communist and nationalist. Tito did not consider himself a nationalist, however, and later in the 1950s the Yugoslav Communists attempted to prove why theirs was the true internationalist position.

A hierarchical system such as that created domestically and internationally by Stalin required a powerful center, and the justification for one was provided in a 1951 article in the party journal *Bolshevik* (Sobolev, 1951).[2] This is considered to be the most significant theoretical statement after Dimitrov's (Skilling, 1961; Brzezinski, 1967; Kase, 1968) and was notable for its assertion that the People's Democratic revolutions had begun as bourgeois-democratic, but had "grown over" into socialist revolutions. This settled a long-running debate among Soviet ideologues as to whether these "revolutions" had been socialist from the beginning, or whether they had started as something lower on the Marxist continuum, and thus had lesser prestige ideologically.

Many of the most vocal proponents of the latter school of thought came from the Institute of State and Law, and by early 1952 were forced to recant in the face of the endorsement of Sobolev's position (compare Kotok, 1951, and 1952). In April 1952 a Central Committee decree criticized the State Juridical Literature Publishing House for "unscrupulousness" in only publishing works by a narrow group of scholars on People's Democracy. Such authors were said to be "sometimes even politically doubtful," their views on People's Democracy were characterized as "incorrect," and the director and editor of the publishing house were removed ("O ser"ëznykh nedostatkakh," 1954: 625). (Just before Stalin's death in 1953, the editorial board of the Institute's journal, *Soviet State and Law*, was also reorganized. Compare the listing of editorial board members in nos. 1 and 2–3, 1953. See also the article on the journal's "shortcomings" in nos. 2–3.)

Sobolev's 1951 article was significant in a number of respects. First, its venue of publication, the Central Committee theoretical journal *Bolshevik*, gave it the stamp of authority. Secondly, Sobolev was a "responsible worker" in the Propaganda Department ("Sobolev," 1981)[3] headed at the time by Suslov.

In content, too, Sobolev's article was noteworthy. In his discussion of the relevance of the experience of People's Democracy for Great Britain, he broached the notion that "parliamentary paths" to socialism were possible in Western Europe. Sobolev quoted the new Communist Party of Great Britain Program to assert that a parliamentary majority could be won, and a "people's government" established on the basis of Parliament (Sobolev, 1951: 35). This contradicts the notion that the Soviet Union was unalterably opposed to such theoretical innovation under Stalin.

Of course, one may protest that these were mere words; especially in the Stalin period, the use of ideology to conceal true intent was rampant. But at the same time, this suggests that the experience of People's Democracy significantly influenced later Soviet theoretical development by demonstrating the viability of other forms of transition to socialism. Another noteworthy aspect of this article is that an explanatory note printed on the first page stated it was based on a lecture given in the party office of the Moscow party organization, which at that time was headed by Nikita Khrushchev (Hough, 1979: 200). This raises a number of possibilities, the most interesting of which is that this may have been where Khrushchev was first exposed to the notion of parliamentary paths to socialism and gave it his stamp of approval.

Other authors have also sought to dispel the myth of monolithic Stalinism (see D'Agostino, 1988; Hahn, 1982; Hough, 1985; Ra'anan, 1983), but the general view of this as a sterile period remains. Decisions which with the hindsight of the 1950s (at the height of the cold war) appeared part of an insidious plan to extend Soviet domination to Western Europe and Greece are now considered by some to have been made despite Stalin's desire for a lessening of international tension with the West. Such a foreign-policy line – essentially, peaceful coexistence – would allow the ripening of contradictions within and between capitalist nations, bringing on inter-capitalist war, which was still seen as inevitable (D'Agostino, 1988: 165).

In one of the first major revisionist works questioning basic assumptions about the cold war, Marshall Shulman traced the development of an increasingly pessimistic Soviet view of the international situation after 1948. Whereas at one point Stalin feared the possibility of a war between East and West, by 1952 he asserted even more strongly the inevitability of inter-capitalist war (Shulman, 1985: Chapter 10). What have been interpreted in the West as aggressive foreign policy actions, in this view, were aimed not so much at extending Soviet power as consolidating it.

For example, the Greek civil war was pursued most vigorously by Tito, who was reportedly told angrily by Stalin to end it (Dijilas, 1962).

For Stalin, the October 1944 "percentages" agreement with Churchill had clearly placed Greece outside the Soviet orbit, and the civil war there threatened to wreck what was left of Allied cooperation. Enough work has been done in the West, meanwhile, to plausibly demonstrate connections between the more militant Soviet leaders and their foreign counterparts (Shulman, 1985: 48–9). Andrey Zhdanov, executor of the cultural campaign to reassert party orthodoxy after the war, shared with the Yugoslavs and the Bulgarians a desire to spread communism through violent revolution, and seemed to work against Stalin's purposes at times (Ra'anan, 1983). It may well be that Zhdanov's political disgrace in 1948 resulted from the Soviet break with Yugoslavia.

This is not the prevailing perception of the post-war course of events in Western scholarship, but it merits attention for the credible arguments it makes in proposing that we view much of what occurred not as part of any grand design but rather as manipulation of events by rival factions.

For instance, the refutation of the economist Yevgeniy Varga's views on the prospects of the survival of capitalism after the war is often seen as a manifestation of the enforcement of Stalinist orthodoxy. Varga had written at the end of 1945 that capitalism had emerged from the Second World War in good position to avoid an immediate collapse due to overproduction. His argument was that the state had sufficient capacity to intervene on behalf of the capitalist class as a whole in order to save the system, rather than acting only in the narrow interests of monopoly capital (Lynch, 1987: 20–2). What is more, despite being of an obviously lower type than Soviet democracy, bourgeois democracy was said to provide sufficient scope for progressive elements within these societies to influence the state. This also implied that a parliamentary path to socialism was possible.

When Stalin refuted these notions in 1952 with his *Economic Problems of Socialism in the USSR*, he perhaps took this position out of expediency rather than conviction. He had professed views more or less in line with Varga's in an interview with Harold Stassen published in *Pravda* in May 1947, for example (Stalin, 1947), and in other forums as well, suggesting that he viewed neither post-war tensions with the West nor its imminent collapse as inevitable. The attention of many Western authors is drawn to the fact that this conversation took place the day after the beginning of discussions on Varga's book; it would seem to be just as significant that it was published on the eve of the anniversary of the victory over Germany, suggesting a desire to continue the wartime relationship.

It seems to be the case that Stalin originally may have agreed with Varga's assessment, but that by the early 1950s to do so no longer served policy needs, given the tensions of the cold war. Some have suggested that Varga was attacked for other than ideological reasons, namely as a function of factional or bureaucratic politics. Hahn and McCagg, in fact, make the excellent point that Varga's detractors, such as Voznesenskiy (the deputy prime minister and head of Gosplan), fared worse than the economist himself. Voznesenskiy was arrested and shot; Varga merely had his institute and its journal shut down, and published little else beyond self-criticisms for the rest of the Stalin period. Even in these self-criticisms, he rarely admitted he was wrong. Even when he finally did acknowledge the supposed validity of the criticism levelled against him, he was so obsequious as to imply he really did not agree (for example, see Varga, 1949). He then re-emerged after the death of Stalin to become a prominent theorist of international relations (Lynch, 1989: 23–5).

We should also keep in mind that Varga made his prediction of the stabilization of capitalism for about ten years in late 1945; thus, when Stalin published his view in 1952 in favor of its imminent collapse, he may have been in fact agreeing with Varga.

Varga's assessment of capitalism's chances was rather favorable, in that he proposed it could avoid short-term collapse through government direction of the economy (that is, planning) (Lynch, 1987: 21–2). In addition, calling the East European regimes "new democracies," as he had in 1947, implied something distinct from both the Soviet Union and the Western democracies. This in turn suggested that mixed economies – the dreaded "third path," perhaps – could survive in Eastern Europe, thus doing away with the need to follow the Soviet example.

As already mentioned, however, by 1947 (in light of the growing tensions of the cold war) and certainly by 1948 (with the Soviet–Yugoslav dispute in full bloom), an analysis of capitalism which suggested the opposite was necessary. One danger of a "third path" between capitalism and socialism was that it came too close to the Soviet New Economic Policy of the 1920s. Successful experiences of this type could raise the uncomfortable question of why such an experiment was not allowed to continue in the Soviet Union instead of being ended bloodily and abruptly by collectivization.

The public repudiation of Varga's views in 1947–9 should therefore be seen for both its domestic and foreign relevance. On the one hand, it helped to solidify the notion that there were only two "camps" in the world, as Andrey Zhdanov had claimed at the opening of the Cominform in 1947: there was no possibility of a third way, distinct from capitalism and socialism. It also foreclosed any possible discussion of the merits of the New Economic Policy and the slackening of state control over the economy within the Soviet Union.

What were the ideological functions which theoretical elaboration of the notion of People's Democracy fulfilled? The function of legitimation was undoubtedly important, although it does not appear to have been so much a question of legitimating the existing social structure to its inhabitants as for communists of other countries who looked to the Soviet Union for support and to Eastern Europe for an example. The 1951 Sobolev article, for example, had clearly suggested that for British Communists, People's Democracy was the path to socialism (Sobolev, 1951: 34). In addition, the identification of People's Democracy with the Soviet Union and the application of the Soviet experience to Eastern Europe was important for its legitimating effect domestically in the Soviet Union. Combined with victory in the war, the rise of similar regimes validated the Soviet system and made up for its shortcomings.

The role of explanation, meanwhile, was important in this period as well. If we look at what was actually being said by Sobolev and his opponents about the establishment of the People's Democracies, the debate appears part of a process by which Soviet elites defined their worldview. Sobolev's suggestion that the East European regimes were not really socialist until sometime in 1947–8 corresponded to, and explained, reality better than his opponents' view.

Sobolev, writing in *Bolshevik* in 1951, gave official sanction to the view that the People's Democratic revolutions had begun as bourgeois-democratic and then "grown over" into socialist revolutions by 1947–8 (Sobolev, 1951: 29). Those who took the opposite point of view argued that these revolutions had been socialist from the beginning (for example, Mankovskiy, 1949: 7; Kotok, 1951: 44); the state structure had been smashed in the course of the war, and all traces of parliamentary democracy had been removed. Sobolev, however, suggested that parliamentary forms were retained and used by the new regimes, and the state structure was smashed only in the period of the socialist revolution (Sobolev, 1951: 29).

This debate therefore was not only over the nature of the East European states, but also about the proper revolutionary strategy. A "socialist from the beginning" school of thought implied more straightforward attempts at taking power and quicker transformation.

On the other hand, the "growing over" school suggested there were important tasks to be taken care of before socialist transformation could start. Given such concerns, this debate should be seen in important ways as fulfilling the function of explanation.

Another interesting aspect of post-war ideological debates is the similarity of Varga's views on capitalism to those of Mikhail Gorbachev, given in the October Revolution anniversary speech in 1987 (Gorbachev, 1987c). Both spoke of the ability of capitalism to survive without militarism; the main difference between them was that Gorbachev was even less pessimistic on capitalism's chances for survival.

At the same time, the function of rationalization was also fulfilled by the ideological construct of People's Democracy. As noted above, the major ideological statement by Dimitrov emerged after policy had taken a specific direction. Only after the establishment of single-party systems in Eastern Europe in 1948 did Dimitrov announce that People's Democracy qualified as a form of the dictatorship of the proletariat. Theoretical elaboration of the concept in the following period then served to explain the creation of similar states while asserting the superiority of the Soviet Union. This was done in a number of ways, for example by asserting the applicability of the Soviet experience in Eastern Europe or by the promotion of the image of the Soviet Union as the leader of the world communist movement.

Nonetheless, we should keep in mind the political context of the time and acknowledge that to most communists, leadership of the Soviet Union and specifically of Stalin was an article of faith. For them, to suggest that the Soviet Union should be the head of the socialist camp was their worldview, not a rationalization. Use of internationalism to rationalize Soviet leadership of the bloc only became primary once the East Europeans began to assert and defend their own national interests.

The function of communication in this case is the most problematic. Pervasive terror in the Stalinist system made open alliance-building dangerous, but scholars and politicians nonetheless spoke relatively freely within bounds and identified themselves in terms of certain issues (see Hough, 1985). In foreign policy, ideology was used in a more symbolic manner. For example, East European leaders quickly parroted Dimitrov's version of the theory of People's Democracy in early 1949, thereby professing allegiance to the new line (Brzezinski, 1967: 77).

The limits of autonomy, 1953–1956

Stalin's death in March 1953 brought an almost immediate relaxation of terror throughout the bloc, and a change of policy as well. The "Doctor's Plot," fabricated in the last months of the old dictator's life in order to initiate a new wave of terror throughout the Soviet Union, was renounced within weeks of his passing. Mass releases from the camps had to wait for proper de-Stalinization but the avoidance of a new purge was undoubtedly a great relief to many in the leadership and the bureaucracy.

The "New Course," meanwhile, was adopted in the Soviet Union under new Prime Minister Georgiy Malenkov's auspices and soon imitated in Eastern Europe as well. Its main feature in domestic policy was increased investment in consumer goods after their long neglect under Stalin, and a certain lessening of tension with the West (Brzezinski, 1967: 158–68). The struggle to settle the Soviet succession led to Malenkov's defeat, however, mainly over the issues of the inevitability of nuclear war and investment priorities. In February 1955 Malenkov lost his position as prime minister, leaving Khrushchev and Foreign Minister Molotov as the dominant figures in the leadership. One author has noted a difference of views between these two later that year in their assessment of the role of the Warsaw Pact, signed in May. For Khrushchev, the Pact was a "reflection of his drive toward détente with the West ... [and] an asset in the Cold War." For Molotov, meanwhile, the Pact represented "a vehicle for socialist consolidation, military preparedness, defense" (Remington, 1971: 26–7).

Another of the first steps of the new Soviet collective leadership was to attempt reconciliation with the former object of vilification, Yugoslavia. The difficulty of such an effort was compounded by the fact that for the remaining Stalinist leaders of Eastern Europe, acceptance of Yugoslavia back into the bloc threatened legitimation of the "national communism" which had been so bloodily suppressed in the final years of Stalin's rule. Political struggles and show trials within Eastern Europe were decided in favor of "Moscow" communists who had been trained in Moscow in the 1930s and 1940s. The victims were largely "local" communists who, like Tito, had spent the war years in-country and therefore had sources of legitimacy independent of the Soviet Union. (It should be pointed out that Tito himself was a Comintern *apparatchik* in Moscow before the war, however; wartime experiences were the crucial factor.) They also tended to have different priorities than the Soviets – national rather than international. The revival of various forms of national communism would seriously jeopardize the positions of those who owed their political fortunes to Stalin.

Khrushchev's attempts to build a bloc based on ideological ties seemed to stem from Leninist faith in the goodwill and internationalist camaraderie of communists. He may therefore have been ideologically blind to the attendant dangers. He envisioned a bloc held together through formal party ties rather than the informal, personalistic relations typical of the Stalin period. Considerable domestic autonomy would consolidate the regimes domestically, while a common ideology backed by economic mechanisms would bind them together on the international level.

The Yugoslavs, however, would not lightly re-admit themselves into what they perceived to be a Soviet-dominated bloc. The declarations made in 1955, on inter-government relations and, in 1956, on the re-establishment of party ties, reflected in ideological terms Yugoslav unwillingness to forfeit their independence ("Deklaratsiya," 1955; "Ob Otnosheniyakh," 1956a). They are worth examining at some length, especially because as official documents, they became part of the Marxist-Leninist "codex", so to speak, and were often quoted by reform-minded Soviets and East Europeans to promote reform agendas.

An interesting indication of how far the Soviets were willing to go to mollify the Yugoslavs is that according to well-placed Yugoslavs, both of these documents were based on Yugoslav drafts (Brzezinski, 1967: 177, 198).[4] In an effort to appear conciliatory, Khrushchev and his Prime Minister Nikolay Bulganin travelled to Yugoslavia in an act of contrition for the sins of Stalin. The statement on principles between the Soviet and Yugoslav governments characterized the basic principles of their relations as "respect for sovereignty, independence, territorial inviolability and equality," as well as "mutual respect and non-interference in internal affairs for any cause – of an economic, political or ideological character" ("Deklaratsiya," 1955).

Another indication of Soviet willingness to concede to Yugoslav desires was the dissolution of the Cominform in April of 1956 (Leonhard, 1979: 78). The Cominform had been the source of the most vitriolic attacks on the Yugoslavs, and despite its relative powerlessness, was still seen as symbolic of Soviet desire to control the communist movement. Tito and the Yugoslav leadership returned to Moscow for the first time since before the Soviet–Yugoslav break, and signed an agreement on interparty relations, signalling the formal restoration of party ties. The June 1956 statement on the principles governing inter-party relations made fleeting reference to the "internationalist principles of Marxism-Leninism," but was more notable for its acknowledgment that a "richness of forms of the development of socialism facilitates its strengthening" ("Ob Otnosheniyakh," 1956a). This was in stark contrast to the theory of People's Democracy, which held that the general patterns of the construction of socialism as exhibited in the Soviet Union were of universal significance. In both statements those principles which were stressed bore striking resemblance to what Soviet reformers in the 1970s called "common-democratic" principles.

Combined with the de-Stalinization campaign launched at the 20th Congress of the CPSU by Khrushchev in February 1956, these statements were seen in Eastern Europe (perhaps mistakenly) as suggesting that diversity in the construction of socialism would now be tolerated in Moscow. The ideological revisions proclaimed by Khrushchev at the Congress reinforced this perception. The intensification of class struggle after success of the socialist revolution was rejected, and Khrushchev stated explicitly that "many paths to socialism" were possible, holding up Yugoslavia as an example. He also admitted the possibility, given favorable conditions, of non-violent, parliamentary means to make the transition to socialism, confirming from the highest rostrum of the CPSU what had already been suggested in the pages of the party press some years before (Khrushchev, 1956: 4). The difference between "many paths to socialism" and a "parliamentary path" is that the former refers to socialist development after a successful socialist revolution, whereas the latter is the non-violent equivalent of the socialist revolution itself.

Within eight days of the 1956 Soviet–Yugoslav declaration on party relations, however, worker dissatisfaction in Poland manifested itself in riots in Poznan, setting in motion events that would demonstrate the limits of Soviet tolerance for reform in Eastern Europe. The dual crises in Poland and Hungary in October 1956 indicated that domestic autonomy, such as was allowed to develop in Poland, could not be combined with a perceived challenge to the security interests of the Soviet Union, as in Hungary. The Soviets, although combining threatening troop movements with political intimidation at the highest level, in fact were not overjoyed at Gomułka's return to power but did not intervene.

In Hungary, meanwhile, a protracted government crisis led to the replacement of the Stalinist Ernö Gerö with Imre Nagy as Prime Minister in response to the demands of rebellious crowds in the capital, Budapest. The Soviets first intervened in response to a Hungarian Politburo request on October 23, and dispatched a delegation headed by Suslov and Anastas Mikoyan to take stock of the situation as well (Brzezinski, 1967: 228). A cease-fire was negotiated, and the withdrawal of Soviet troops began. This was followed by an October 30 statement in *Pravda* which attempted to satisfy East European demands for a clarification of the relationship in light of the Soviet–Yugoslav declarations and Khrushchev's ideological revisions. Unlike the Soviet–Yugoslav declarations, however, the *Pravda* declaration specifically cited "proletarian internationalism" and the "common ideals of the construction of socialist society" as the principles uniting the countries of the socialist "community." At the same time, the document claimed that relations could be built "only on the principles of full equality, respect for territorial integrity, state independence and sovereignty, [and] non-interference in the internal affairs of one another" ("Ob Otnosheniyakh," 1956b). This statement was published while the leading Soviet ideologist, Suslov, was out of Moscow, which may explain its less than categorical stance. It was taken to suggest much more latitude for the East Europeans, but was sufficiently ambiguous in many ways to allow any interpretation. This most likely reflected a Soviet dilemma rather than a cynical ploy: Khrushchev needed to display tolerance of diversity in Eastern Europe in order to entice Yugoslavia back into the bloc. At the same time, the Soviet Union wished to remain, for its own purposes (legitimation, the superpower relationship) the recognized leader of the bloc. This statement should therefore be seen as an accurate indication of a confused Soviet reaction to the Hungarian uprising.

In the June Soviet–Yugoslav declaration on party relations, the independence demonstrated by Yugoslavia had made it impossible to describe relations as being based on proletarian internationalism, the euphemism for Soviet-defined limits on a socialist country's sovereignty and acknowledgment of Soviet leadership. In the case of Hungary, however, the attempt to assert similar independence prompted the Soviets to explicitly include both proletarian internationalism and the assertion of "common ideals" for the construction of socialist society. The latter recalled Soviet claims of ideological superiority by virtue of the fact that they had thirty years' accumulated experience in the building of socialism.

The ambiguous tone of this statement was settled practically, by the Soviet invasion of November 4, and ideologically, by Suslov's speech on the 39th anniversary of the October revolution. After the October 30 statement, two events changed the Soviet perception of the situation in Hungary and contributed to the decision to intervene a second time. First, France, Great Britain and Israel launched their ill-fated bid to prevent nationalization of the Suez Canal, creating an international crisis of equal magnitude to the Hungarian uprising. Second, Hungarian Prime Minister Imre Nagy lost control of the situation and gave in to increasingly radical demands. (The Soviet ambassador, future KGB chief Yuriy Andropov, had in fact warned his superiors some months before that neither Nagy nor Gerö would be able to cope with the situation (Burlatskiy, 1990: 114).) Nagy's declaration on November 1 that Hungary would declare neutrality and withdraw from the Warsaw Pact was the last straw for the Soviets, who had already seen the "general laws" of socialist construction breached with the announced restoration of parliamentary democracy the previous day. The parliamentary path was a means to an end (socialist revolution), not an end in itself. For the Soviets, this represented a dangerous precedent for the reversability of the historical process throughout the bloc.

Suslov's October Revolution anniversary speech therefore should be seen in this light. He spoke of four "general features and patterns" (*cherty i zakonomernosti*) of the socialist revolution: the establishment of the power of the working class; the worldwide strengthening of the union of the working class with the peasantry and other laborers; the liquidation of capitalist ownership and the planned nature of the economy; and the "decisive defense of the gains of the socialist revolution from the attacks of the former ruling exploitative classes" (Suslov, 1956: 1). The watchdog of Soviet ideology came out very strongly for the application of these patterns throughout the world socialist system, obviously in an attempt to avoid future upheaval. His addition of "defense of the gains of the socialist revolution" was fairly novel; earlier in 1956 a book by Soviet theoreticians on People's Democracy had listed the fourth general pattern of socialist construction simply as "cooperation with other socialist and peaceloving states" (quoted in Skilling, 1961: 423).

Suslov did come out in favor of different paths to socialism, with due respect for national features; he also urged the exchange of experience between the countries of the world socialist system on the basis of the "principles of equality and proletarian internationalism." He stressed this point again when he stated that in light of the 20th Congress' concept of the variety of forms of the transition to socialism, "the communist parties attentively analyze the national conditions of their countries ... standing on the firm foundation of Marxism-Leninism, [and] the principles of proletarian internationalism" (p. 3). Suslov did mention the October 30 statement but, despite his assertion of its "great meaning," gave it much less attention. Suslov's speech indicated that the Soviets would be much less forgiving of national experimentation in the future.

1957–1960: An end to revisionism?

One way to control such behavior would be to keep track of it through increased party ties. In the wake of the Hungarian rebellion, the Soviets created a special department devoted to relations with its allies, called the Department for Liaison with Communist and Workers Parties of Socialist Countries (Teague, 1980: 14) (referred to here for brevity as the Liaison Department). Its first head was the former ambassador to Hungary, Yuriy Andropov, who had warned the Soviet leadership of the possibility of violent outbreaks and the probable inability of the Hungarian leaders to handle them (Burlatskiy, 1990: 114). It would therefore seem that he was rewarded both for his prescience before the crisis, and his conduct during it.

Andropov then proceeded to gather about him a cadre of the "best and brightest," so to speak. Consultant, and then deputy chief, of the department was Lev Tolkunov (Burlatskiy, 1990: 45), who then chose his friend Fëdor Burlatskiy to take his place as head of the consultants' group. (In his first meeting with Andropov, Burlatskiy protested that he had no specialized knowledge of the socialist countries; Tolkunov replied that his writings for *Kommunist* showed he had a good knowledge of the Soviet system, "which is a good base for mastering the experience of the other countries of socialism" (Burlatskiy, 1990: 50)).[5] It is significant that Burlatskiy and a number of future reformers – Anatoliy Butenko, Georgiy Arbatov, and Aleksandr Bovin – all worked in *Kommunist* in the late 1950s and early 1960s, and it was here they formed their initial contacts (see Appendix). During the Khrushchev period, then, *Kommunist* was one of the breeding grounds of future "*shestidesyatniki*" – committed communists, usually in their mid-thirties, who had had their hopes raised by de-Stalinization and then dashed by the retrenchment of the Brezhnev period. The *shestidesyatniki* (literally, the "sixties people," from the Russian word for 60) were an important source of ideas and sometimes political support for the development of Gorbachev's "new political thinking."

Despite the imposition of strict limits on the autonomy of bloc members, ideological debate within the Soviet Union and between it and Eastern Europe over several issues continued. This should be seen as attempts by the East Europeans to achieve a measure of domestic autonomy and legitimacy, based on their own interpretations of the fundamental principles guiding the relationship. The Soviets themselves made some slight revisions in the theory of People's Democracy before the 20th Party Congress. The biggest change was that Soviet theory now assumed a middle ground on the question of the character of these regimes; the People's Democratic revolutions were graced as socialist from the beginning, with the provision that the dictatorship of the proletariat had not been established immediately (see Skilling, 1961: 421).

However, this did not stop theorists from Bulgaria and Czechoslovakia from questioning the prevailing Soviet theory of the formation of their states. Writing at first in their own journals and then in the Soviet philosophical journal *Voprosy Filosofii*, they challenged the periodization of the People's Democratic revolutions developed by Sobolev in 1951 (who was by now a deputy editor of the CPSU theoretical journal *Kommunist*) (Skilling, 1961: 245). Both writers asserted that their revolutions had always been socialist, with a form of the dictatorship of the proletariat in existence from the beginning (Bystřina, 1957; Pavlov, 1956). The Czechoslovaks seemed insulted that Soviet theoreticians would suggest that there had been important "democratic and feudal tasks" to be accomplished in the immediate post-war period, given the country's level of development. Pavlov, meanwhile, claimed that Bulgaria had begun straightaway in September of 1944 to realize socialist tasks, and creatively developed the Stalinist slogan of "national in form, socialist in content" to suggest that the revolution in Bulgaria was "people's-democratic in form, socialist in content" (Pavlov, 1956: 57). Pavlov's article was especially significant in view of his position as head of the Bulgarian Academy of Sciences (*Sovetsko–Bolgarskiye otnosheniya*, 1981: 547). Both singled out Sobolev by name, which was a serious move by the rules of the ideological game. The fact that their articles were printed in a Soviet journal also suggested support for their views among influential Soviets. In addition, Bystrina's 1957 book on People's Democracy in Czechoslovakia was translated into Russian and published by the Soviet Juridical Literature Publishing House in 1961. As mentioned above, this press had been censured in 1952 by Central Committee decree for publishing politically dubious views of People's Democracy. In an example of the use of ideology as a vehicle for communication,

Bystřina thanked Pavlov and a Soviet legal scholar, B. S. Man'kovskiy, for their help (Bystrina, 1961: 7).

This debate shows an interesting parallel with those over contradictions and internationalism thirty years later. In the 1950s as in the early 1980s, the debate was between the defenders of orthodoxy, represented in the pages of the party press, and challengers writing in the journal of the Institute of Philosophy. As Skilling (1961: 427) has pointed out, the East Europeans at first glance seemed to be promoting a "rightist" or revisionist line by stressing the national features of their revolutions, but in fact were "leftist" in that they promoted a more radical interpretation. In the 1980s, however, those writing in *Voprosy Filosofii* took clearly revisionist positions against those of the party apparatus. This is simply an indication of how the political center had shifted in 25 years. Nonetheless, we see that in both cases challenges to the prevailing line came from within the intellectual establishment.

The debate of the 1950s also illustrates how fundamental principles – in this case, the concept of national features – can be variously interpreted to promote different political objectives. This also seemed an attempt by the East Europeans to assert their legitimacy, apart from the Soviet Union, through the suggestion that they too had begun as socialist regimes, instead of drifting purposelessly into a higher stage of development (in other words, "grown over").

The Soviets would not relent on this issue, and important rejoinders were published in *Voprosy Filosofii* (Stepanyan, 1957; Pushev, 1958) and in *Kommunist*. Stepanyan, who at the same time was active in defining the proper interpretation of contradictions (see above) weighed in with a definitive article which ended the debate in favour of the Soviet view. He claimed that "in new historical conditions, a peaceful transition to the second, socialist stage of the revolution was accomplished in all the countries of People's Democracy" (Stepanyan, 1957: 10). Basing his argument on Lenin's "predictions" about such peaceful transitions, he specifically singled out Czechoslovakia to show that the revolution had taken on a socialist character only after 1948 (p. 11). Another Soviet author, meanwhile, asserted that due to the existence of slave-labor and semi-feudal production relations in occupied Czechoslovakia under the Germans, the pre-war achievements of bourgeois democracy had been wiped out. Therefore, the revolution had indeed accomplished "democratic and feudal" tasks in the first stages (Pushev, 1958: 96–7).

Sobolev also continued to publish his views in authoritative books and articles, most notably in his own journal (Sobolev, 1956, and 1958).

More importantly, after the decision by the November 1957 Conference of Communist Parties to create a new theoretical journal for the
world communist movement, he was sent by the CPSU Central Committee to become one of its responsible secretaries ("Sobolev," 1981).
Problems of Peace and Socialism (or *World Marxist Review* in its English
version) was based in Prague, and the despatch of Sobolev to the
Czechoslovak capital appeared to be a purposeful slight to those
Czechoslovaks who had challenged the Soviet view.

The year 1957 also witnessed the first major challenge by Soviet
conservatives to Khrushchev's rule. Alarmed by his ideological
revisions of the 20th Party Congress, and especially by the outbreaks in
Poland and Hungary, what was dubbed the "Anti-Party Group" made
an attempt to unseat Khrushchev at a June meeting of the Politburo
(then called the Presidium). Khrushchev demanded a plenary meeting
of the Central Committee, and Soviet Defense Minister Georgiy
Zhukov helped by allowing the use of military aircraft to fly CC
members in from all parts of the Soviet Union. Suslov chaired the
meeting, and there is some suggestion (Petroff, 1988: 99–103) that he
acted as an "impartial broker," or even perhaps supported Khrushchev against his opponents (Hough, 1979: 217). As a result, Molotov,
Malenkov, Lazar Kaganovich, and Dimitriy Shepilov were ousted
from the Politburo and the Central Committee, followed in later years
by others who had opposed Khrushchev (Hough, 1976: 218).

The political counterpart in foreign affairs to these debates was seen
at the November 1957 conference of communist parties in Moscow.
The twelve ruling communist parties issued a declaration which
attempted to define the tasks of the world communist movement and
lay down a general line. Growing differences between the Chinese
and the Soviets were seen in the former's attempts to play down the
importance of the ideological revisions of the previous year. The
declaration stressed proletarian internationalism as the basis of relations among socialist states, as well as the leading role of the Soviet
Union. The declaration also proclaimed the principles of "complete
equality, respect for territorial integrity and state independence and
sovereignty" between socialist states, but then even more firmly
endorsed "fraternal mutual aid" as the "effective expression" of socialist internationalism ("Deklaratsiya," 1957). This was one of the first
documents to make a distinction between proletarian and socialist
internationalism, and implied that one of the cardinal tenets of the
latter was mutual aid as seen in Hungary the previous year.

The declaration also attempted to clarify the "general laws" of socialist development, which differed little from those announced by Suslov a year earlier ("Deklaratsiya," 1957). A reference to the "gradual socialist reorganization of agriculture" was added, as a concession to the Poles (Brzezinski, 1967: 305). In addition, the declaration also added a call for a "socialist revolution in the sphere of ideology and culture" to the general laws of socialist development.

The Soviets, for their part, managed to include criticism of both "revisionism" (the Yugoslavs) and "dogmatism" (the Chinese), although condemnation of the former was considerably harsher. Revisionism was said to be the "main danger," and a "manifestation of bourgeois ideology that paralyzes the working class" ("Deklaratsiya," 1957: 2). The Yugoslav delegation (with Tito noticeably absent) refrained from signing the document, and the field was left to the Chinese, who attempted to tie the Soviets to a more radical and aggressive foreign-policy line. The Yugoslavs made something of an attempt to live up to this charge the following year with the publi-cation of the Theses for their 7th Party Congress, which codified their heretical views (see below).

An important article dedicated to the 1957 conference by the chief of the CC International Department (responsible for relations with non-ruling communist parties), Boris Ponomarev, clearly laid out the Soviet interpretation of revisionism. He listed seven elements of revisionist thought: (1) "smoothing over and underestimating the aggressive essence of imperialism ... (2) denial of the leading and guiding role of the communist parties ... (3) denial of the basic laws of class struggle ... (4) slipping down to the positions of social-democra-tism ... (5) denial of the universal meaning of the Leninist theory of the dictatorship of the proletariat ... (6) revision of the Leninist prin-ciples of party construction ... (7) rejection of proletarian inter-nationalism and slipping down to the positions of 'national commun-ism'" (Ponomarev, 1957: 15–16).

These were all sins which the Yugoslavs more than any other member of the world communist movement had committed. The new Program of the League of Communists of Yugoslavia adopted at their 7th Congress the following March signalled that they would not be bound to Soviet-defined ideological tenets. The Yugoslavs attempted to promote themselves as the "true" Marxist-Leninists, and in a lengthy statement of their worldview challenged the prevailing notions at every turn (see the discussion in Fedoseyev, 1958). In a twist which foreshadowed later efforts in both Eastern Europe and the Soviet Union, the Yugoslavs attempted to redefine internationalism rather than reject it outright. They denied the Stalinist test of inter-nationalism in one's attitude to the Soviet Union, or even in the display of mutual assistance. Instead, they suggested it meant those principles which had been stressed in the June 1956 Soviet–Yugoslav statement on relations between communist parties. They would be joined by the Romanians and Eurocommunists in the 1960s and 1970s, who would attempt to promote a "new internationalism" for the world communist movement, and also by Soviet reformers, who for their part stressed "common-democratic" values (see next chapter).

With the revisionist pole removed from the world communist movement with the departure of Yugoslavia, only the dogmatist Chinese were left to challenge Soviet ideological authority. By the time of the Conference of Eighty-one Communist Parties in 1960, the Sino-Soviet rift had grown so wide as to be unbridgeable, although neither side wished to precipitate an open break. About a dozen parties sided with the Chinese, however (Brzezinski, 1967: 412), and the final document was so broad a synthesis of Soviet and Chinese views as to negate its effectiveness as a guide for bloc policy. Later Chinese exclusion from the bloc meant that Moscow alone would retain the prerogative to determine acceptable adherence to the principle.

Internationalism, proletarian and socialist, 1960–1968

Nonetheless, while the Soviets attempted to retain this prero-gative for themselves, the East Europeans were becoming more assert-ive in bloc affairs. The Soviets began to use "socialist internationalism" more and more in the theoretical literature to describe relations between socialist states, although proletarian internationalism was still used, largely to describe relations between communist parties.

One example of this growing tendency was an article in *Kommunist* (Tolkunov, 1961) which gave something of a condensed treatment of all the tendentious issues in inter-socialist relations, and therefore deserves to be examined at length. As mentioned above, Tolkunov was deputy chief of the Liaison Department at the time (Burlatskiy, 1990: 45); therefore, he was more constrained than less senior figures in the interpretations he could give to the principle of socialist inter-nationalism.

First, Tolkunov went to great lengths to define the proper relation-ship between the socialist camp, system, and commonwealth. For this author, the three seemed interchangeable: "Mutual relations have risen to a new level in the framework of the socialist camp – the social, economic, and political *commonwealth* of free sovereign peoples" (p. 19, original emphasis).

More notable was the assertion (p. 19) that the "new type of international relations" represented by those between socialist states included both "common-democratic" (*obshchedemokraticheskiye*) and socialist principles. In the first category Tolkunov included equality and mutual respect for sovereignty, but said they were filled with a "new content." Socialist principles, on the other hand, included "the voluntary combination of efforts in the struggle for socialism, fraternal mutual assistance and support" (p. 19). Even the fact that he mentioned common-democratic principles, however, set him apart from later Soviet officials, who would usually mention these principles only in order to belittle their significance when compared to those of internationalism.

Tolkunov characterized socialist international relations as based on the principles of Marxism-Leninism and proletarian internationalism, and went on to state in an italicized passage that one of the "main objective bases" of the unity of socialist countries was "the necessity of joint defense of socialist achievements [and] the struggle against imperialism" (p. 20). Light (1988: 181) has pointed out the similarity of a statement made later in the article to the "Brezhnev Doctrine" of 1968: "Every Marxist party, every socialist state has responsibility not only for the fate of socialism in their own countries, not only for its fate within the boundaries of the entire commonwealth, but also for the fate of socialism in the entire world" (Tolkunov, 1961: 25). Thus, not only were socialist states made beholden to defend the Soviet Union, but also to defend socialism in other countries. This was one more example of the creation of the "ideological menu;" as with Sobolev's 1951 discussion of the notion of the parliamentary path to socialism, the concept was available in the literature, later to be chosen and given a leader's *imprimatur* (see below).

Finally, in yet another echo of later debates, Tolkunov utilized the term socialist internationalism to reject the notion that differences between socialist states could become antagonistic:

> There is no doubt that with the proper policy of the communist parties, which assumes the combination of the principles of socialist internationalism with national interests, there can be no conflicts or aggravations in mutual relations between socialist countries. It is necessary to underscore with full force the significance of this political factor in the conditions of socialism. (Tolkunov, 1961: 24)

This strong assertion of the role of internationalism in overcoming the tension between national and international interests did little to convince the other members of the world communist movement. All in all, this article was one of the clearest statements of the principles over which later debates would develop.

Socialist internationalism became a barometer of Soviet–East European relations; its absence or appearance in joint statements could be an indication of which side had prevailed on an issue. The Romanians, for example, stridently refused to be bound by the principle. A 1964 statement of neutrality in the Sino-Soviet split was at the same time a strong assertion of Romania's independence. Romania declared bluntly that "there are not and there can be no unique patterns and recipes" to be followed in the construction of socialism. More to the point, they stated: "There is not and cannot be a 'parent' party and a 'son' party, parties that are superior and parties that are subordinate" (quoted in Daniels, 1987: 308, 309).

Despite Khrushchev's effort to mold a commonwealth of interests after exclusion of the Chinese from the bloc, the Romanians used the "interested-member" principle to opt out of participation in many CMEA projects. This was a clear clash of worldviews; the Soviets were in favor of a socialist international division of labor in which each country would specialize in what it did best. Romania perceived this as an attempt to establish Soviet hegemony, and instead favored autarkic development of its national economy, preferring to continue in the Stalinist mode of self-reliance.

Romania's unwillingness to be bound by the principle of socialist internationalism found support in certain Soviet circles. One important sign of support came from a consultant in Andropov's Liaison Department (better known in the 1970s and 1980s as a columnist for the Government newspaper *Izvestiya*), Aleksandr Bovin. The department's group of consultants was a veritable hotbed of reformism in the early 1960s, and included such anti-Stalinists as Fëdor Burlatskiy, Georgiy Shakhnazarov, and Oleg Bogomolov, in addition to Bovin (Burlatskiy, 1990: 250–5).

In a 1965 booklet on internationalism, Bovin reflected the initial uncertainty in Soviet foreign policy as a result of the ousting of Khrushchev the previous year. Much as with Tolkunov's 1961 article, a certain ambiguity is evident, due most likely to their positions as party officials. Bovin, for example, speaking of the Comintern, noted that "the formula of 'subordination' of national interests to the international is valid, [but] was applied too mechanically without account of the great quantity of nuances which unavoidably arise at every stage of the historical process" (Bovin, 1965: 9). He included criticism of

Stalin, despite growing signs that a more accepting view was beginning to prevail on this issue in the Soviet bureaucracy. Finally, he
extended his analysis of the relationship between national and international interests to the present day with the observation that "socialist states may have non-coinciding interests in various areas of political
and economic life" (p. 23). He was to take these views farther in a book
published with Butenko and others in the mid-1970s (see next
chapter). For now, however, we should see his views as choices on the
ideological menu which did not prevail in 1968.

As with the case of Hungary twelve years earlier, in 1968 the
meaning of socialist internationalism was decided by armed force. The
invasion of Czechoslovakia settled the argument in favor of the definition of internationalism as consistent with limitations on the sovereignty of individual countries. The new line was announced the
month after the invasion in *Pravda*, and by Brezhnev in Poland in
November (Brezhnev, 1968; Kovalëv, 1968). Under a new dimension of
the principle of proletarian internationalism, it became not only the
right of the Soviet Union and other socialist states, but their *duty*, to
intervene whenever it was determined that socialism was threatened.

At the Fifth Congress of the Polish United Workers Party, Brezhnev
talked of the existence of "general laws of socialist construction" and
stated that when socialism was threatened, "this becomes not only a
problem of the people of a given country, but also a general problem, a
concern of all socialist countries." His remarks appeared to have been
based on the most authoritative attempt to explain the invasion,
published in *Pravda* in September. Above the name of S. Kovalëv, this
article had claimed that it was "impossible to oppose the sovereignty
of the individual socialist countries to the interests of world socialism,
of the world revolutionary movement" (Kovalëv, 1968). Both statements seemed to be based on the interpretation, mentioned above,
offered by then-deputy chief of the Liaison Department, Lev Tolkunov, in 1961. The crisis in Czechoslovakia merely provided the opportunity to confirm this interpretation in practice.

For all its profound ramifications in the world communist movement, the crushing of the Prague Spring was not without its effects
within the Soviet Union as well. The Institute of the Economics of the
World Socialist System (IEWSS) had been originally established in 1961
as a kind of supra-planning agency for the socialist bloc, but never
lived up to this role, especially in light of East European recalcitrance
to participate in CMEA planning and division-of-labor schemes. Its
failure in 1968 to give the leadership any kind of warning of the

impending crisis in Czechoslovakia led to the replacement of its director, Gennadiy Sorokin, and a secret Central Committee resolution ordering its reorganization in order to provide more political information.[6] The Central Committee sent a new director from the Liaison Department, Oleg Bogomolov, who had succeeded Burlatskiy as head of the consultants' group. Bogomolov and Anatoliy Butenko, a sector head at the IEWSS since 1964, were very well connected politically, and proceeded to collect a group of intelligent and reform-minded scholars, providing them with a creative atmosphere and a place of refuge from the ideological stagnation which prevailed during the Brezhnev era.

In the Liaison Department itself, meanwhile, a number of important changes had taken place. Andropov left the Department to become head of the KGB in 1967, and more or less dropped out of sight as far as the open element of Soviet–East European relations was concerned. Even before his departure, however, his group of analysts had begun to disperse: Burlatskiy and Tolkunov left the Department in 1965, while Arbatov left to become Director of the newly created Institute of the USA and Canada in 1967. Finally, Shakhnazarov was sent off to become a responsible secretary of *Problems of Peace and Socialism*, also in 1967, succeeding Aleksandr Sobolev. In essence, then, only Aleksandr Bovin was left of the original group of Andropovite reformers, and he was to depart in 1972.

These people were all replaced with men of considerably less imagination and creativity by the new collective leadership under Brezhnev. Konstantin Katushev, with little experience in foreign affairs, became Secretary for bloc relations in early 1968 after reportedly giving hard-line criticism of the reforms in Czechoslovakia (Hough, 1979: 464). The new chief and first deputy of the Liaison Department, Konstantin Rusakov and Oleg Rakhmanin, were both China specialists appointed in early 1968, perhaps indicating that the Soviet leadership desired to repair the relationship with China rather than to devote more intellectual energy to Eastern Europe (Teague, 1980: 18, 20).

Such personnel changes undoubtedly sent mixed signals to Eastern Europe. On the one hand, the breakup of an obviously reform-minded group suggested that a new line of domestic conservatism was in the offing. Yet, the appointment of China specialists to head the Liaison Department, combined with Brezhnev's remark to Czechoslovak leaders in December 1967 that personnel changes at the highest echelon were their own affair (Dawisha, 1984: 16), must have indicated that the Soviets were too concerned with domestic issues and the problem of China to take much interest in Eastern Europe. That such was not the case, of course, became evident during the course of the Prague Spring, but this initial confusion may have contributed significantly to miscommunication between the two sides.

Conclusions

The invasion of Czechoslovakia capped a two-decade period in which the Soviet Union repeatedly utilized armed force to support socialist regimes in Eastern Europe, accompanied by ideological argumentation which often seemed to be aimed solely at rationalizing it ex-post facto. The Soviet sacrifice in the Second World War allowed many in the post-Stalinist leadership to justify the maintenance of Soviet influence in the region at any cost; in addition, Eastern Europe was a valuable asset, seen in the context of the superpower relationship.

At the same time, ideological argumentation between the Soviet Union and Eastern Europe can be seen as the process of staking out political positions in a common language. The Soviets justified their leading role in the bloc by claiming themselves as the first and most experienced socialist state, and by suggesting that the East European states had only gradually developed into socialist states. Then, combined with the notion of the historical process and the laws of history, the East European regimes were obligated to follow the Soviet model of development. When Khrushchev attempted to create a more viable bloc by loosening the ideological reins and suggesting a multiplicity of forms of socialist development, he was also attempting to woo back the Yugoslavs. Therefore, he specifically pointed to their form of socialism as acceptable, and in so doing unleashed forces he may not have expected. The backlash at home (in the form of the attempted coup by the Anti-Party Group) and abroad (in the form of open challenges to Soviet rule in Poland and Hungary) forced him to re-impose stricter control and search for a new formula which would still allow the Soviet bloc to accommodate states as diverse as Yugoslavia, Poland, and China. His efforts failed, but the resulting ideological debates over the definition of ideological tenets should be seen as efforts to construct a political center in the world communist movement through the language of ideology.

Soviet efforts to unify the bloc under its leadership, however, invariably foundered on a nominal commitment to the equality of states in international affairs. More importantly, the Soviets used the principle of proletarian (and later socialist) internationalism to stress that divergences between the socialist countries' national interests and those of the bloc could only be resolved on the basis of Marxism-Leninism. Given that the Soviet Union abrogated to itself the right to define the "proper" interpretations of Marxism-Leninism, the Soviet Union was thus the ultimate arbiter of ideological tenets which were said to lie at the basis of the Soviet–East European relationship.

Interpretations of the fundamental principles of Marxism-Leninism continued to perform important political functions for the system. Ideology communicated the sentiments of the Soviet leadership to Eastern Europe, for instance prior to the invasion of Czechoslovakia (see Dawisha, 1984). In the context of a relationship with loosely defined norms, it served as a medium of communication between like-minded Soviets and East Europeans, as in the debate over the nature of the East European regimes. Finally, it served as the political language in which the rules of conduct in the Soviet–East European relationship were defined, especially in a period of growing diversity within the world communist movement.

The Chinese and Yugoslav influence on Soviet–East European relations is an example of how an increase in the number of participants in ideological discourse can affect the outcome. Both provided an alternative pole to which either neo-Stalinists or revisionists in Eastern Europe could appeal for support. The Chinese, for example, provided ideological ammunition especially to the Romanians in the latter's resistance to Khrushchev's schemes for a "socialist division of labor" within the bloc. Most importantly, the prestige and ideological independence of China and Yugoslavia aided East European efforts to gain autonomy within the bloc and to find a voice for themselves even after the Chinese excommunication and the failure of reconciliation with Yugoslavia. When the Soviets were forced to appeal to other communist parties for support, this conferred greater status on the junior partners.

Legitimation, too, had its role, especially after the exclusion of Yugoslavia and China from the bloc. Legitimacy in Soviet eyes was defined in terms of adherence to Soviet-defined "regularities" of socialist construction. Ideological debate in the Soviet Union focused on what these regularities were in the 1970s, and over their very existence in the 1980s.

Internationalism served as the vitally important rationalization of the invasion of Czechoslovakia after 1968, of course. The invasion of

Hungary was justified to some extent by use of the principle of internationalism, but not as elaborately as under what came to be known as the "Brezhnev Doctrine." It seemed that the intervention in Hungary was just as important as a seminal event in the development of Soviet leaders' worldview. They claimed to have learned certain lessons from that experience, namely that the West had developed new techniques of "sneaking counterrevolution," preferring sub-version from within rather than the instigation of open rebellion. In their view, the invasion of Czechoslovakia was an appropriate response.

In the following chapters we will examine the use and further interpretation of the theoretical principles at the basis of the Soviet–East European relationship. We shall continue to concern ourselves with the important question of socialist internationalism, and shall examine as well a question which is basic to a Marxist worldview – the issue of antagonistic contradictions within a society.

3 Contradictions and internationalism in the 1970s: the Eurocommunist challenge

The invasion of Czechoslovakia augured profound changes within the Soviet Union, as well as in its relations with the world communist movement. What little hope remained for the realization of reform from within the system was dashed by the ascendancy of Brezhnev and the consolidation of a conservative domestic line. One of the first acts of the Brezhnev leadership was the appointment of Sergey Trapeznikov to head the Central Committee Science Department, which gave responsibility for the social sciences to one who was known for his almost Stalinist outlook. As mentioned in the last chapter, the Institute of the Economics of the World Socialist System was reorganized by secret Central Committee decree. Oleg Bogomolov left the Liaison Department to become head of the IEWSS, and proceeded to gather a well-trained and reformist cadre of theoreticians who challenged many of the prevailing notions of the basis of Soviet–East European relations.

This chapter examines the response of the international communist movement to the invasion of Czechoslovakia and the initial stages of this re-assessment as seen in the development of views on socialist internationalism and contradictions. In addition to an analysis of the major theoretical statements on socialist internationalism, I examine how the concept was used in official multilateral documents at international communist party conferences and Warsaw Pact Political Consultative Committee (PCC) meetings.

To examine the importance of socialist internationalism for the Soviet Union and its East European allies, we must keep in mind the international and domestic milieux after 1968. Despite a brief hiatus after the invasion of Czechoslovakia, détente proceeded apace and in fact accelerated under the administration of US President Richard Nixon. For their own reasons, each superpower pursued accommodation. The United States wanted to gain Soviet help in reaching a settlement in Vietnam, and to modify Soviet behavior abroad and at home. The Soviet Union, meanwhile, saw détente as a way to legitimate its own superpower status, and increased trade with the West as a means of avoiding politically painful economic reform (see Garthoff, 1985: 24–68).

Détente did offer significant scope for a relaxation of international tensions and increased cooperation, but at the same time Western economic and political penetration presented serious challenges to the maintenance of Soviet hegemony in Eastern Europe. Nixon's visits to the region in the early 1970s – he visited Romania in 1969, Yugoslavia in 1970, and Poland in 1972 – suggested what became known as the Sonnenfeldt Doctrine after the confidential speech of the US Department of State Counselor by the same name in 1976: the United States, while not recognizing the legitimacy of Soviet hegemony in the region, recognized the fact of it and attempted to promote what autonomy it could in Eastern Europe, in the hope of making that relationship more "organic" and thereby influencing Soviet behavior (Garthoff, 1985: 495–6). The Soviets, however, saw mainly the negative side of this, and responded by increasing efforts aimed at ideological and political homogeneity (see Hutchings, 1983: 206–28). Meanwhile, superpower competition in the Third World also continued despite détente, requiring further economic sacrifice on the part of the Soviet Union, and political support and economic cooperation on the part of its allies.[1]

An examination of PCC documents issued from 1969 and 1980 (in other words, between the Czechoslovak and Polish crises) is useful for several reasons. First, the Pact itself was the major instrument used to bring multilateral pressure on recalcitrant allies in this period (see Jones, 1981, and d'Encausse, 1987). Second, Warsaw Pact documents more accurately reflected the Soviet–East European bargaining process than, for instance, those of the Council for Mutual Economic Assistance (CMEA), in which three non-European members could also influence the discourse.

It is important to keep in mind how PCC documents were drafted. According to a Central Committee official involved in the process for many years, the practice was for the host country to prepare a draft document, usually two weeks before the meeting, and to circulate it to the other countries. Mid-level representatives then would meet and work out the text, operating under the rule of consensus. This explains much of the non-definitive character of PCC statements.[2]

Interestingly, the formulation "socialist internationalism" itself did not appear in any of the Warsaw Pact PCC documents examined.[3] This was surprising, given that this was the one forum in which we would expect the Soviets to have been able to secure forthright expressions of allegiance to the principle.

When analyzing these documents, we look first of all at how the goals of Pact cooperation are characterized. PCC declarations or communiqués usually contained a characterization of the basis of the socialist countries' foreign policy, or the goals of their foreign-policy activity. These characterizations could be oriented either to Soviet or autonomist formulations, or, more often, a compromise of both. Among the euphemistic phrases used by the East Europeans (and sometimes by Soviet theoreticians) to call for greater autonomy included the following: "national-state interests"; "common-democratic principles;" and "new internationalism." When the Soviets or conservative East Europeans desired to show loyalty to Soviet leadership of the bloc, they had these euphemisms to choose from: the "common interests" of the bloc; the "harmonious combination" of national and international interests; "unity," be it "monolithic," "unshakeable," or "indestructible;" and, more simply, "internationalism," whether "socialist," "proletarian," or even "proletarian socialist." Finally, terms such as "international solidarity" or "international relations of a new type" were considered sufficiently inoffensive by all concerned to be used as compromise terms when necessary. (Of course, the use of diplomatic language in the true sense is also important; that is, we look to see whether a meeting passed in "full understanding and unity" or simply in "a spirit of fraternal friendship," for example.)

Much of the history of ideological debate between the Soviet Union and the rest of the world communist movement concerned the proper definitions of terms such as these. Yet, as Vernon Aspaturian has pointed out, with the growth of truly independent European communist parties in the 1970s, the situation began to change:

> One of the truly innovative behavioral characteristics of the Euro-communists is their refusal to engage in this bizarre charade of retaining rhetorical loyalty to principles whose content and context have radically changed. Instead, they have resorted to the more honest approach of repudiating certain "durable" principles whose durability was in semantic form only. (Aspaturian, in Aspaturian, 1980: 9)

Before the Eurocommunist parties brought themselves to the outright rejection of terms they saw as obsolete, however, they went through a period of attempting to gain acceptance of their own interpretations within the movement. Reformist Soviet scholars, living under another set of rules and faced with obstinate refusal on the part of their conservative colleagues and leaders to change, did not have the luxury of being able to reject the prevailing interpretations. If they wanted to act within the system, they were forced to continue the "bizarre charade," developing alternative understandings of the prevailing ideological principles.

The meanings of internationalism

As we saw in the previous chapter, socialist internationalism was a contentious issue in Soviet relations with the world communist movement, affecting relations with Eastern Europe as well. By 1969, the concept[4] contained a number of propositions presenting certain theoretical and practical problems for members of the international communist movement. Four key issues were associated with it: (1) acknowledgment of the Soviet Union as the *center* of the movement; (2) the legitimacy of *pluralism* within the movement and the question of its unity; (3) the existence of a *model* or "regularities" (*zakonomernosti*) of socialist development; and (4) the question of national versus international interests and, accordingly, of sovereignty.

The first issue which had divided the world communist movement essentially since the death of Stalin was the question of whether or not there should be an acknowledged center of the movement. International conferences of communist parties were invariably divided over this issue, and the 1970s also witnessed serious disputes over this question. An article by Konstantin Katushev, the CPSU secretary responsible for relations with socialist countries, for instance, claimed that although there was no accepted center of the movement, "a special responsibility devolves on the Soviet Union" by virtue of its economic, military and political might (Katushev, 1973a: 5).

This was related to the question of political and economic pluralism. Any suggestion of ideological pluralism within the movement was fiercely resisted by the Soviets and some of their East European allies, especially the Bulgarians. It is notable that the East Germans were also staunch defenders of the bloc solidarity which a rejection of pluralism implied. For them, unity helped to ensure against abandonment by the rest of the bloc in the pursuit of détente and West German credits. Acceptance of pluralism within social systems also implied a multiplicity of views largely incompatible with the communist parties' leading role within these societies.

Perhaps most pressing in the 1970s was the third issue, the question of the universal validity and applicability of the Soviet model of socialism. For years, Soviet theoreticians and leaders had used the writings of Lenin to promote the notion that all societies passing from capitalism to socialism had to do so by way of the dictatorship of the proletariat. Lenin had written in 1917 in "State and Revolution" that the transition from capitalism to communism would undoubtedly yield a variety of political forms, "but the essence will inevitably be the same: *the dictatorship of the proletariat*" (Lenin, 1975: 262, original emphasis). This was the accepted justification for the establishment of the "People's Democracies" in Eastern Europe after the Second World War (see Chapter 2).

The historical experience of dictatorship, however, associated with both fascism and Stalinism in the Western mind, made continued adherence for the West European communist parties difficult. In the Soviet case, many saw the embodiment of dictatorship in the Stalinist tenet that the class struggle (manifested as purges and terror) intensified as socialism grew stronger. In addition to that aspect of socialist internationalism which stressed the need for a dictatorship of the proletariat, there was also that element which held that the success of socialism in the Soviet Union and its status (continually stressed) as the most "developed" socialist society suggested that its experience revealed the general laws of socialist development (see Terry, 1984b: 242–3).

Finally, there was of course that element of socialist internationalism which came to be known in the West after the invasion of Czechoslovakia as the Brezhnev Doctrine, or doctrine of limited sovereignty. CPSU General Secretary Leonid Brezhnev's detailed discussion and endorsement of socialist internationalism as the basis of intersocialist relations three months after the invasion of Czechoslovakia at the Polish United Workers Party Fifth Congress (see Chapter 2) was an important endorsement at the theoretical level of that which had already been confirmed at the level of practice, and served as the basic statement of the official Soviet position on the issue until the early 1980s.

1969–1975: Last gasp for internationalism?

By early 1969, the international environment in many ways had impressed upon Soviet leaders the necessity for a further consolidation of the bloc and the world communist movement. Yet, throughout the first half of the 1970s, the principle of socialist internationalism was resisted by or subjected to criticism from three sides: from Romania and Yugoslavia, the East European renegades; from the independence-minded West European communist parties; and from Soviets within the intellectual establishment.

The March 1969 PCC session reiterated its call made in Bucharest in 1966 for an all-European conference on security and cooperation which would guarantee the post-Second World War order ("Obrashcheniye," 1969). Growing contacts between East and West Europe, as seen in the diplomatic recognition of the Federal Republic of Germany by Romania in early 1967, required a strategy on the part of the Soviets to manage that process and to insure that any West German inroads into Eastern Europe went through Moscow. In the first place, this meant obtaining recognition of the German Democratic Republic, with all that this implied in terms of the German–Polish border and the existing status quo in Europe.

In addition to calling for a European security conference, the PCC also created three bodies designed to increase the Pact's military unity – a Committee of Defense Ministers, a Military Council, and a Technical Council (see Herspring, 1980: 5). The Committee of Defense Ministers and Military Council soon began to meet regularly and to coordinate Warsaw Pact military policy (see also Hutchings, 1983: 69–73). While these changes had all been prepared well in advance, their significance was heightened by the fact that the meeting took place during continuing heavy border clashes between the Soviets and Chinese; the communiqué claimed that the measures adopted would "facilitate a still greater strengthening" of the socialist countries' armed might ("Kommyunike," 1969). The meeting reportedly was delayed for five hours while the Soviets attempted to convince their allies (particularly the Romanians) to acquiesce in a verbal show of support, with the implication of participation by non-Soviet Warsaw Pact troops in action against China. The Romanians refused, relying on the letter of the Warsaw Treaty, which limited their responsibilities to Europe (Hutchings, 1983: 70).

With growing differences within the international communist movement, the document adopted by the Moscow Conference of Communist Parties in June 1969 was only a general endorsement of the Soviet position on the key issues of socialist internationalism ("Zadachi," 1969). Here, on the threshhold of détente, the Soviets succeeded in achieving a fair measure of consensus and unity within the movement, while minimizing the effects of the Warsaw Pact invasion of Czechoslovakia. The conference had been proposed as early as 1963, by Khrushchev, with the aim of asserting Soviet leadership of the bloc (Hutchings, 1983: 56). His ouster forced preparations to lag, while the invasion of Czechoslovakia caused a postponement of the scheduled November 1968 meeting.

When finally convened, the basic document adopted by the 75 parties which attended the conference made repeated references to the "unity of the international communist movement." This phrase was included in its title, and seemed the most the parties could agree on. The Italian Communist Party (PCI), for instance, signed only one part of the four-part document, that dealing with East–West relations. Sixty-six parties did sign the document, but several added their qualifications orally. Among the latter were the Romanians, who took a middle position and did not join several of the West European communist parties, such as the Spanish and Italians, in denouncing the invasion of Czechoslovakia at the conference (Hutchings, 1983: 57). The Yugoslavs did not attend at all, and many of the Asian communist parties followed the lead of the Chinese and stayed away as well (Leonhard, 1979: 124).

The second section contained an analysis of the "world system of socialism," in which the key issues of socialist internationalism and their meaning in the current international situation were defined and elaborated upon. The Soviets gained acquiescence to the assertion that "the defense of socialism is the international duty of communists" ("Zadachi," 1969: 3). This was not a ringing endorsement of socialist internationalism. Strong statements were, however, made in favor of the "regularities" (*zakonomernosti*) of socialist construction: "The successful development of (socialist construction) presupposes a strict observation of the principles of proletarian internationalism" (in effect in favor of Moscow). This was a fairly straightforward endorsement of Soviet positions.

In a premonition of later debates over the concept of contradictions, the document stated that although in socialism "there are no such antagonisms as are peculiar" to capitalism, "divergences" (*raskhozhdeniya*) between socialist countries could indeed arise. These, however, "could and should be successfully resolved on the basis of proletarian internationalism." The document also warned against these divergences breaking the "united front of the socialist countries against imperialism."

In the final section of the document, devoted to the world communist movement, it was acknowledged that there existed no center of the international communist movement. In a significant concession to the independence-minded parties, the participants of the conference declared that the basis of relations between communist parties was "the principles of proletarian internationalism, solidarity and mutual support, respect for independence and equality, [and] non-interference in each others' internal affairs" (p. 4). The document also stated unequivocally that "each party has equal rights." At the same time, however, what has been called the doctrine of dual responsibility was proclaimed. In language essentially similar to the Brezhnev formulation of the previous year, the document stated:

> Each communist party is responsible for its activity before its own working class and people and at the same time – before the international working class. The national and international responsibility of each communist and workers' party are inseparable. (p. 4)

These are but a few of the examples of how the Soviet Union succeeded in gaining qualified endorsement for its interpretation of socialist internationalism at the conference and in the basic document, and it is against this understanding that we may measure subsequent changes in interpretation over the next two decades. It was significant that at every turn in the 1969 document, autonomy-oriented interpretations were counterposed to Soviet understandings of the basic principles guiding intercommunist relations. The 1969 Conference was an important way-station on the road to the independence of what later became known as the Eurocommunist parties. It demonstrated that despite nominal unity, they could promote their own views and even oppose the Soviets.

Following the conference, in October 1969 Willy Brandt became Chancellor of the Federal Republic of Germany and inaugurated a policy based on an acknowledgment of the existence of the GDR and the post-Second World War territorial changes. Known as *Ostpolitik*, it offered West German credits and economic assistance in return for recognition of the FRG by Eastern Europe and the Soviet Union. A Warsaw Pact summit statement issued in December met this development with guarded optimism, no doubt reflecting East German leader Walter Ulbricht's fear of being isolated as the rest of the bloc pursued its own interests ("Vstrecha," 1969).

A meeting of Warsaw Pact foreign ministers in June of 1970 declared their countries' willingness to allow the United States and Canada to join in preparations for the upcoming pan-European conference (Garthoff, 1985: 113). This was followed by the signing of a non-aggression treaty between the Soviet Union and the FRG in August, and a tersely worded statement describing the PCC meeting at which the Soviets and East Europeans debated their policy on *Ostpolitik* and détente ("Zasedaniye," 1970).

Despite East German foot-dragging, relations continued to improve between the FRG and the rest of the bloc. In early December, the FRG and Poland signed a treaty which recognized the border between the GDR and Poland as the permanent German border. This was a long-standing objective of the Poles and the Soviets, inasmuch as it signalled acceptance by the Federal Republic of the territorial changes wrought by the Second World War. The West Germans made ratification of both treaties contingent on the Western powers reaching agreement with the Soviet Union over the status of Berlin; it had been a source of tension in the center of Europe since the end of the Second World War. Berlin technically remained an occupied city, in which the sovereignty of the GDR was not recognized by the West, nor was the West German claim of its half of the city as a constituent part recognized by the East.

With tentative agreements reached between West Germany and the USSR and Poland, the December 1970 PCC meeting in East Berlin issued a declaration which revealed disagreement within the bloc:

> The participants of the conference expressed the determination of the parties and governments of their countries henceforth to realize coordinated joint activities in the international arena in the interests of reliably guaranteeing security in Europe and the whole world. ("Zayavleniye," 1970)

The phrasing in this particular declaration was perhaps the most negative of all PCC documents; note that there was no mention of working for socialism (or even peace and progress), as was sometimes seen in other documents. Such a formula reflected what one Western author has called "thinly veiled" Soviet–East German differences over how best to develop bloc policy *vis-à-vis* West Germany (Hutchings, 1983: 138). Within six months, in May 1971, the East German Leader Walter Ulbricht had been removed, probably under Soviet pressure, to facilitate the process of détente. His interpretation of internationalism required the rest of the bloc to sacrifice its interests in favor of East German interests, resisting Soviet efforts to reach agreement with the West over Berlin, for example. With Ulbricht gone, agreement on the Quadripartite Agreement regulating the status of Berlin was reached and signed in September 1971.

One of the first manifestations of Soviet attempts to rethink socialist internationalism appeared in *Problems of Peace and Socialism* in 1971. Many of the major Soviet specialists on Eastern Europe were present at a symposium devoted to examining the regularities of the world socialist system. The East Europeans were also well represented, and the Czechoslovaks, for example, spoke strongly in favor of socialist internationalism and the defense of "socialist gains," given their experience with precisely that aspect of internationalism in 1968 ("Laws," 1971: 8–9). The Romanians, meanwhile, remained steadfast in their opposition to any application of the general laws of socialism.

The presentations of former Liaison officials Oleg Bogomolov and Georgiy Shakhnazarov were notable for the assertion that not all of the "regularities" of socialist construction which had been confirmed at the domestic level operated at the international level. Bogomolov, by this time director of the IEWSS, came out in favor of the "law of internationalization" as the most fundamental of the "regularities" governing the development of the world socialist system. Somewhat at odds with the prevailing ideological climate of the time, however, he noted that a "regularity" and a "principle" were not quite the same, and suggested that socialist internationalism was better thought of in terms of the latter category. This suggested that internationalism was a principle on which to base relations, rather than a scientifically observable product of those relations (pp. 9–10).

Shakhnazarov, a former Central Committee colleague of Bogomolov in the 1960s who had been sent as a responsible secretary of *Problems of Peace and Socialism*, also distinguished himself. He made a statement at odds with the 1969 Declaration of Communist Parties when he stated that

> seen from the standpoint of the dialectics of the national and international in the socialist world system, the fact that the fundamental interests of the peoples of the socialist countries coincide *did not rule out differences, contradictions, and the like,* over separate points. (p. 35, emphasis added)

The 1969 document, it will be recalled, had admitted only "divergences" between socialist countries and within the movement. Shakhnazarov said that what was important was the approach to solving such clashes of interest, and came out in favor of application of the principle of socialist internationalism with "the utmost patience and concern." Such strong professions of allegiance to internationalism were often a form of camouflage in which the most vocal proponents of a concept were really less than enthusiastic adherents.

The official announcement in 1971 (neither a communiqué nor a declaration) of the first of what were to become a series of meetings between Soviet and East European leaders in the Crimea prominently noted the "close all-around cooperation between (socialist countries) on the basis of the principles of Marxism-Leninism and socialist internationalism" ("Druzheskaya vstrecha," 1971). The Romanians did not attend the meeting, and the entire announcement, in fact, was very much oriented to Soviet needs and interpretations of the overriding foreign-policy concerns of the day. It once again called for a European security conference and for ratification of the agreements between the FRG and the Soviet Union and Poland. This suggested that the rule of consensus by which these documents were composed did indeed constrain the Soviets in some respect.

By contrast, the announcement of the 1972 meeting of socialist countries' leaders in the Crimea was almost devoid of information; beyond listing those who attended, there were really only two short paragraphs of substance, which mentioned only "an exchange of opinions on the course of socialist and communist construction" and discussions on further cooperation ("Druzheskaya vstrecha," 1972). It seemed likely that the Romanians had once again thrown a monkey-wrench into the proceedings, this time by attending. Nicolae Ceausescu prefaced his arrival in the Crimea with a call at a Romanian Communist Party Conference two weeks beforehand for a "better definition of the principles that should govern relations among all socialist countries" (quoted in Hutchings, 1983: 100). It would appear that his refusal to agree on those principles made the publication of a final statement impossible.

No PCC meeting took place in the year between the 1972 and 1973 Crimea meetings, so the announcement of the latter took on added importance as an indicator of the state of affairs in the bloc. In a sign that the Soviet Union attached great importance to ideological unity in the face of improvements in the East–West climate, this announcement of the annual "friendly meeting" included a reference to the "cohesion of the international communist movement on the basis of the principles of Marxism-Leninism and proletarian internationalism" ("Druzheskaya vstrecha," 1973). This was notable as one of the few times that the Romanians allowed the inclusion of proletarian internationalism in a document over which they presumably had some veto-power.

A similar theoretical concession seems to have been made about this time by the Soviets. A surprising statement in favor of a more nuanced understanding of the relations between socialist states was published in November 1973 by Konstantin Katushev, the Central Committee

Secretary responsible for bloc relations. Speaking before a gathering of the Soviet Union's highest scientific bodies, Katushev used the term "contradictions" to refer to what were usually labelled "differences," or, at best, "divergences" (Katushev, 1973b: 3). The rest of Katushev's speech, reprinted in the theoretical journal *Kommunist*, was less notable, but his inclusion of the term seemed to reflect a growing awareness on the part of at least some in the Soviet leadership that their approach to relations with Eastern Europe was in need of flexibility.[5] In Brezhnev's speech before the 24th CPSU Party Congress in 1971, for example, the prevailing line was that only "difficulties" in relations between socialist countries were possible (Brezhnev, 1971: 10).

The April 1974 PCC session was marked by Ceausescu's adamant refusal to endorse measures to reorganize the Warsaw Pact command structure more closely under Soviet aegis, and by a renewal of his call for a rotation of the post of Warsaw Pact commander-in-chief among all seven allies (Hutchings, 1983: 138) (the position was held by a Soviet throughout the history of the Pact). Given that the Romanians were traditionally most opposed to socialist internationalism as a basis of socialist inter-state relations, it was not surprising that this session of the PCC also did not result in a clearer endorsement of the Soviet position than passing mention of "international relations of a new type."

The communiqué issued for this PCC meeting pointed to the "new type of international relations" as an example for other nations to emulate ("Kommyunike," 1974). It also stated that the members of the Warsaw Pact would "strengthen their indestructible friendship in the interests of socialism, progress and peace." Although compared to the statement quoted above from the December 1970 PCC conference this was a glowing endorsement of the Soviet conception of the basis of the Soviet–East European relationship, it still fell far short of a bold statement of willingness on the part of the East Europeans, in fact, to be bound by the strictures of socialist internationalism.

The invasion of Czechoslovakia caused changes not only in certain European communist parties' willingness to acknowledge Soviet leadership of the world communist movement, but also in individual parties' political strategies. The invasion and subsequent criticism by a majority of the European communist parties had the effect of freeing them from the straitjacket of Soviet tutelage. While the needs of participation in electoral systems drove much of the rejection of Soviet-inspired theoretical principles, it is undoubtedly the case that the emergence of Eurocommunism as an independent phenomenon was also the result of massive disillusionment with the Soviet model of socialism. Much as Khrushchev's denunciation of Stalin caused serious disillusionment among Soviets, so the invasion of Czechoslovakia caused many West European communists to see the Soviet Union in a different light.

By the early 1970s, the major European communist parties (the French, Italian, and Spanish) had adopted strategies and programmatic party statements which put them largely at odds with the Soviet conception of the world.[6] The development of autonomous views within the Italian Communist Party began already in 1956, when Palmiro Togliatti suggested in the wake of the invasion of Hungary that the Soviet model should not be mandatory for all communist parties. The invasion of Czechoslovakia caused outspoken criticism on behalf of the PCI by Luigi Longo, who had succeeded Togliatti as Secretary General. Finally, with the development of the "historic compromise" between 1973 and 1975, the PCI under Enrico Berlinguer proposed a strategy to gain widespread support for social change by promoting a broad alliance with all political forces (Leonhard, 1979: 168–79).

In 1973, the Spanish Communist Party denied the necessity for the dictatorship of the proletariat after the revolution, signalling rejection of a fundamental principle of Marxism-Leninism and even more outspoken criticism to come (Leonhard, 1979: 231–2). Meanwhile, the French Communists' refusal to explicitly condemn the invasion of Czechoslovakia betrayed an inability to fully and finally break with the Soviets, but an agreement with the Socialists on a program of government in June 1972 led to a certain degree of electoral success (Leonhard, 1979: 194–207). But the PCF continued to vacillate, officially rejecting the dictatorship of the proletariat at its 22nd Party Congress in 1976, while joining a Soviet-led conference of European communist parties in April of 1980 (Hutchings, 1983: 215).

The third direction from which the prevailing understandings of bloc relations were subjected to attack was, of course, the Soviet. A book on *Socialism and International Relations* published in Moscow in late 1975 demonstrated continuing disagreements among Soviet theoreticians concerning the principles on which bloc relations would be based. This book was rather schizophrenic in that the authors included well-known conservatives as well as reformers; each more often than not seemed to be criticizing views found in the neighboring chapter. Anatoliy Butenko and Richard Kosolapov, later to clash over the notion of contradictions in socialism (see Chapter 5), co-authored the first chapter and were both listed among the editors of the volume. Other notable figures included Vadim Pechenev, later an advisor to Konstantin Chernenko; Aleksandr Dashichev, who would write policy-papers on Soviet policy toward West Germany for Gorbachev; and Yuriy Novopashin, who would become one of the leading critics of socialist internationalism in the early 1980s. In addition, a very unorthodox article was written by Aleksandr Bovin, who by this time had left the Central Committee to become a columnist for the Government newspaper *Izvestiya*. There, he worked with Lev Tolkunov, the former first deputy chief of the Liaison Department who had become editor of *Izvestiya* in 1965 (see Appendix). Bovin's article was the most noteworthy, not least because he had recently left (or been removed from) his position as head of the consultants' group in the Liaison Department. Much of Bovin's article was taken from an earlier pamphlet on internationalism, written soon after the ouster of Khrushchev, while he was still a Central Committee official (see Chapter 2). Bovin in fact may have written this chapter while still in the Central Committee[7] and, if so, it suggests just how long it took to rid the Central Committee of reformers.

In his 1975 work, Bovin was even more outspoken than previously. Speaking of contradictions, Bovin posed the following questions and answers:

> Is it really necessary to pass through the purgatory of contradictions in order to acknowledge the variety of paths to socialism and of forms of socialist society; is it really necessary to pass through a struggle of opinions in order to create on a voluntary basis firm and stable ties between socialist states? Arguing abstractly and theoretically, it is possible to answer: No, it is not necessary. But the historical experience, the practice of relations between the countries of socialism attests otherwise. The principles of intergovernmental ties in the world system of socialism are established in the course of utilizing the advantages of socialism, *but also in the struggle with elements of nationalism and great-power chauvinism*, that is, in the process of overcoming contradictions, brought into play by these elements. (Bovin, 1975: 255–256, emphasis added)

This was a surprising quote to encounter in the mid-1970s. He does not qualify the statement in any way to suggest that he had any country other than the Soviet Union – a great power – in mind. As far as the possibility of antagonistic contradictions was concerned, he maintained they were an "anomaly" of inter-socialism relations, and could only occur due to subjective factors (that is, through the activities of individuals or groups). At the same time, he urged compromise in the solution of non-antagonistic contradictions between socialist countries; while compromises were a "temporary, palliative" solution, they allowed political actors "to win time so that deeper factors can create a basis for the resolution of contradictions not only on a political, but also on a solid social-economic basis" (p. 254). In other words, he was suggesting that the Soviet Union find solutions other than the "harmonious combination" of national and international interests, the euphemism for subordination of the former to the latter. More to the point, he was urging that the Soviet Union develop a more organic relationship with Eastern Europe in which each side's interests were not guaranteed primarily by "political factors."

As mentioned above, this book was inherently contradictory in that it contained chapters by authors of both conservative and reformist persuasions. For instance, one author criticized those who stressed "common-democratic" principles such as sovereignty, stating that this minimized the role of socialist internationalism (Yakimovich, 1975: 234–5). Such a criticism seemed aimed at the likes of Novopashin, who in his contribution to the book pointed to the "complete independence and initiative in carrying out national policy" by socialist states as one of the basic principles of relations between them (Novopashin, 1975: 163). Meanwhile, the contribution by Butenko and Kosolapov indicated that the latter had influenced the book to some extent, since this chapter lacked much of the sharp reformist language usually associated with Butenko's writings.

1975–1980: A plethora of internationalisms

As usual, these differences of opinion among Soviet theoreticians were a microcosm of such views within the world communist movement as a whole. This was achingly apparent in the negotiations in the run-up to the 1976 Berlin Conference of European Communist Parties. In the course of between twelve (Leonhard, 1979: 142–4) and sixteen (MacGregor, 1978: 339) meetings between October 1974 and June 1976, the Eurocommunists, joined by the Yugoslavs and Romanians, steadfastly defended inclusion of autonomist interpretations of fundamental principles in drafts of the conference document.

The Soviets, for their part, continued to put forward their views of the proper revolutionary strategy. The seventieth anniversary of Lenin's pamphlet, "Two Tactics of Social-Democracy in the Democratic Revolution," conveniently came in mid-1975, and the Soviets used the occasion to remind the world communist movement of the "universal" meaning of Lenin's conclusions. An article by the editor-in-chief of *Problems of Peace and Socialism*, Konstantin Zarodov, was clearly aimed at two audiences: the European communist parties which did not follow the Soviet lead, and the Portuguese communists, who did.

In April 1974, the overthrow by the military of the successors to the Portuguese dictator Salazar initially indicated a rightist trend in Portugal, but this trend was arrested by the resignation of General Antonio de Spinola, and his replacement by a regime of left-leaning military officers and communists. Portugal was drifting leftward (one result was the decision to shed its remaining colonies, including Angola and Mozambique), and had already experienced an attempted right-wing coup in March 1975. Elections in April gave the Socialists and Popular Democrats 64.2 percent of the vote, while the Communists and their allies received 17.5 percent. (The Christian Democrats were barred from the election, and smaller leftist parties split the rest) (Szulc, 1975: 16). Continued tension between the unorganized Socialists, the Communists, and rightist forces over the formation of a government cabinet created a fluid and chaotic situation in July and August. This prompted the Communist leader, Alvaro Cunhal, to attempt to swing the armed forces behind him in early August by engineering the arrest of a commander of the elite forces. Adroit political maneuvering by the left-leaning chief of the security forces, Ortelo de Carvalho, led to Cunhal's humiliation (see Szulc, 1975: 51–2).

This obviously confused situation prompted Zarodov to turn to Lenin's teaching on the "growing over" of the bourgeois-democratic revolution into the socialist, as in Russia in 1905. As seen in the previous chapter, this was the Soviets' preferred interpretation of the rise of socialist regimes in Eastern Europe after the Second World War, and now was being used to urge a similar expansion of the revolution. Zarodov wrote that "demands of a common-democratic character ... mobilize the masses, drawing them into joint struggle with the proletariat against the dominance of the exploiters," noting that "the battle for democracy becomes a prologue of the socialist revolution" (Zarodov, 1975: 2). In other words, "common-democratic" tasks were somehow of a lower order than socialist. By extension, this meant that common-democratic principles should be subordinate to internationalist principles in international relations.

Zarodov's article was also notable for its emphasis on the dictatorship of the proletariat and criticism of "modern opportunists" and "conciliators" who wanted to dissolve Marxist-Leninist parties into "any ideologically amorphous organization" which declared "unity for the sake of unity" (p. 3). Such a phrase seemed aimed at communist parties such as the Italian and Spanish, which by this time were exploring new avenues of cooperation with other leftist parties. (And whose leaders had also attempted to dissuade Cunhal from following his revolutionary line; see Szulc, 1975: 48.) The Eurocommunists responded with their own protests and criticisms of Zarodov's views, prompting Brezhnev to meet with him in a demonstrative show of support in September (Valenta, 1980: 110).

Such strong statements in favor of more aggressive tactics on behalf of communist parties were also striking in the wake of the Conference on Security and Cooperation in Europe (CSCE) and the signing of the Helsinki Final Act the previous summer. This illustrated how East and West adhered to different conceptions of détente, which contributed in large measure to its decline in the late 1970s.

Repeated calls for a European security conference, combined with the bloc's offer in 1970 to include Canada and the United States, led to North Atlantic Treaty Organization acceptance of such a conference, in conjunction with negotiations on conventional force reductions in Europe which NATO had been urging since 1968. The CSCE was seen by the Soviets as an important step in gaining multilateral endorsement of the post-Second World War status quo, and managing the development of détente. For the Soviets, the Helsinki Final Act codified the status quo in Europe by obligating the signatories to respect the sovereignty and territorial integrity of other countries, and by obtaining pledges of non-interference in internal affairs and supporting the fulfillment of international responsibilities (Garthoff, 1985: 474). The Final Act also promoted economic and cultural interaction, promoting détente in general and, specifically, Soviet attempts to obtain the Western credits necessary to avoid economic reform.

The Helsinki process also, however, had its drawbacks for the Soviets; namely, it required them to put their signature to many Western understandings of such concepts as freedom of travel, information and speech which could later be used against them, both at home and against the East European regimes. The principle of non-interference in internal affairs, of course, was meant to deflect Western criticism in these areas, but the fact that the Warsaw Pact states had signed the Final Act certainly opened them to criticism from within. Just as importantly, it provided a forum for the East European states to make known their entry onto the world stage, as they became political actors in their own right and not merely satellite appendages of the Soviet Union.

The growing independence of the Eurocommunist parties was underscored in speeches by French and Italian leaders at the 25th CPSU Party Congress in February of 1976. At the same forum at which Brezhnev gave a spirited defense of internationalism and optimistic appraisal of world socialism, Enrico Berlinguer spoke only of "internationalism," neither proletarian nor socialist (Berlinguer, 1976: 8). Speaking generally in favor of Soviet foreign policy, Berlinguer even more strongly came out for "full independence of any country," and distinguished the Italian vision of socialism as one in which "all individual and collective freedoms" would be guaranteed (p. 9). PCF Politburo member Gaston Plissonier, meanwhile, spoke to the Soviets of his party's congress earlier that month, which had endorsed a broad union of leftist forces and rejected the dictatorship of the proletariat. He did, however, endorse proletarian internationalism, reflecting the mixed feelings of the PCF on complete dissociation from Soviet positions (Plissonier, 1976).

Brezhnev's remarks at the congress on the course of relations between socialist countries was an even more glowing characterization than he had given in 1971. He failed to mention even the possibility of divergences, much less serious differences or contradictions between socialist countries (Brezhnev, 1976b: 8–15). The general secretary did, however, make a special point of putting "special emphasis" on proletarian internationalism against some in the world communist movement (the Eurocommunists) who "openly" suggested renouncing it (p. 37).

Then, two weeks after the Soviet congress, Mikhail Suslov responded to such assertions of independence with a scathing (if veiled) attack on the Eurocommunists. In a speech to the yearly general meeting of the Soviet Academy of Sciences, he lashed out at the "opponents of Marxism ... who have begun more often to dress themselves in Marxist clothing," who misinterpreted Marxism-Leninism and attempted to rob it of its "revolutionary essence" (Suslov, 1976). The watchdog of Soviet ideology was unequivocal in his praise for proletarian internationalism as the "holy of holies," and the "most valuable achievement and inexhaustible source" of the world communist movement. In order to make it clear who was being referred to, the Academy of Sciences awarded the Gold Karl Marx award posthumously to Jacques Duclos, the French Stalinist party leader who had died the previous year. A French academic was awarded another medal at the end of the ceremony. The lavishing of such honors was obviously meant to indicate the real target of Suslov's remarks.

In the face of Eurocommunist opposition, however, the document adopted at the 1976 Berlin Conference of European Communist Parties in June contained no reference either to proletarian or socialist internationalism, stating only that the participants would "develop their international comradely voluntary cooperation and solidarity on the basis of the great ideas of Marx, Engels and Lenin in strict observance of the equality and sovereign independence of each party" ("Za mir," 1976). Such a statement represented a significant concession by the Soviets to the Eurocommunist parties compared to the 1969 conference document. It included phrases meant to mollify both sides – the "great ideas" (not principles) of Marxism's founding fathers for the Soviets and their allies, "equality and sovereign independence" for the Eurocommunists, Yugoslavs, and Romanians.

During the conference, each party attempted to clarify its position on internationalism in the speeches of the heads of delegations. From the Soviet and conservative East European point of view, the important aspect of the document's treatment of internationalism was that it was said to be "solidarity" based on Marxism-Leninism. The Bulgarian leader Todor Zhivkov, for example, stated: "Our sacred duty is to preserve the great heritage of Marx, Engels and Lenin, enriched by the theory and practice of revolutionary struggle and the construction of socialism . . ." He was, in fact, more vocal than the Soviets in his denunciation of left and right revisionism, and in his support for the "general laws" of socialist development and the dual responsibility of communist parties before their own people and before the rest of the movement (Zhivkov, 1976).

For the Eurocommunists, Romanians, and Yugoslavs, on the other hand, the critical characterization of internationalism contained in the conference document was "international comradely voluntary cooperation . . . in strict observance of the equality and sovereign independence of each party."

Romania's Nicolae Ceausescu expressed the view of many other conference participants when he spoke of a solidarity based on something other than Marxism-Leninism:

> It is possible to understand the concept of international solidarity only in an organic connection with the struggle in defense of the interests of the working class of each country, of the national interests of each people, [and] of the independence and sovereignty of each nation. (Ceausescu, 1976)

The "international duty" of Romania's communists, meanwhile, consisted only in "widely developing cooperation with the socialist countries." Such "wide" cooperation was not directed primarily at the rest of the bloc; Romania's trade with the West grew steadily during this period, and Romanian theorists took every opportunity to stress the independence of individual communist parties. What is more, Romania used the "interested member" principle to opt out of many CMEA development schemes since the early 1960s (see Zimmerman, 1984: 142).

The speech by CPSU General Secretary Brezhnev was rather less strident than those by delegates loyal to the Soviet position. He chided those who suggested that proletarian internationalism was "outmoded," or that calls to strengthen internationalist ties meant re-creation of an organized center (Brezhnev, 1976a). He characterized proletarian internationalism as "the solidarity of the working class, of communists of all countries in the struggle for common goals, their solidarity in the struggle of the peoples for national liberation and social progress, [and] voluntary cooperation of the fraternal parties with strict observance of the equality and independence of each" (Brezhnev, 1976a: 2). This obviously watered-down version of internationalism failed to include the "dual responsibility" and "mutual assistance" which had been considered mandatory in earlier incarnations. With such an approach, Brezhnev attempted to assume a middle-of-the-road posture in the context of the world communist movement. Much as the Yugoslavs two decades before, however, many of the European communist parties would not adhere to Soviet interpretations of the principles guiding relations between communists.

Thus, no single understanding of the concept of internationalism prevailed at the conference. Full, uncensored speeches of those delegates who did not share the loyalist position were published only by the East Germans, as hosts of the conference; the Soviets printed a disingenuous disclaimer in *Pravda* that the speeches were published in a "shortened" form. The Yugoslavians later protested that the proceedings and outcome of the conference had been misrepresented by the Soviets, who claimed more consensus than had actually been reached (Hutchings, 1983: 212). The fact that the document was issued without the signatures of the participating delegations further emphasized the differences within the movement.

In the aftermath of the conference, various interpretations of internationalism surfaced in the movement's theoretical journals. The Italian Communist Party reiterated its position on internationalism shortly after the conference in *World Marxist Review*, stating: "With the new scope of the [communist] movement developing in the world, we believe that the definition of internationalism as 'proletarian' has become restrictive and does not accord with the new social reality" (Rubbi, 1977: 127). Explaining the absence of proletarian internationalism from the document, Rubbi, the PCI secretary for foreign relations, stated that "we rose above this formula, because, objectively, it would have restricted the [document's] unitarian appeal." The PCI's assertion of a "new internationalism" within the world communist movement was obviously designed to expand its electoral base beyond the traditional sources of support, in line with the "historic compromise."

What is more, the new internationalism also threatened the model of socialism which had developed in the Soviet Union and Eastern Europe: "We are working on the premise that the development of socialism in the world is a process that will proceed in different forms and will have a different content . . ." (Rubbi, 1977: 128). And, in a direct challenge to growing Soviet demands for heightened orthodoxy within the bloc and the movement more generally, he stated that "social, political, cultural and ideological pluralism" (p. 129) would be guaranteed in any West European form of socialism.

Eurocommunism posed a threat not only to Soviet leadership of the international communist movement, but also to the East European states. The danger of Eurocommunism for the Soviets was that it offered an alternative model, both in how to attain state power, and in how to build a socialist society. Both threatened Soviet legitimacy domestically, and more broadly within the bloc, by questioning the Soviet monopoly on truth. The new internationalism, meanwhile, threatened the East European regimes for the same reasons, while at the same time challenging their legitimacy by questioning the necessity, for example, of the dictatorship of the proletariat. As we saw in the previous chapter, "People's Democracy" was said to be in essence a form of the dictatorship of the proletariat, in which the construction of socialism closely followed the Soviet pattern. Challenging adherence to either of these notions struck to the very heart of the theory on which these regimes historically had attempted to base their legitimacy.

To underscore orthodox opposition to the new internationalism, Rubbi's article was preceded by a piece condemning "ideological and political pluralism" by the Bulgarian writer Asen Kozharov, who had already published a strident, book-length criticism of pluralism at the time of the Berlin conference (Kozharov, 1976). Ostensibly aimed at "bourgeois pluralism," the article reserved its harshest criticism for those who came out in favor of a multiplicity of models of Marxism and socialism: "This is not substantiated by experience, which shows that for all the different roads to socialism, and all the different forms of the new society, the essence of socialism remains the same" (Kozharov, 1977: 116). This statement clearly contradicted the new internationalist position because it asserted that the "essence" or "content" of socialism could not be different from the "general laws of socialist development." Thus, Kozharov's article also asserted the universality of the dictatorship of the proletariat, said by Lenin to be the essence of the socialist revolution.

The Italians, however, did not relent theoretically. In early 1977 they also called for a serious study of contradictions in socialism, attacking the Soviet refusal to do so through criticism of the Soviet scholar Mikhail Iovchuk (Spriano, 1977: 51). Gian Carlo Spriano, the second-ranking Italian communist leader, urged delving into the contradiction between production forces and "the statized and bureaucratic organization of the economy." Using harsh language, he also suggested that dissent in the Soviet Union was a genuine contradiction rather than manifestations of "immature" ideological viewpoints, as Iovchuk had argued in *Voprosy Filosofii*. Even in respect to real "ideological infection," then, the Eurocommunists could be a threat to Soviet and East European societies.

The spring of 1977 saw a certain deepening of the Eurocommunist phenomenon in two respects. First was the March "Eurocommunist summit" of French, Italian, and Spanish leaders in Madrid, at which they reiterated their determination to build socialist societies which differed fundamentally from the Soviet. They refrained from direct criticism of the Soviet Union and Eastern Europe, however (Willenz, 1980: 254).

The second aspect which drew a significant amount of attention from the Soviets was perhaps the most well-argued theoretical elaboration of Eurocommunism, Santiago Carillo's *Eurocommunism and the State*. Appearing in April of 1977, this book by the PCE Secretary General provided a theoretical basis for the refutation of much of what the Spanish had already rejected. Carillo claimed that the invasion of Czechoslovakia was "the straw that broke the camel's back and led our parties to say: 'No.' That kind of internationalism had come to an end as far as we were concerned" (p. 132).

Most bitingly, he denied that a "genuine workers' democracy" had been built in the Soviet Union (Carillo, 1977: 157). He characterized the

Soviet state as "bureaucratized" and relatively free to act, coming close to an autonomous understanding of the state (p. 164). In addition, Carillo captured one of the core problems of the Soviet system, namely, the gap between proclaimed ideology and reality (p. 160). In this he came very close to the criticisms of some East European dissidents who saw alienation as one of the defining features of Soviet-style socialism. The support of the Eurocommunists for democratic change in Eastern Europe and for fledgling dissident movements, such as Charter 77 in Czechoslovakia, was perhaps the most alarming element of the challenge which development of a distinct brand of Marxism posed to the Soviets (see Valenta, 1978).

The Soviets responded quickly to Carillo's book with an article in mid-1977 directed specifically at the Spanish communist leader. Appearing as an unsigned editorial in the magazine *New Times*, the article echoed many of the same themes voiced by Suslov and Brezhnev the year before. It attempted to reject the very notion of "Eurocommunism" by suggesting that there could only be one "true, scientific communism," as Suslov had said ("Contrary," 1977: 10). It also accused Carillo of being a Marxist who objectively served the interests of imperialism which, in an echo of Brezhnev's speech at the Berlin conference, "actively co-ordinates" its "anti-Soviet activities" ("Contrary," p. 13).

Amidst this increasing debate within the movement following the Berlin conference, various party secretaries (usually for ideology or international relations) of the five East European countries loyal to the Soviet interpretation of socialist internationalism all stated their countries' allegiance. These displays of fealty more often than not also contained harsh attacks on the Eurocommunist position, betraying East European elites' fear that "new internationalism" and the political pluralism it implied threatened their own positions.

Along with Bulgarian and East German attacks on the Eurocommunist position (see Yotov, 1978, and Axen, 1977), the Czechoslovak press carried the most strident criticisms of new internationalism (see, for example, Kudrna, 1977). A somewhat pathetic appeal for international support was made by the Czechoslovak Communist Party (CPCz) ideology secretary, Vasil Bil'ak, in 1977:

> The present situation in our country and the problems with which we are struggling in the building of our socialist society, however, have at the same time caused an urgent need for international support of the CPCz on the part of other sectors of the revolutionary workers' movement ... Therefore, we would appreciate it if the fraternal

parties in capitalist countries intensify their struggle against such imperialist propaganda [directed against Czechoslovakia] ... (Bil'ak, 1977: 21)

Polish and Hungarian statements from this period were notably less critical of the Eurocommunist position, (see, for instance, Vass, 1978), while the Romanians heartily endorsed the Eurocommunist new internationalism. The Hungarians, in fact, not only refrained from overly harsh condemnation of new internationalism but maintained rather warm relations with the West European communist parties, hosting visits by the PCI general secretary and other leading figures (see Hutchings, 1983: 214, and Pajetta, 1980).

The PCC and internationalism

Disintegration of the unity of the world communist movement and failure to secure backing for its position on socialist internationalism at Berlin, it seems, caused the Soviet Union to turn inward and seek compliance within the Warsaw Pact.

As mentioned above, socialist internationalism did not appear in any Warsaw Pact PCC document adopted between 1969 and 1980. Internationalism did, however, appear twice in descriptions of bloc "summits," the meetings between the leaders of socialist countries in the Crimea in the early 1970s.

A careful reading, however, shows that internationalism in one form or another was not completely absent from later PCC documents. After 1976, the Soviets tended to succeed in gaining acceptance of certain phrases which were used to endorse their understanding of socialist internationalism. Documents before 1976 were much more circumspect. This suggests that after the Berlin conference, in the context of a worsening international situation, the need for unity within the bloc and clear expressions of loyalty to internationalism arose once more. But the Soviet inability to achieve the Eurocommunists' clear endorsement of the principle further complicated efforts to enforce allegiance to the principle closer to home.

The document adopted at the Berlin conference, as mentioned above, contained a formulation of internationalism vague enough to be acceptable to all. Each party was therefore free to interpret the meaning of internationalism as it wished. With such different understandings on either side of the issue, it is interesting to note that the declaration of the November 1976 PCC session in Bucharest, which was preceded by three days of negotiations between Brezhnev and

Ceausescu to work out acceptable compromises (Hutchings, 1983: 103–4), contained a rather favorable characterization of the basis of bloc relations. In a special section devoted to relations between the socialist countries, it stated that they would

> continually strengthen cooperation between them on the basis of the principles of Marxism-Leninism and international solidarity, respect for the equality and sovereignty of each state, non-interference in internal affairs, [and] comradely mutual aid. ("Za novyye," 1976: sec. IV)

This was very close to the formulation of internationalism reached at the Berlin conference earlier in the year, and seemed to represent a concession on the part of the Romanians in terms of including a description of the basis of inter-socialist relations as the "principles of Marxism-Leninism," a formulation not included at Berlin that summer. The phrase "comradely mutual aid," too, was often taken as a euphemism for the Brezhnev Doctrine. The remaining descriptions were all considered less offensive terms.

If the 1969 Bucharest PCC meeting witnessed creation of a number of organs to increase military cooperation within the Pact, the 1976 Bucharest meeting saw a similar effort in the political realm. The communiqué for the meeting stated that in order to "perfect the mechanism of political cooperation," the PCC had decided to create a Committee of Foreign Ministers and a unified secretariat ("Kommyunike," 1976). As mentioned above, Brezhnev negotiated for three days before the meeting with Ceausescu, and it seemed likely that one area of discord was the creation of these political bodies. Another example of how the 1976 declaration was toned down to make it more palatable to the Romanians was that a 1974 reference to the socialist states as being true to their "international duty" was dropped (see "Kommyunike," 1974: 2, and "Za novyye," 1976: 2).

Disagreements also surfaced at the 1978 PCC meeting in Moscow. Soviet relations with China after the death of Mao had not improved, and the Soviets hoped to arrange for its condemnation by the Warsaw Pact. In addition, strains were also developing within the alliance over the issues of the burden of aid to Vietnam, increased defense spending, and heightened cooperation within the Pact itself (Herspring, 1980: 13). Both the 1976 and 1978 declarations, in fact, expressed the intent of the socialist countries to "develop all-round cooperation and comradely interaction with the young states of socialist orientation," the first time such a reference had been included in PCC documents ("Kommyunike," 1976, and 1978). Significantly, the 1976 statement to this effect was followed by a sentence which noted the multiplicity of forms for the "new society," a phrase presumably included at the behest of the Romanians. In any case, such a statement could have been written much more strongly, for instance as in the reference to "international duty" included in the 1974 communiqué.

As in earlier documents, these differences were reflected in the communiqué describing the meeting. Whereas the communiqué following the 1976 meeting had described it positively, as proceeding in "full mutual understanding, fraternal friendship and close cooperation" ("Kommyunike," 1976) (most likely reflecting the three days of negotiation beforehand), the 1978 version could say only that it took place in "fraternal friendship and comradely cooperation" ("Kommyunike," 1978). In other words, "full mutual understanding" (or any other kind) had not been reached. That this was certainly true was seen by Ceausescu's blunt expressions of dissatisfaction upon his return to Bucharest. Ceausescu revealed that one of the Soviet Union's demands at the meeting had been for an increase in defense spending on the part of its allies, in order to respond to the NATO decision in May to increase defense spending by 3 percent per year (see Hutchings, 1983: 107; Herspring, 1980: 10).

There were other signs that the meeting had not succeeded (from the Soviet point of view) in reaching the desired consensus. One indication was patently obvious: Ceausescu's refusal to join the rest of the bloc and sign a declaration on the Middle East condemning the Camp David accords. The general PCC declaration adopted at the session, which in 1976 had listed Marxism-Leninism and "international solidarity" as the first two elements of inter-socialist relations, in 1978 dropped international solidarity to *eighth* (and last) in a list of principles on which relations were said to be based ("Deklaratsiya," 1978).

The Romanian disinclination to participate in Soviet-sponsored gatherings extended to the academic field as well. They rarely attended international gatherings of socialist scholars held in Bogomolov's Institute of the Economics of the World Socialist System, for example. At one such conference in October 1978 Butenko and Novopashin co-authored the speech which served as the basis for discussion, and came under criticism both from conservative East Europeans and their fellow Soviets. The two IEWSS scholars clearly set themselves apart, for instance, from "other authors" who suggested that "the general law of drawing together (*sblizheniye*) is an all-encompassing complex law, including other patterns (such as the 'dawn of nations' or the 'strengthening of sovereignty')" (Butenko, 1979b). The deputy director of the IEWSS, Il'ya Dudinskiy, said he found this "hard to agree with," but it is likely that the Romanians would have hastened to give support to such a view. "Drawing together" was the term used (along with the slightly less offensive "socialist economic integration") by the Soviets to urge closer cooperation among the CMEA countries, usually to the detriment of the East Europeans. Brezhnev had declared at the 25th CPSU Party Congress that drawing together was an "objective law" (Brezhnev, 1976b: 9), which did not prevent the East Europeans from seeing it mainly as an attempt to bind their economies more tightly to the Soviet. Here, Butenko and Novopashin were suggesting that neither the "dawn of nations" (that is, national features) nor sovereignty should be subordinated to the process of drawing together. Statements such as these indicated that some Soviet scholars were making an attempt to break out of the straitjacket of conformist thinking imposed by the stagnation of the Brezhnev period.

The practical expression of internationalism, of course, is often taken to be armed intervention on behalf of a socialist state perceived to be in danger of collapse. The December 1979 invasion of Afghanistan may or may not technically have been a manifestation of socialist internationalism, since the young Afghan regime could hardly have been called "socialist." The overwhelming perception, however, is that the invasion was yet another manifestation of Soviet-style internationalism (see Mitchell, 1982), and as such it was roundly condemned by the Italian, Spanish, Yugoslav and Romanian parties, among others. In addition, some Soviet authors also held that the invasion was a demonstration of a now-condemned internationalism (Ambartsumov, 1989, and Sheynis, 1989). In the next chapter we examine the theoretical re-assessment of socialist internationalism which took place in the 1980s in the context of a need to re-examine the objectives of Soviet foreign policy.

Conclusions

Examination of the use of the concept of socialist internationalism in the wake of the invasion of Czechoslovakia reveals an interesting pattern.

First, we see that socialist internationalism took on a distinctly ritualistic or symbolic character in this period. After its endorsement as the justification for the invasion of Czechoslovakia, it was accepted in 1969 as the principle governing relations within that part of the international communist movement which took its lead from the Soviet Union. At the same time, it became a term laden with meaning, most of it negative.

The aspect of socialist internationalism stressed most often in this period, as may be expected given the centrifugal tendencies unleashed in the bloc by détente, was the need for coordination of foreign policies. This may be seen as a use of a theoretical concept to rationalize a policy: the coordination of bloc policy was undertaken not primarily out of conviction, but rather for reasons of power politics. The East European states followed policies, such as the orientation of trade toward the Soviet Union rather than the West, which appeared to contradict their best interests.

Soviet interest in promoting the acceptance of socialist internationalism was threefold. In the first place, there was the desire to maintain ideological uniformity in the interests of protecting the bloc (and hence the Soviet position within it) from outside influence. Secondly, there was the need to present the image of a united front of socialist states which supported the political initiatives and international activity of the Soviet Union. From the Soviet point of view, the border clashes with China in 1969 had also underscored the need for "unshakeable unity" with its allies.

A third motivation for Soviet insistence on East European allegiance to socialist internationalism was the legitimating aspect of the concept. Leadership of the bloc and the world communist movement conferred significant prestige, both historically and in the context of superpower competition.

It is worth pointing out as well that the ideology of internationalism provided a coping mechanism for exactly those kinds of hardships which the population of the lesser superpower in global competition would experience. In other words, the Soviet Union's drive for parity with the United States necessitated the creation of a mighty military-industrial complex, diverting significant resources from other sectors of the economy which could be used to satisfy the needs of Soviet consumers. One way to address discontent with the continuing lack of consumer goods was to portray the Soviet Union as "selflessly" fulfilling its "internationalist duty," similar to how promises of a brighter communist future were used throughout Soviet history in attempts to justify shortcomings and inadequacies in the present. That is, knowing that the revolution was being advanced abroad was meant to help people cope with the miserableness of their existence at home, brought on by "selfless" assistance or the neglect of consumer industries for the sake of investment in military industries. "Imperialist subversion," meanwhile, was a constant theme which also demanded unity of the bloc and justified economic hardship at home, oftentimes through a search for scapegoats, as in the Stalin period. These should be seen as sociological aspects of the Soviet ideology of internationalism (see the discussion of sociological theories of ideology in Geertz, 1973: 204-5).

Seeking compliance with the principle within the bloc, however, the Soviets ran into a number of difficulties. The most obvious was the refusal of the Romanians to acknowledge the validity of socialist internationalism in Warsaw Pact documents. In the case of PCC documents, the Romanians could effectively foreclose any hope the Soviets may have had in securing Pact recognition of the principle.

At the same time, other East European states may have had an interest in refusing to endorse socialist internationalism in the framework of the Warsaw Pact against the background of a deteriorating international environment. In this case, it may be appropriate to see the Romanians as the "lightning rod" of the bloc, taking positions unpopular with the Soviets which other states shared but found politically impossible to express openly. The Hungarians, for example, were not ardent proponents of the concept during the 1980-1 Polish crisis (Volgyes, 1986: 327). Later in the 1980s, they implicitly challenged socialist internationalism and Soviet leadership of the bloc by asserting the special role of "small states" in the maintenance of inter-European détente.

As far as the East European stake in socialist internationalism is concerned, we should distinguish between the positions of those who vigorously supported it and those who just as vociferously rejected it. Among the former were all of the Soviet Union's Warsaw Pact allies, with the exception of Romania. Opponents of the concept were the Romanians, Yugoslavs, and Albanians. The West European communist parties were divided, with the French decidedly more willing to declare allegiance to the Soviets by supporting proletarian internationalism on occasion.

Why would East European states have been loyal to a concept which supposedly limited their sovereignty, among other unpalatable aspects? In the first place, we should understand that after 1969 among the most vocal adherents of internationalism was a narrow circle of Czechoslovak elites; in other words, precisely those who had been installed as a result of adherence to the principle and thus had the most to lose should it be abandoned. The same applied, if to a lesser degree, to the other East European regimes, inasmuch as socialist internationalism served to legitimate their own domestic systems of rule in the face of the Eurocommunist challenge.

As mentioned above, the East Germans were especially interested in maintaining bloc unity, since the GDR would be isolated and exposed as illegitimate if the rest of the bloc rushed to embrace détente and the benefits of economic relations with West Germany. During the 1960s, the GDR enjoyed a veto over any East European attempt to establish relations with the FRG, until the defection by Romania in February 1967. Thus, East European states at times had their own interests to guarantee in promoting socialist internationalism.

Secondly, professions of loyalty to the concept may also have been part of a broader competition for Soviet favors. In other words, by being seen as the favorite junior ally, an East European state could secure for itself a privileged position within the bloc. Bulgaria was the most vocal supporter of the Soviet interpretation of socialist internationalism, especially against the challenges of the Eurocommunists.

We should also keep in mind that détente and the Helsinki process "marked the diplomatic debut of the East European socialist states as actors, albeit with limited roles, on the international stage" (Hutchings, 1983: 97). For Marxist-Leninist elites and the bureaucracies on which they relied, socialist internationalism offered an avenue for the legitimation of national identities distinct from their pre-war incarnations.

Finally, the five East European states ostensibly loyal to the principle were not bashful in declaring their allegiance for domestic audiences. The motivations at work here included the rationalization of alliance with the Soviet Union to a populace which generally harbored little love for the Soviets; or between historical enemies such as Hungary and Romania, or East Germany, Poland, and Czechoslovakia.

By the late 1970s, however, the international environment which had earlier served to reinforce East European interests in adhering to socialist internationalism had changed. Détente was beginning to unravel as a result of mutual superpower misunderstanding as to the meaning of "peaceful coexistence." The addition of two less-developed members to CMEA (Cuba and Vietnam) also disinclined the East Europeans to voice support for an internationalism which could be used to garner their cooperation in sharing the burden of development aid to those countries.

At the same time, a downturn in US–Soviet relations adversely affected the East European economies. Renewed tension led to further demands on the part of the Soviets for increased military spending in the context of Warsaw Pact obligations. Thus, for all these reasons the

East Europeans had an interest in not professing loyalty to socialist internationalism at multilateral forums. The East European interest in maintaining détente despite frosty US–Soviet relations led in the early 1980s to repeated assertions by the Hungarians and East Germans that smaller states had a "special responsibility" to continue the process (see next chapter). This was firmly denied by Soviet conservatives, who perceived this as disintegration of the supposed unity which they had worked for so long to guarantee.

The fact that the East Europeans at times vociferously defended internationalism does not contradict the observation that they tended to reject the concept at international party conferences. Rather, it instead illustrates that the interpretations given a theoretical principle can be put to more than one political purpose. In the context of multilateral bloc forums, socialist internationalism meant several things: the right and obligation of the Soviet Union to intervene on behalf of a "threatened" regime, even if the regime itself saw no danger; acknowledgment of the leading role of the Soviet Union within the bloc; applicability of general laws of socialist development which constrained East European autonomy; and sharing the burdens both of supporting the less-developed members of the socialist community, under the euphemism of "internationalist duty," and of increased military spending. When directed at domestic audiences, however, internationalism meant the following: the applicability of general laws (notably the leading role of the communist parties); a denial of the validity of any domestic pluralism; recognition of the leading role of the Soviet Union, insofar as this legitimated its presence in Eastern Europe; and verbal and material backing from the rest of the community for the maintenance of the regime.

We also see that the speeches given at the 1976 Berlin conference by the East European "loyalists" were particularly strong statements of support for socialist internationalism and harsh attacks on the Euro-communists. Such statements are consistent with the different motivations for either expressing loyalty to the principle or not; at Berlin, the Eurocommunists represented a visible challenge which had to be addressed or to whom the renegade Romanians could appeal. At PCC meetings, the perceived threat was no longer from the Euro-communists, but from the Soviets. Therefore, the responses changed.

Similarly, Romanian and Yugoslav refusal to be bound by socialist internationalism also acted as a legitimating device, both at the elite and popular level. In Romania, a categorical rejection of the Soviet interpretation of internationalism went hand in hand with a virulent nationalism which sought legitimacy in an identification of socialist Romania with its pre-communist and even medieval predecessors (see Dawisha, 1990: 51–5). A more concrete interest in rejecting socialist internationalism can be identified for Romania and Yugoslavia as well: a refusal both (a) to recognize the "general laws" of socialist develop- ment as manifested in the Soviet Union, and (b) to allow any interven- tion, open or covert, in their internal affairs.

Finally, the Eurocommunist position on socialist internationalism was motivated by a similar desire not to submit to Soviet control, which had proved so disastrous earlier in the century for other parties. It was also vital to develop electoral platforms which would successfully appeal to Western voters already suspicious of concepts such as the "dictatorship of the proletariat" and the Soviet "model" of socialism. The Euro- communist decisions in the 1970s to jettison the dictatorship of the pro- letariat (despite some waffling by the French) did in fact help their electoral performance, albeit temporarily (Leonhard, 1979: 181, 207).

But the rise of Eurocommunism was also, and perhaps more impor- tantly, a part of the disillusionment of some West European communist parties to the crushing of the Prague Spring. Czechoslovak aspirations for a more "humane" socialism corresponded closely to the desires of many in Western Europe, and especially the Italian and Spanish com- munists. Mikhail Gorbachev's declaration of support for "new think- ing" in international relations in the mid-1980s in fact seemed to be a way of promoting the Eurocommunist "new internationalism" and perhaps even socialism "with a human face" (see Chapter 4).

In the 1970s, some Soviets continued to develop alternative interpreta- tions of the basic principles of bloc relations, within the constrained environment of the Brezhnev era. The 1975 book by a group of authors associated with the IEWSS suggested that among certain segments of the intellectual community, there was a willingness to examine creatively the processes taking place in Eastern Europe and the Soviet Union. IEWSS scholars wrote a number of unasked-for *zapiski* – memo- randa to the Central Committee on current topics – in which they attempted to give a realistic appraisal of the situation in Eastern Europe (Bogomolov, 1990). These were largely ignored because of a bureaucracy which had a vested interest in maintaining a stable (if stagnant) environment, domestically and in Eastern Europe.

In the next chapter we shall examine how Soviet theoreticians responded to the dual challenges of "new internationalism" and the rise of Solidarity to intensify their own re-assessment of the meaning of socialist internationalism.

4   Socialist internationalism, 1980–1989: demise of a concept

Historically, a great degree of uncertainty as to the final policy line has been associated with periods of leadership succession in the Soviet Union. Policy toward Eastern Europe was no exception, and socialist internationalism in the early 1980s was subject to the same pressures for redefinition seen in other areas of Soviet theory. The continuing stagnation in all spheres of Soviet life was increasingly obvious, especially to liberal intellectuals familiar with other societies, even if only superficially. A hostile international environment in the wake of the invasion of Afghanistan and the imposition of martial law in Poland, however, mandated attempts at even stricter control over innovative thought by the central authorities.

Already in the late 1970s, Leonid Brezhnev had criticized the level of ideological work in the Soviet Union, and a Central Committee resolution aimed at promoting a higher level of ideological work was published in 1979 (Brezhnev, 1978: 2; "V Tsentral'nom Komitete," 1979). The result was a campaign which even more pointedly displayed the shortcomings it was meant to address, such as "formalism," "twaddle," and a "gray, official style of materials" ("V Tsentral'nom Komitete," 1979: 1). These measures were aimed mainly at the mass media, but the point is that there was a recognition even by Soviet leaders that ideology no longer answered either their needs or those of the populace at large.

Efforts by the Soviet propaganda apparatus to overcome the gap between reality and its official presentation took the form of attempts to re-assert "orthodox fundamentals" (see Remington, 1988: 5), a style very much in keeping with the approach of the guardian of ideology, Mikhail Suslov. In such a situation direct questioning of official policy was extremely risky, but nonetheless certain "aesopian" techniques could be used to air views at odds with those of Soviet officialdom. More importantly, the proponents of heretical views often had important protectors within officialdom itself. With Suslov's death in January 1982 and a subsequent loosening of ideological control, however, some Soviet intellectuals began to openly question the official interpretations of Marxism-Leninism. In this chapter and the next I examine the development of such views in the 1980s, which became increasingly forthright and open with the ascent of Mikhail Gorbachev to the post of CPSU General Secretary. The present chapter examines the demise of socialist internationalism as a concept governing relations between socialist states, while the following chapter concentrates on the simultaneous debate on the notion of contradictions within socialism.

In the 1970s the key issues of socialist internationalism had been the questions of the existence of more than one "model" of socialism; the leading role of the Soviet Union within the bloc; ideological pluralism; and, of course, the question of sovereignty. The debate in the 1980s revolved more or less around the same questions but in a different language, through the use of different concepts.

After the death of Brezhnev in November 1982, Soviet authors continued to debate the relationship between "common-democratic" (*obshchedemokraticheskiye*) and internationalist principles within socialist internationalism, and the "harmonization" of national and international interests of socialist states; now, the role of non-superpowers in international relations became an issue as well. The first question appears in retrospect to have been a premonition of the struggle carried out at the highest levels of the Soviet leadership later in the 1980s over whether "class" values or "common human" values should be the basis of Soviet foreign policy, a debate examined in this chapter. The possibility that smaller states may play an independent role in international relations, meanwhile, called into question the cohesion of the bloc on questions of foreign policy, as well as the right of the Soviet Union to define that policy.

Discussing the harmonization of national and international interests was another way of posing the question of how to balance the interests of individual states as opposed to those of the bloc (defined largely by the Soviet Union). By the late 1970s, "interests" had become an important topic in the nascent field of political science in the Soviet Union; at issue was whether or not different groups within classes could legitimately possess different interests (see Hill, 1980: 90). Prominent among the Soviet theorists who tackled the issue was Georgiy Shakhnazarov, deputy chief of the Liaison Department and also president of the Soviet Political Science Association. Shakhnazarov discussed the issue largely in the context of the development of democracy within the

Soviet Union, and from the early 1970s had claimed that the interests of different social groups were not always easily reconciled in socialist societies. In a book on socialist democracy, he came close to an admission of the possibility of antagonisms when he stated that contradictions between interests "may on occasion become extremely sharp unless prompt and sensible steps are taken to resolve them" (Shakhnazarov, 1974: 43). It was inevitable that such concerns should spill over into the study of international relations among socialist states (see Light, 1988: 305).

This also illustrated that since their inception in the late 1950s and early 1960s, the two institutions most responsible for relations with socialist countries in fact spent much of their time analyzing the domestic Soviet situation. Fëdor Burlatskiy gives ample evidence that while he headed the group of Liaison Department consultants in the early 1960s, one of its main concerns was how to reform the Soviet Union (see Burlatskiy, 1990). Anatoliy Butenko of the Institute of the Economics of the World Socialist System, meanwhile, also devoted many of his writings to general questions of socialist development.

Point-men and trailblazers: Novopashin and Butenko

The early 1980s were relatively devoid of open debate over the meaning of the concept of socialist internationalism. Some intimations of liberal dissatisfaction with the traditional interpretation of the term could be seen, however, in symposia held by the IEWSS in the early 1980s, and in a collective work published in 1979 under the joint editorship of Butenko and several East Europeans.

Initially, Soviet scholars tended to limit their efforts at re-interpretation of fundamental principles to scientific symposia, the proceedings of which were printed in small numbers. These conferences were important mainly in that as part of the output of Soviet Academy of Sciences scientific institutions, the proceedings were sent to the Central Committee departments with responsibility in these areas. Such conferences also afforded liberals the opportunity to be more outspoken than they could be in the press or even the scientific journals although, as we saw in the last chapter, this sometimes opened them up to more criticism as well. The notion of "networking," as in building contacts with like-minded members of other countries' scientific establishments, may have been important; it seems more the case, however, that the East European regimes sent their least open-minded scholars to these conferences.[1]

The joint work by Butenko and others (Angelov, 1979) listed Yuriy

Novopashin as the author of two sections of a chapter on "Principles of international relations of a new type" (Novopashin, in Angelov, 1979: 98–135). Again, in the constrained ideological environment of Brezhnev's Soviet Union, open questioning of the principles of bloc relations was politically impossible, but we can see that Novopashin did choose to stress certain aspects of the "new type" of international relations while downplaying others. In the first section (the second section was authored by a worker in Novopashin's sector, Dmitriy Fel'dman), Novopashin relied on the October 1956 Soviet statement of principles governing relations between socialist countries (see Chapter 2) to suggest that "mistakes" had been made in the development of inter-socialist relations. It was significant that he used this document to express the conviction that "respect for sovereignty" was one of the "general democratic" principles underlying bloc relations. Since it appeared between the first and second Soviet invasions of Hungary in 1956, this implied that one such "mistake" was the Soviet invasion which followed this declaration.

More importantly, Novopashin distinguished between "common-democratic" and "internationalist" principles within socialist internationalism (pp. 102–8). Among the internationalist principles he listed "comradely mutual aid and solidarity," "fraternal cooperation," and "joint defense of the achievements of socialism." The last had often been used as a euphemism for the Brezhnev Doctrine, but Novopashin quoted the 1976 Berlin Conference of European Communist Parties document to make the point that this principle is "inseparable from the responsibility of each socialist state [and] ruling party for the fate and policy of its own country." In other words, he made no attempt to claim that communist parties had a "dual responsibility" before their own people and before the rest of the world communist movement.

Among the "common-democratic" principles, Novopashin listed "respect for sovereignty," "equality of socialist states and nations," "non-interference in internal affairs," and "mutual aid." Most importantly, he did not include the prevailing view in official Soviet publications that respect for sovereignty implied the "harmonization" of national and international interests, a euphemism for the notion of the subordination of national interests to those of the Soviet Union.

By themselves, such statements amounted to little more than theoretical hairsplitting. In the context of what had been commonly accepted by Soviet authors as the basis of bloc relations, however, and in the context of the unsettled question of the post-Brezhnev succession, such statements represented the first stirrings of debate over the meaning of internationalism and hence over policy toward Eastern Europe.

"Full mutual understanding" was achieved again at the May 1980 Political Consultative Committee (PCC) session in Warsaw, devoted to the Warsaw Pact's 25th anniversary ("Kommyunike," 1980). "International solidarity," however, remained a distant goal, appearing as the last of the governing principles, as in the 1978 communiqué (see Chapter 3). Since the previous meeting, serious strains had continued to develop within the alliance, this time over the Soviet invasion of Afghanistan and its effect on East–West relations. This intervention, unlike the Soviet invasion of Czechoslovakia in 1968, was not to be followed within a year by an upswing in détente, and the East Europeans feared it would wreck what was left of détente.

Among the disturbing developments in Eastern Europe in 1980, to Soviet eyes, was the growing crisis in Poland. Periodic crises there were nothing new, of course; unrest in 1956, 1968, 1970, and 1976 had made Poland something of an anomaly even within bloc. The crisis of 1980–1, however, differed from other East European crises in that it was led and organized primarily by workers, going to the very heart of the legitimacy of Soviet-style socialism. What is more, the notion of free trade unions provided an alternate center of power and legitimacy outside of party control. In the face of apparent indecisiveness by the Polish United Workers Party, Solidarity challenged the "leading role" of that party, and eventually came to challenge the socialist system itself. By implication, Solidarity's threat to the PUWP was a threat to the leading role of the Soviet Union within the bloc. All in all, the crisis was a challenge to socialist internationalism.

The crisis began, as had those of 1970 and 1976, with strikes and unrest in response to price rises announced by the Polish leadership in the summer of 1980. In August, Lech Wałesa jumped a fence to join the Gdańsk shipyard strikers and formulated a list of demands including free trade unions and the right to strike. By the end of the month, in the face of a wave of worker unrest, the PUWP and Solidarity reached agreement on these demands, explicitly including recognition of the party's leading role in order to re-assure the Soviet's (see "Government strikers reach agreement," 1980). In September, a PUWP Central Committee plenum replaced the party leader Gierek (who himself had replaced Gomułka in 1970 as a result of unrest over price rises). The crisis continued, mainly as a result of the paralysis of the PUWP, split between those who recognized the need for reform and those who urged the imposition of order.

The Soviets therefore called an emergency meeting of Warsaw Pact leaders in Moscow in December of 1980 to discuss the Polish situation in a multilateral context. The result of the meeting was to give the Polish leadership more time to deal with the situation. The official announcement of the meeting reflected this willingness, stating that the participants of the meeting "expressed their certainty that the communists, working class, [and] fraternal laborers of Poland will be able to overcome the difficulties which have arisen, [and] will facilitate the further development of the country on a socialist path." The Warsaw Pact countries also pointedly declared that the PUWP and Poland could "firmly rely" on the support of the fraternal countries; for their part, the Polish leaders professed their determination "that Poland was, is and will be a socialist country." Finally, in keeping with the general practice of Warsaw Pact documents, socialist internationalism was not mentioned, although international solidarity returned to figure prominently ("Vstrecha," 1980). It appeared the Soviets had achieved the acquiescence of the East Europeans to include this reference more prominently than had recently been the case in an effort to demonstrate their resolve to defend the socialist regime in Poland. Presumably, even Romania's Ceausescu could agree with that use of the term.

Despite the crisis in Poland and growing dissatisfaction at home with socialist internationalism, the interpretations of internationalism given by the conservative party apparatus continued to prevail as the Brezhnev era drew to a close. Pseudonymous articles by the first deputy chief of the Liaison Department, Oleg Rakhmanin, in the journal *Questions of the History of the CPSU* in 1980 and 1981 maintained an obstinate refusal to countenance change. In 1980 he criticized mainly the Chinese and West European communist parties, but harshly attacked those who "only in words acknowledge internationalism" (Borisov, 1980: 7). This may have been aimed at his fellow Soviets, since the Eurocommunists had long since ceased to acknowledge internationalism even in words.

At what was to be the last of his four reports to CPSU congresses, Brezhnev the following February gave a notably less optimistic account of the development of the world socialist system than he had in 1976. Admitting that he could not "paint the picture of the present-day socialist world in exclusively radiant colors," he urged the study and utilization of other socialist countries' experience (Brezhnev, 1981: 10–11). He also retracted his claim of "drawing together" as an objective law, and acknowledged that national features, too, were important (p. 15). But he refused to characterize either the crisis in Poland, or problems in the bloc as a whole, as anything more than "complications" (p. 10), or the product of imperialist interference which capitalized on subjectivist "mistakes" (p. 14).

One attempt to promote a more nuanced relationship between the Soviet Union and Eastern Europe was the suggestion by Oleg Bogomolov in 1981 that a "socialist partnership" between socialist countries be developed. He claimed that the intensification of democracy and the development of such a partnership would be the "dominating tendency" in the 1980s (quoted in Novopashin, 1983: 76). Rakhmanin, however, talked only in tired platitudes of "strengthening the unity and solidarity" (*splochënnost'*) of the socialist countries, and of "difficulties" in their development (Borisov, 1981: 17, 20). Just as the main object of his 1980 article was China, Rakhmanin in 1981 devoted the most attention to Poland. It was most significant that he singled out as the main cause of the crisis "the separation of the vanguard from the masses" (p. 26). This separation, he wrote, had been caused by a retreat from Marxist-Leninist principles in the Polish party. With such a statement he appeared to place himself between those who saw the cause of the crisis in the fact that the PUWP had lost contact with the "masses," such as Konstantin Chernenko, and those such as Suslov who viewed the problem as the lack of discipline within the PUWP (Brahm, 1989: 7).

In the wake of the imposition of martial law in Poland, Soviet scholars turned to an examination of the crisis through debate on the question of whether social antagonisms could develop in socialist societies (see Chapter 5). Within the Warsaw Pact, what could be justifiably described as contradictions between national and international interests continued to grow. The breakdown of US–Soviet détente exacerbated these differences, as the East Europeans had little interest in sacrificing their access to the Western economies for the sake of the Soviets' need to close ranks. Romania had been oriented to the West for some time but, by the early 1980s, the East Germans, for example, had an interest in détente independent of the superior relationship. Inter-German détente was both a means of legitimizing the GDR and of subsidizing it with West German economic assistance.

That there was a desire within the socialist community for something more along the lines of Bogomolov's partnership was apparent from the documents adopted at the January 1983 Prague PCC meeting. As in earlier years, no mention was made of either proletarian or socialist internationalism. What was more surprising was the characterization of "international relations of a new type," which were said to be based on "voluntary equal cooperation and international solidarity of sovereign socialist states" ("Politicheskaya deklaratsiya," 1983). Although "international solidarity" was a concession to Soviet attitudes, even more significant was the substitution of "voluntary equal cooperation" for "Marxism-Leninism," the usual phrase in earlier documents.

In addition, a special paragraph was devoted to the assertion that "each people has a sovereign right freely to decide, without any kind of interference from outside, how to live, how to establish [its] social order, equivalent to the legal right to defend its choice." This statement appeared in a section which attempted to respond to hostile criticism from the West, particularly the Reagan administration. As such, it can be seen on one level as a rejection of Western criticism. At the same time, it was the strongest statement of sovereignty to appear in a PCC document, and obviously was included as a concession to East European concerns. What is more, it seemed to stress exactly those "common-democratic" principles to which scholars such as Novopashin had referred. It was perhaps significant that Georgiy Shakhnazarov, well known for his liberal views, appeared behind CPSU General Secretary Andropov in the picture of the Soviet delegation on the front page of *Pravda* on the day of the communiqué. The two had, of course, worked together many years before in the Liaison Department, and Andropov seemed to be making a point about Soviet–East European relations by including Shakhnazarov, a reformer, in the delegation.

The communiqué itself, meanwhile, could claim only that the meeting had passed in an atmosphere of "friendship and comradely mutual understanding" ("Kommyunike," 1983). Although not marked by the open dissent seen in some earlier meetings, there nonetheless was opposition from the East Europeans, notably the East Germans, to the Soviet decision to proceed with the deployment of intermediate-range missiles in the event of failure to prevent the placement of similar US missiles in Western Europe.

The growing tendency to contrast socialist internationalism with "common-democratic" principles, as done by Novopashin, came under direct and open attack from defenders of the Brezhnevite order. One such article, appearing in the same journal as had many pseudonymous Rakhmanin articles (and at the same time as one of Novopashin's clearer statements in favor of a rethinking of socialist internationalism – see below), attempted to show that the two groups of principles were not incompatible – as "certain Soviet authors" had suggested (Savinov, 1983: 46). Among those who were mentioned as having committed the sin of division was the very same Dmitriy Fel'dman whose section appeared between those two authored by Novopashin discussed above. Savinov's mention of Fel'dman may in fact have been an example of singling out for criticism a less important figure as a means of attacking the views of someone more noteworthy, but who enjoys some kind of protection. (Fel'dman was a colleague from the IEWSS, and also appeared as joint author of a literature review with Novopashin and Arkadiy O. Lapshin, another outspoken critic of socialist internationalism – see *Voprosy Filosofii*, no. 3, 1986).

This illustrates that the debate among Soviets over the character of relations with Eastern Europe was beginning to heat up by 1983. Novopashin returned to the fray with an even more direct condemnation of the contemporary character of Soviet–East European relations with an article which broached the subject of contradictions between socialist countries (Novopashin, 1983). Of course, these had always been held to be non-antagonistic, if present at all. What is more, such differences as did arise were to be "successfully resolved on the basis of proletarian internationalism," as in the words of the 1969 Declaration of the international meeting of communist parties. This document even denied that contradictions between socialist countries could develop, and spoke only of "divergences." During this period, in fact, the characterization of intersocialist differences as divergences rather than contradictions quite often was a reliable indicator of either a conservative or liberal position.

Novopashin, on the other hand, rather forthrightly suggested the possibility of real contradictions not only within but between socialist states. In so doing, he challenged the whole basis of the supposed unity of the socialist community. Noting that there were valid objective factors which created differences between socialist states, he rejected the opinion of other Soviets that views such as these would mean the recognition of ideological pluralism and "political polycentrism" of the socialist community (Novopashin, 1983: 21).

Novopashin also took a position very close to that of the "new internationalism" discussed earlier in the last chapter when he stated that

> the solution to the problem of the further improvement of socialist international relations is primarily connected to a fuller realization in them not only of common interests *but also of the interests and requirements of each socialist country.* (p. 24, emphasis added)

This is strikingly similar to the Eurocommunist claim that each communist party can make the greatest contribution to the common cause by answering its own concerns first.

Finally, Novopashin continued to counterpose democratic and internationalist values. He stated that a world socialist system was possible only when its members based interaction on "common-democratic principles of noninterference in internal affairs, respect for territorial integrity and the development of mutually beneficial cooperation" (p. 17).

Such implicit and open criticism of the official Soviet position from within the Soviet Union – from its leading institute devoted to the study of world socialism, no less – represented a basic challenge to the whole conduct of Soviet relations with Eastern Europe since the end of the Second World War. Since 1968, the concept of socialist internationalism had been used to justify both the invasion and the leading role of the Soviet Union within the bloc. Questioning of this concept was tantamount to calling into question the entire Soviet system of control in Eastern Europe.

Between the Soviets and East Europeans, meanwhile, certain issues also came to be argued under the rubric of socialist internationalism. For their own reasons, both the East Germans and the Hungarians pursued the theoretical and practical line that small states could promote inter-European détente even in the face of deteriorating superpower relations.

In the case of East Germany, this line took the shape of continued efforts by Erich Honecker to expand inter-German contacts, and to become the first East German leader to pay an official visit to West Germany. Such a visit had been first scheduled for 1984, only to be cancelled under Soviet pressure (Dawisha, 1990: 146). As mentioned above, the East Germans were unhappy at the prospect of hosting additional Soviet missiles, for a number of reasons. Some of the cost would be borne by them, and in addition they created yet another obstacle to inter-German détente.

The Hungarian position was expressed most forcefully by Mátyás Szürös, the party secretary for international relations and a former ambassador to the Soviet Union. In a series of articles and even radio call-in shows, Szürös promoted the notion of national interests as the most important determinant of a state's foreign policy. In his most important statement, which appeared in the Hungarian Socialist Workers' Party (HSWP) theoretical journal, Szürös noted that before 1957 the movement was guided first by a "decision-making center" (the Soviet Union), and between 1957 and 1969 by world conferences of communist parties. (He pointedly did not include the decisions of the 1976 Berlin conference as binding.) In such conditions, he wrote, national interests "necessarily played a secondary role and generally had to be subordinated to interests and objectives that were seen as common ones." But in contemporary conditions, Szürös claimed: "There is no question of this kind of unconditional subordination today" (Szürös, 1983: F6). Not content to leave anything to the imagination of his readers, the HSWP secretary was quite blunt in pointing to "bilateral economic relations between the socialist countries and within the framework of the CMEA" as areas in which it was not an "easy task" to reconcile "very diverse national interests" (p. F7).

Such diverse interests even extended to the question of the relationship between the common laws of socialist construction and national characteristics. Szürös contradicted much of the conventional teaching of the time and directly challenged the continuing applicability of the Soviet experience by asking whether or not "all of the laws rated as being common ones have stood the test of time?" (p. F7). His belief was that they obviously had not, especially in light of the relatively successful Hungarian reform.

The Borisov/Vladimirov articles

Unorthodox views such as these and Novopashin's threatened not only the conduct of Soviet relations with the rest of the bloc, but also the conductors – the communist party bureaucracy. Acknowledging the possibility of pluralism would mean accepting as legitimate political expression outside the purview of the CPSU, with the attendant threat to political control.

Accordingly, the harshest response came precisely from those whose positions would be threatened in the case of a collapse of party authority. Once again, Rakhmanin semi-officially and pseudonymously addressed the problem of relations with the socialist world. An article which appeared in April 1984 under the slightly different pseudonym of "O. V. Borisov" was a vivid response to what were evidently growing inclinations among sections of the intelligentsia for a rethinking of socialist internationalism (Borisov, 1984). Rakhmanin addressed all the issues in turn – contradictions, national models of socialism, the role of small states, and the continuing validity of socialist internationalism. Speaking directly to the principles which underlay the latter concept, he listed "equality, independence, non-interference in internal affairs, solidarity and mutual support," and aimed his barbs at unnamed "revisionists" (such as the Poles and Hungarians) who attempted to "substitute the international interests of the revolutionary struggle for narrowly and falsely understood national interests" (Borisov, 1984: 45).

One of Mikhail Gorbachev's first official appearances in his new capacity as CPSU General Secretary was to head the Soviet delegation to ceremonies marking the renewal of the Warsaw Pact in April 1985. For one of the few times in his tenure, Gorbachev professed the Soviet Union's allegiance to socialist internationalism as the basis of bloc relations, but left much unsaid in his speech on the occasion (Gorbachev, 1985b). Unlike Polish leader Wojciech Jaruzelski, Gorbachev endorsed socialist internationalism but left it undefined. Jaruzelski, meanwhile, defined the concept in the following terms:

> The combination of the principle of socialist internationalism and the community of national interests leads to this: all things that are general are national, and that which is national serves the entire [socialist] commonwealth. (Jaruzelski, 1985)

This somewhat convoluted statement implied that Poland would look after its own interests first, and felt that in so doing it would serve the interests of the bloc. Such an interpretation of socialist internationalism, however, was at odds with the position so painstakingly developed by conservative Soviets over the previous two decades.

As with earlier Warsaw Pact documents examined in this study, the communiqué issued for this meeting also did not mention socialist internationalism ("Kommyunike," 1985). Instead, it spoke only lukewarmly of the "important meaning" of the Warsaw Pact, and the fact that for thirty years it had served "the development and strengthening of all-round cooperation [of its members], the guarantee of their sovereignty, security, and inviolability of their borders, [and] the joint working out and realization of their peace-loving foreign-policy course." This was hardly a ringing endorsement of either international relations of a new type or socialist internationalism. It may have reflected the rumored disagreements over the renewal of the Pact.

Jaruzelski's remarks and Gorbachev's ritualistic and passing reference to socialist internationalism virtually begged clarification from the *apparat*. This was provided by another pseudonymous article by Rakhmanin (this time under the name "O. Vladimirov") which appeared in *Pravda* the following summer, which was seen by some as an attempt to put a hard-line "spin" on Gorbachev's passing reference to internationalism (see Dawisha, 1990: 203). Many sections of this article were taken almost word for word from the 1984 article, and the themes were the same as well: denial of a special role for "small states" and of "national models of socialism," for example. A notable addition was the attack on "anti-communist theoreticians and opportunists, who slander proletarian internationalism, declare it outdated, [and] try to present themselves as the trailblazers of some kind of 'new unity'" (Vladimirov, 1985). Given that Rakhmanin's use of pseudonyms was a common secret, many in Eastern Europe wondered as to the purpose of this article.

One possible variant of the "new unity" to which Rakhmanin disdainfully referred was a concept which was being put forward at this time by the IEWSS scholars. Novopashin and his colleague Arkadiy Lapshin, in a review of four books put out by the "Peace and Socialism" publishing house in Prague, suggested characterizing relations between the socialist countries as a "socialist partnership," as had Bogomolov in 1981. They described this partnership as

> a form of international relations based not only on comradely solidarity and mutual assistance, but also on real (*fakticheskiy*) equal rights of the cooperating countries, that is, on the equality of their laws and obligations which is guaranteed [even] in the conditions of the continuing objective inequality of these countries under socialism. (Lapshin and Novopashin, 1984: 157)

As for the "harmonization" of national and international interests, "flexibility and a readiness to compromise" were said to be the necessary condition – "not a subordination of the interests of certain countries to the interests of the rest, nor an imposition of the will of the majority on one country or another." These comments displayed a marked similarity to statements such as those by Szürös, for instance, and in fact seemed to represent a form of communication between like-minded elites. Another example of communication was a statement by Bogomolov himself in July, in an article in the theoretical journal *Kommunist*. Bogomolov very closely repeated Jaruzelski's view that the East European socialist states served the interests of the wider community by serving their own interests first (see Bogomolov, 1985: 90).

Novopashin reiterated his call for a "socialist partnership" later in the year (Novopashin, 1985: 56), in an article whose first two sentences were very similar to a section at the beginning of Rakhmanin's, almost as if to highlight the differences in views which were to follow.[2] Novopashin as well added a new element of criticism, that of "great power ambitions, in whatever subtle and disguised forms they are expressed." Most importantly, he called democratic centralism into question as a principle of bloc relations: "In the sphere of the socialist countries' interstate relations ... democratic centralism does not determine the nature and prospects of these relations" (p. 57). In language presaging that used by Mikhail Gorbachev not more than six months later at the CPSU 27th Congress (see below), Novopashin asserted that "there can be no hierarchy and no system of seniority among [socialist states]," as was necessary when the concept of democratic centralism was applied in a domestic context (Novopashin, 1985: 58).

Novopashin's increasingly outspoken statements semed to correspond to growing uncertainty as to the direction of Soviet policy toward the bloc. In 1979 his writings criticized the basis of the Soviet–East European relationship only indirectly. With the passing of Leonid Brezhnev, however, and as the drift in policy associated with transitory leadership figures continued through 1983 and 1984, he became bolder. Certainly, we should not place too much importance on Novopashin as an individual; it is more appropriate indeed to think of theoreticians such as him as "trailblazers" or "point-men," testing the limits of permissible expression and exposing themselves to criticism. It is also fruitful to see such articles as illustrating the creation of an "ideological menu."

At the PCC meeting in October 1985, Gorbachev's first as Soviet leader, the declaration which was adopted took a markedly conservative tone ("Za ustraneniye," 1985). Unlike previous documents, this declaration noted that the socialist community was united "by a commonality of vital interests and the tasks of the construction of socialism and communism, [and] by a Marxist-Leninist worldview." What is more, the declaration also asserted that cooperation between the socialist countries should be based on the "harmonious combination of their national and international interests."[3] Statements such as these might have suggested that conservatives among the Soviet delegation succeeded in pushing through relatively hard-line interpretations of the principles underlying bloc relations, perhaps because of the inexperience of the new leadership. At the same time, it may be the case that the location of the meeting determined much of the language in that the Bulgarians, as hosts of the meeting, would have composed the first draft of the statements to be issued at the meeting. Todor Zhivkov had always been among the most loyal adherents of socialist internationalism, and in his remarks at the official dinner for the delegations, he declared the Pact members' desire to instill with a "richer content [their] fraternal friendship and mutual cooperation, on the basis of Marxism-Leninism and socialist internationalism." Hungary's Kádár, speaking on behalf of the visiting delegations, spoke only of a "firm unity" (both speeches in "V serdechnoy obstanovke," 1985).

It would be surprising if the inclusion of such conservative formulations was Gorbachev's doing, given later developments in Soviet–East European relations. It is likely, as has been suggested elsewhere (Dawisha, 1987), that at this time Gorbachev simply was more concerned with domestic problems than foreign policy. What is more, the new foreign minister Eduard Shevardnadze had been on the job only since the summer and undoubtedly still lacked clout within the ministry. A number of conservatives were listed as members of the official delegation: former foreign minister and then-President Andrey Gromyko; Defense Minister Sergey Sokolov; the party secretary responsible for relations with socialist countries, Konstantin Rusakov; and Boris Aristov, then minister of foreign trade. Conservative figures such as these surely could have influenced the proceedings to some extent, perhaps in collusion with the Bulgarians.

Unfortunately, this still does not explain how the Soviets could succeed in achieving in 1985 what they supposedly wanted to achieve at earlier meetings – stronger endorsements of their understanding of internationalism. One possible explanation is that Gorbachev intended these strong statements to serve notice that the Soviets would still insist on the applicability of models, only now to urge similar reform efforts in Eastern Europe.

The Party Congress and its aftermath

At the 27th Party Congress, Gorbachev was able to more clearly state his position, perhaps at odds with that of the central *apparat*. "Reports of the Central Committee" to party congresses throughout the Brezhnev period were seen as ritualistic and normative barometers of Soviet attitudes toward different regions of the world. For instance, as mentioned above, Brezhnev stated in 1976 that the continual "drawing together" (*sblizheniye*) of socialist countries was an "objective law" governing their relations (Brezhnev, 1976: 5). Such a statement reflected not only Soviet-led efforts in the early 1970s to more closely integrate the socialist community, but also the intent to continue the process according to Soviet-interpreted "regularities." In every report, socialist internationalism was said to be at the basis of relations with the bloc countries.

Gorbachev, however, pointedly referred not to socialist internationalism as the basis of Soviet foreign policy, but to "strict respect in international practice for the right of each people to choose the ways and forms of its development independently" (Gorbachev, 1986: 86). Although characterizing differences within the community as "disagreements and divergences" rather than contradictions (p. 84), he did state that "unity has nothing in common with uniformity, hierarchy, interference by some parties in the affairs of others, or the striving of any party to have a monopoly over what is right" (p. 85). Such statements clearly indicated his intent to restructure not only the domestic environment, but also the international.

Whereas Gorbachev made clearer reformist statements in his speech to the congress, the characterization of bloc relations which appeared in the new edition of the party program (produced by the collective efforts of the bureaucracy) was not nearly as re-assuring, stressing socialist internationalism and indicating that the bureaucracy remained a bastion of conservatism. For instance, one of the "most important factors" in the success of world socialism was said to be "the building of relations with other fraternal countries on the principles of socialist internationalism" ("Program," 1986a: 204). This suggested a lack of enthusiasm among the *apparat* and an apparent ability to frustrate change.

Accordingly, after the congress the forces of reform moved quickly against such soapboxes for conservative positions as *Kommunist*, and against the *apparat* itself. Richard Kosolapov was removed as editor-in-chief of the party journal at the time of the Congress (compare the lists of editorial board members in nos. 2, 3, and 4, 1986), to be replaced by Ivan Frolov (who was to become editor of *Pravda* in 1989 in an attempt to make the party newspaper a more ardent proponent of reform). Yevgeniy Bugayev, who, as we shall see in the next chapter, harshly criticized the position of those who held that socialist contradictions could become antagonistic, was also removed from the *Kommunist* editorial board by the end of the year after a long tenure. Less conservative figures who joined the editorial board included Karen Brutents, a deputy chief of the International Department and, in a case of poetic justice perhaps, the party philosopher Pëtr Fedoseyev. (Fedoseyev and Kosolapov had clashed behind the scenes in the debate on contradictions; see Chapter 5). Finally, Oleg Rakhmanin seemed to hold on to his position until late 1986, when he was replaced as first deputy chief of the Liaison Department by the reform-minded Shakhnazarov (*Directory of Soviet Officials*, 1987: 17). Rakhmanin also lost any opportunity to promote conservative views in the official party press with his removal from the editorial board of *Partiynaya Zhizn'* (Party Life) in early 1987; he was replaced by Ivan Skiba, also closely associated with the pro-reform team (again, see the lists of editorial board members in nos. 4 and 5, 1987).[4]

Nonetheless, an article published in *Kommunist* after Kosolapov's departure showed that conservative opponents of *perestroika* could still air their views. In a report on the Socialist Unity Party of Germany (SED) party congress, Aleksandr Martynov, the Liaison Department section head responsible for relations with East Germany, spoke quite favorably of the East German reform experience (Martynov, 1986).

Opposition to a liberal re-interpretation of socialist internationalism came not only from within the bureaucracy, but from East European conservatives as well. If the Soviet–East European element of the debate earlier in the decade had centered on the question of the role of small states in the détente process, now the question was more clearly focused on whether the East Europeans would adhere to the Soviet model to embark on a reform course. The aspect of socialist internationalism which came into question, then, was the issue of the universality of the Soviet model.

In previous debates, however, East European refusal to acknowledge its universal applicability had been used to argue in favor of reform, despite Soviet disinclinations to do so. By the mid-1980s, on the other hand, denial of the existence of a model of socialism or of "general laws" of socialist development was used to deny the necessity of reform, along Soviet lines or otherwise. This clearly illustrates how theoretical concepts could be interpreted for various political purposes.

For instance, in 1986 East German and Czechoslovak officials made numerous attempts to demonstrate that the contemporary Soviet experiments held little relevance for their countries. The editor-in-chief of the SED youth organization newspaper claimed that although the Soviet Union deserved recognition for its defeat of fascism, "in technology and progress it is no model to us" (quoted in Radio Free Europe Research, 1986a). A similar and more authoritative position was taken by SED ideology secretary Kurt Hager, who said that the inter-party exchange of experience between the CPSU and SED did not mean "copying everything" (Hager, 1986). The East Germans felt they had been relatively successful in reforming their economic system through the introduction of "combines," a limited decentralization in which research, design, and production were placed under the control of one enterprise (Martynov, 1986: 100).

The Czechoslovak leaders, a group still composed largely of those who came to power as a result of the Warsaw Pact invasion in 1968, also resisted *perestroika*, feeling that they had been installed not to promote reform but to prevent it. The head of the Czechoslovak Communist Party's (CPCz) Agitation and Propaganda Department used the Khrushchevite notion of "different paths" to claim that the socialist countries did not need to emulate Western development in order to be successful (Bejda, 1986). Instead of interpreting Khrushchev's idea to mean that there should be more than one model of socialism, Bejda instead asserted that market mechanisms and other Western-inspired reforms (as were being discussed in the Soviet Union) were little more than retrogressive and "disruptive," as his country had learned in 1968. "Different paths" therefore meant paths distinct from capitalism as well as within socialism, as in the prerogative to reject reform.

In addition to views such as these which appeared in the pages of the East European party organs, in the Soviet Union the press throughout 1986 continued to print articles by East Europeans which gave only lukewarm endorsements to reform. The most prominent of these were by Czechoslovaks, implying support for their unwillingness to reform among Soviet conservatives who still maintained some control over the central press.[5]

Only the Poles and Hungarians greeted Soviet *perestroika* with any vigor. Like the CPSU, the Polish United Workers Party adopted a new party program in 1986. The PUWP Program clashed with the Soviet view of the world on a number of points, the most notable of which for our purposes was its acknowledgement of the existence of "social contradictions based on classes" in Polish society ("Program," 1986b). This frank admission went farther than the corresponding Soviet document, but along with Gorbachev's statements at the congress demonstrated that elements in both parties were coming to recognize that their societies had deep-rooted problems which needed to be addressed.

In an article published shortly after the Soviet congress, the Hungarians also displayed views at odds with the Soviets. Writing on behalf on the Hungarian Socialist Workers Party, Szürös levelled a veiled criticism of the Soviet tendency to promote generally applicable laws of socialist development. Noting that debates between communist parties had subsided in recent years, he wrote:

> Such debates create problems in inter-party relations only if, having advanced a new concept, a party tries to elevate it (and the corresponding political practice) to the rank of a universal law ... Specific-

ally, such was the case with some views on the historical paths to socialism and the current practices of the socialist countries ... It is our firm conviction that there is no universally applicable or binding model of socialism or way to socialism. (Szürös, 1986a: 37)

With his reference to "universal" laws and the "current practices" of socialist countries, Szürös was obviously criticizing the recent state of affairs in Soviet–East European relations. While claiming that the HSWP did adhere to proletarian internationalism, Szürös pointed out that "the important thing is what meaning is read into the concept" (p. 36). That the Hungarians did not read Soviet meanings into the concept was evident from a speech given by Szürös in Finland later that year, where he promoted a line which challenged a unanimous bloc foreign policy. Whereas in 1983 he had been criticized by the likes of Rakhmanin for promoting such a policy, however, this time he could rely on the results of the 27th Party Congress to claim that "every country – regardless of its size – has its own responsibility for maintaining peace and developing cooperation" (Szürös, 1986b: 71).

Initial Bulgarian reaction to Gorbachev's restructuring was luke-warm, to say the least. The year 1985 saw virtually no movement toward reform; some first attempts were made, in 1986, but seemed for the most part insincere and halting. Bulgarian leader Todor Zhivkov periodically announced reforms only to withdraw them from further consideration, as in the fall of 1986 with the reform-oriented "Draft Regulations on Economic Activity" (Radio Free Europe Research, 1986b).

There was some indication, however, that change was in the offing for Soviet relations with Eastern Europe when the long-time secretary for relations with socialist countries, Konstantin Rusakov, lost his position at the 27th Congress. While not a fire-breathing reformer like others in the leadership, his replacement, Vadim Medvedev, had made cautious statements in favor of reform in the past (see Chapter 5). What is more, he had presided over an initial loosening of the reins in mid–1983 as head of the Central Committee's Science and Educational Institutions Department (Directory of Soviet Officials, 1984: 16). This department had the main responsibility for monitoring the Academy of Sciences institutes, such as the IEWSS, where many reform ideas were born.

At the PCC meeting following the Soviet Party Congress in the summer of 1986, signs of a change in style in the conduct of Soviet foreign policy were evident. The section devoted to relations among socialist states in the communiqué retreated from the conservative

assertions of the previous year; it returned to the more neutral formulation of "strengthening unity and solidarity" ("Kommyunike," 1986:
2). More than anything, it called for a "broadened exchange of the
experience of socialist construction, and a wide acquaintance with
each others' affairs and problems."

It was most notable that the unity which Szürös and others had
challenged now appeared to be returning, at least in foreign-policy
matters. It no longer seemed that the Soviet Union was out to ruin
détente (and with it the chances for Eastern Europe to pursue its own
interests in East–West relations), as it had appeared in the early 1980s.
Then, the Soviets had walked out of the Intermediate-range Nuclear
Forces (INF) negotiations in the fall of 1983, continuing a downward
trend in East–West relations which had started almost as soon as the
Helsinki Final Act was signed. Now, in 1986, Soviet and East European
interests were beginning to coincide, at least in terms of promoting
improved relations with the West. One summit had been held
between Gorbachev and US President Ronald Reagan in the fall of
1985, and another was in the offing. More importantly, Gorbachev was
talking more and more of reducing defense spending and cutting
arms, which also lessened the demands made on the East European
allies. The June 1986 PCC meeting offered 25 percent conventional
force reductions ("Obrashcheniye," 1986); along with Gorbachev's
January 15 proposal to eliminate nuclear arms, it suggested a willingness to be flexible in the approach to arms control.

Negotiations at the October 1986 Reykjavík summit, however, foundered on Reagan's commitment to space-based strategic defense (SDI)
and Gorbachev's just as adamant determination to see it scrapped.
Gorbachev, of course, linked agreement on INF to a US commitment
not to pursue SDI. At a meeting of Warsaw Pact foreign ministers in
Bucharest after the summit, Ceausescu expressed his disappointment
at the inability to reach agreement and declared that "the issue of
nuclear weapons in Europe can be solved without linking them to the
whole package of problems, and they are in no way connected to the
question of the 1972 [ABM] treaty and virtually can be approached and
solved independently" (Ceausescu, 1986: AA2). Thus, he sided with
the Hungarians and East Germans in terms of promoting a more
varied foreign policy for the bloc.

The basic issue of Soviet insistence on adherence to socialist internationalism was left unresolved throughout most of 1987 as few
Soviets spoke authoritatively on the issue. Again, this supports the
view that Gorbachev, the Soviet leadership and the bureaucracy were

more pre-occupied with domestic issues and with improving the US–Soviet relationship than with forcing reform on recalcitrant East European leaders. Gorbachev himself said as much on a visit to Czechoslovakia in April, when he declared that the Soviet Union would not foist reform on Eastern Europe (Gorbachev, 1987a). At the same time, he seemed to send a signal to Czechoslovak reformers when he suggested that *perestroika* was "in accordance with the very essence of socialism;" any potential reforms should be socialist in nature. The only drawback was that the question of what was "socialism" was by this time becoming quite muddied (see Chapter 5). Gorbachev's reticence to impose reform on Eastern Europe or to criticize East European conservatives seemed to imply that he still believed in the principle of the unity of communist parties, in terms of not casting off allies who may have outlived their usefulness. Thus, internationalism lived on in some respects.

That the concept was not mentioned directly by top Soviet leaders is not to say it was completely neglected. The most important debate within Soviet policy circles in late 1987 and 1988 came to center on the critical question of the proper basis of Soviet foreign policy. The issue became not how to define socialist internationalism, but rather whether or not Soviet foreign policy should continue to be based on "class" values at all and, accordingly, hew an internationalist line.

Comparing the statements made by Gorbachev on the signing of the Declaration on Soviet–Polish Ideological Cooperation and the declaration itself in April 1987 revealed that different sentiments on this issue prevailed among Soviet policymakers. It was indicative of changes in the climate of Soviet–East European relations that in speeches made on the occasion, neither Gorbachev nor Polish leader Jaruzelski made mention of socialist or any other kind of internationalism. Unlike in 1985, Jaruzelski did not try to obfuscate the concept of internationalism; instead, he ignored it. The Polish leader noted that the equality of relations between the Soviet Union and Poland was strengthening, and that their essence was "mutual trust, respect of national dignity, [and] of the independence of means and decisions" (Jaruzelski, 1987). He did refer to the responsibility of communist parties before their own people and "international concern" for unity, but singled out Gorbachev personally for his contribution to the creation of a favorable climate in which these concepts could be redefined.

Gorbachev spoke in a similar vein; in a phrase reminiscent of the IEWSS reformers, he claimed that cooperation between the Soviet Union and Poland was based on "equality [and] *genuinely partner-like relations"* (Gorbachev, 1987b; emphasis added). He also displayed the impact of *glasnost* by referring to the "difficult heritage" which compli-cated relations between the Soviet Union and Poland, and clearly called for the filling in of "blank spots" in the history of their relations. This offer to fill in the "blank spots" – such as the execution of Polish Communist Party leaders in the Soviet Union in the 1930s, or the killing of Polish officers in the Katyn Forest in 1940 – answered a long-standing grievance in Soviet–East European relations more gen-erally. Unfortunately from the Soviet point of view, it also called into question the monopolistic grip on truth that the region's communist parties, especially the Soviet, had in the socialist system. As a result, something of a "floodgate" effect was observed: Polish, Hungarian, and Baltic historians all began to clamor for a revision of the interpreta-tion of history imposed on them by the Soviet Union.

The "Declaration on Soviet–Polish Cooperation in the Fields of Ideology, Science and Culture," meanwhile, prominently declared in its second paragraph that the Soviet and Polish parties were "led by a responsibility for the fate of socialism [and] the principles of socialist internationalism" ("Deklaratsiya," 1987: 1). The stark contrast between the two sets of statements suggests that a conservative bureaucracy had a hand in drafting the latter statement, and attempted to influence the direction of ideological cooperation between the two countries.

As might be expected, all mention of internationalism, solidarity, or even unity had disappeared from PCC documents by this time. At the May 1987 meeting in Berlin, in fact, the communiqué called simply for more "dynamism" in foreign-policy cooperation ("Kommyunike," 1987: 2). More importantly, we can identify the first intimations of the coming reorientation of the basis of intersocialist relations in the strong call for "strict (*neukosnitel'noye*) observation of the principles of equality and mutual responsibility in the system of political relations between the allied states." Previously, any mention of "responsibility" had been tied to consideration of the interests of world socialism, and certainly not in the context of political interstate (rather than inter-party) relations.

A more subtle indication of the changes in store for Eastern Europe was the Soviet Union's acceptance of the principle of assymetrical cuts in conventional weapons ("Kommyunike," 1987: 2). This was accom-panied by the adoption of a new "defensive" military doctrine by the Warsaw pact ("O voennoy doktrine," 1987) which, along with the cuts proposed at the previous PCC meeting, suggested the seriousness of the Soviet Union's desire to cut defense spending. What is more, both the new defensive military doctrine and willingness to negotiate arms reductions demonstrated that the Soviet Union no longer saw the maintenance of large armed forces in Eastern Europe as necessary. This obviously had major implications for the fate of the East European leaders, inasmuch as one of the roles of Soviet troops in the region was always thought to be the propping up of unpopular regimes (if only by the simple fact of their presence).

"Internationalism" or "common human values"?

The most prominent participants in the debate over class versus common values included three Politburo members. Yegor Ligachev was the most vociferous defender of the conservative position, which held that despite an improving international atmosphere (or perhaps because of it), the Soviet Union ought to continue to adhere to a class-based foreign policy. Taking the opposite position were Foreign Minister Eduard Shevardnadze, and Aleksandr Yakovlev. Both forcefully propounded and elaborated the view that the Soviet Union's foreign policy ought to be based first of all on "common human values" rather than class interests. The foreign policy suggested by such a line called for increased cooperation with the rest of the world, both in economics and in the political resolution of pressing problems such as regional conflicts.

Gorbachev in some ways initiated this debate in two speeches at the end of 1987 and the beginning of 1988. The first was one of the more notable and comprehensive statements of his worldview, on the 70th anniversary of the Great October Socialist Revolution (GOSR). Gorbachev's comments on the meaning of socialist internationalism were somewhat ambiguous; depending on one's point of view they could be read as either supporting or rejecting the concept. Given what we knew of Gorbachev's advisors and general intentions, however, he seemed to favor reformist interpretations of the concept. In addition, the conservative-oriented statements which Gorbachev made were most likely included under pressure from party stalwarts in the Central Committee and Politburo. One of the benefits of *glasnost* was the CPSU's greater willingness to reveal its internal workings, and in a speech to the CC plenum which preceded the GOSR anniversary celebrations, Gorbachev went much further in his criticism of Stalin (see *Izvestiya TsK*, no. 2, 1989). In any case, the speech had to be approved by other Politburo members, since he spoke on its behalf.

For instance, speaking of the notion of a model of socialism, Gorbachev stated:

> Life has amended our conceptions of the logical patterns and speeds of the transition to socialism ... We have also become convinced that socialism does not, and cannot have, a model against which all are compared. (Gorbachev, 1987c: 60)

This was a far cry from authoritative Soviet statements made as little as two years before which had maintained that socialism as built in the Soviet Union demonstrated the validity of certain universal laws.

Furthermore, Gorbachev also supported the notion of non-interference in internal affairs when he asserted that "all [communist] parties are fully and irreversibly independent" (Gorbachev, 1987c: 59). Acknowledging that "it took time to free ourselves from the old habits," Gorbachev gave his interpretation of the principles underlying socialist internationalism:

> These are unconditional and total equality, the responsibility of the ruling party for affairs in its state, and for patriotic service to its people; concern for the general cause of socialism, respect for one another, a serious attitude toward what has been achieved and tried out by friends, and the strict observation by all of the principles of peaceful coexistence. The practice of socialist internationalism rests on these. (p. 60)

In other words, socialist internationalism for Gorbachev did not entail any "dual responsibility" before both the national and international socialist communities. His enumeration of the principles of intersocialist relations was in general similar to that used earlier in the decade by scholars such as Novopashin, as described above.

In an article which largely echoed the themes sounded by Gorbachev, the CPSU secretary for relations with socialist countries, Medvedev, also supported the priority of common human values. Writing the lead article for *Kommunist* in January 1988, Medvedev also devoted significant attention to the "renewal" of socialism and the development of the world socialist system. Discussing the question of the relationship between "basic regularities and national peculiarities," with an obvious nod to past practice he noted that "even it has its own history" (Medvedev, 1988a: 11). He described this history in the following terms:

> Once, the acknowledgment of national peculiarities was considered almost a retreat from Marxism-Leninism. A little later they began to interpret this question in such a spirit, that national differences were

unavoidable and permissible at the early stages of socialist construction, but would then be overcome, polished; they would recede into
the past ... In reality, national features are not something alien and
contrary to socialism. (Medvedev, 1988a: 11)

This article sent a clear signal to Eastern Europe that the Soviet Union
would no longer fear experimentation along national lines, from the
CC secretary with responsibility in that area.

At the February 1988 plenum of the CPSU Central Committee, Gorbachev gave another endorsement to a re-orientation of Soviet foreign
policy away from its traditional bases. "The fundamental theoretical
question," he said, "topically arising before both Marxists and their
opponents is the question of the combination of class and common
human sources in real world development and, accordingly, in politics" (Gorbachev, 1988a: 3). He even went so far as to claim that the
"new role of common human values is the central link of new thinking," and identified their "objective basis" in the "processes of internationalization taking place in the world."

A concrete expression of new thinking and the reliance on common
human values was seen in the Yugoslav–Soviet declaration signed the
following month ("Yugoslav–Soviet Declaration," 1988). The document was notable in several respects, not least for the venue of its adoption. Soviet policy toward Yugoslavia had always been taken as something of a litmus test for the former's willingness to tolerate diversity in
the rest of Eastern Europe. After all, regardless of other sources of the
conflict (namely Stalin), the Soviet–Yugoslav dispute really was an
issue of East European independence from Soviet control and tutelage.

Seen in this light, the Yugoslav–Soviet declaration was also important because, in the first place, it specifically reinforced the validity of
the Soviet–Yugoslav declarations of 1955 and 1956 (see Chapter 2)
which were meant to entice Yugoslavia back into the communist fold
with promises of non-interference and autonomous development. The
1988 declaration clearly ruled out interference in internal affairs "in
any form whatsoever"; it also represented Gorbachev's further
endorsement of the concept of "specific paths and forms" of socialist
development ("Yugoslav–Soviet Declaration," 1988: 46).

Perhaps most importantly, in a section devoted to inter-party relations the declaration stated that the League of Communists of Yugoslavia and the CPSU re-affirmed

the universal significance of democratic principles in relations among
communist, workers', socialist, social-democratic, national-liberation
and other progressive parties and movements, based on their inalien-

> able right to decide independently their own roads of social develop-
> ment. ("Yugoslav–Soviet Declaration," 1988: 46)

This was a clear statement of the intent to re-orient Soviet foreign policy around commonly recognized principles of international conduct rather than toward a Soviet-defined internationalism. It is worth remembering that milder statements in 1956 in the same context had been taken by independent-minded Poles and Hungarians as a clear endorsement of what was then known as "national communism."

The 19th Party Conference in June 1988 provided the "new thinkers" in the Soviet leadership an opportunity to proclaim the priority of common-democratic principles and common human values once again, this time from the second highest rostrum of the CPSU next to party congresses. Gorbachev repeated that such values were the "core" of new thinking (Gorbachev, 1988b: 11). In addition, he stated that "sovereignty, independence, equal rights, and noninterference" were becoming the "generally acknowledged norms of international relations," and that, as a consequence, "the policy of force in all its forms and manifestations has historically outlived itself" (Gorbachev, 1988b: 12). In a phrase surely designed to counter the conservatives' objections with their own language, he stated: "Resisting freedom of choice means placing yourself in opposition to the objective course of history itself." This was a creative use of the materialist dialectic, to say the least, a tactic which Gorbachev was to use again in the fall of 1989 when East German leader Erich Honecker also refused to accept change.

Foreign Minister Shevardnadze, meanwhile, echoed similar sentiments. In his speech to a special "scientific and practical conference" at the Foreign Ministry devoted to the further restructuring of Soviet foreign policy a month after the party conference, Shevardnadze firmly asserted the priority of common human values:

> One must not identify coexistence, which is based on such principles
> as nonaggression, respect for sovereignty and national indepen-
> dence, noninterference in internal affairs and so on, with class
> struggle. The struggle between two opposing systems is no longer a
> determining tendency of the present-day era. (Shevardnadze, 1988:
> 30)

Such a reversal of fundamental principles was enshrined as a basic concept of relations within the Warsaw Pact at the July 1988 PCC meeting. The communiqué adopted at this meeting was unambiguous in its statement of principles:

The participants of the conference proceed from the indivisibility and growing interdependence of the world, [and] from the necessity of *the affirmation of the priority of common human values in relations between all states.* ("Kommyunike," 1988: 1, emphasis added)

With such a statement, Gorbachev had won his allies' formal acquiescence to a restructuring of relations. He was most likely helped in this by Jaruzelski; as the meeting was held in Warsaw, the Poles would have drafted the initial documents. Gorbachev had already made another attempt at patching old wounds and filling the "blank spots" in history before the PCC meeting with a speech to the Sejm (the Polish parliament), in which he condemned the deportation of Poles from the "western districts" of the Soviet Union after the Second World War. These were the areas given by the Soviet Union in the Nazi–Soviet Non-aggression Pact before the war, and again after the war as part of the post-war adjustments of boundaries. Thus, in an ideological slight of hand, he did not at all intimate that these were in any way Polish lands (Gorbachev, 1988c).

Winning acceptance of a new basis for inter-socialist relations was not an easy task. According to a Central Committee official involved in the preparation of the documents, the East Germans and the Romanians were said to have presented the greatest opposition to the inclusion of "common human values" as the basis of intra-socialist relations, and certain "difficulties" were associated with acceptance of ecological problems in the concept. Signalling an intent to deal with ecological issues was problematic for two reasons: (a) addressing ecological problems contradicted many of the East European leaders' pet economic or industrial projects (especially the grandiose plans of Nicolae Ceausescu); and (b) it costs money to deal with these problems and clean them up, and the East European economies were becoming increasingly strapped. The 1988 PCC document included the first reference to ecological problems in Eastern Europe ("Kommyunike," 1988: 2), and an accompanying declaration attempted to develop a unified policy on protection of the environment in a European context (see "Posledstviya," 1988). The problem with common human values, meanwhile, ran a bit deeper: they represented "a threat to their [the East Europeans'] political structures."[6] The communiqué reflected the fact that a less cordial atmosphere had prevailed; whereas the atmosphere at the previous three meetings was said to have been one of "friendship and comradely cooperation," the 1988 communiqué dropped the description of "comradely" ("Kommyunike," 1988: 2).

Winning the cooperation of his conservative opponents proved just as hard. Seeing the potential threat to their positions, some conservative East European leaders (notably the Czechoslovaks and East Germans) reportedly refused to endorse deep cuts in Soviet troop levels in the region at the PCC meeting (see Dawisha, 1990: 212; see also Radio Free Europe, 1989a: 3).

As the standard-bearer of the conservative Soviet *apparat*, Ligachev attempted to defend class values as the basis of Soviet policy in a speech to the party *aktiv* of the city of Gorkiy. He had already promoted the publication of a public attack on Gorbachev earlier in the year (the infamous Nina Andreyeva letter). Now, he himself urged a non-market approach to reform, noting the negative features of markets in capitalist societies such as social stratification and "a concentration of wealth in the hands of a small section of society. Should we really reproduce all that here?" he asked rhetorically (Ligachev, 1988a: 36).

Such opposition to the introduction of Western norms also extended to foreign policy. In a section of his Gorkiy speech broadcast on the national television news program, Ligachev made clear his views on the relation between class and human values in foreign policy:

> We proceed, comrades, from the fact that international relations are particularly class in character, and that is of fundamental importance. Any other way of putting this question introduces confusion into the consciousness of our people and our friends abroad. Active struggle in the solution of general human problems ... by no means signifies any – I would say – artificial braking of the social and national, national–liberation struggle. (Ligachev, 1988b: 42–3)

Statements such as these clearly identified Ligachev with those at home and abroad who found the more radical elements of Gorbachev's reform program unsettling.

One week later, Yakovlev answered Ligachev's remarks by directly placing *perestroika* and Marxism itself into their world-wide context. For the basis of the "self-renewal" of socialism, he said, "we turn anew to the theory and practice of world development, *both socialist and non-socialist*" (Yakovlev, 1988, emphasis added). Taking his remarks even farther, he declared that "Marxism as such is the thinking out of common human interests from the point of view of the history and development of all mankind, and not only certain of its countries or classes, peoples or social groups." He denied that in the process of putting forward the interests of exploited classes and the proletariat – the "bearer of the historic mission of liberation of man and mankind" – the founders of socialism opposed these interests to all the rest. That is, he denied that there could be any separation between the two classes of interests, as Ligachev (and the CPSU for the previous seventy years) had insisted.

For all of its novelty and the obvious debt to "new thinking," this debate was strongly reminiscent of that earlier in the decade over "common-democratic" versus "internationalist" principles within the context of socialist internationalism. The tables now were turned, however; the conservatives argued not from the commanding position of control of the key levers of power, but rather found it necessary to defend their views against the authority of the general secretary himself.

The debate was settled in favor of universal human values at the end of September 1988, when the Central Committee apparatus which had been responsible for implementing class-based policies and which undoubtedly represented an obstacle to their reformulation was reorganized. The most relevant result for our purposes was the absorption of the Liaison Department into the structure of the International Department. The Liaison Department ceased to be an independent entity within the CC structure, reducing its role in policy-making, since the person responsible for relations with socialist countries was no longer head of his own department but a deputy within the International Department. In a move symbolic of the triumph of "common human" values, the International Department itself was made subordinate to one of six Central Committee commissions, headed by Aleksandr Yakovlev. As the "architect of *perestroika*," Yakovlev's views were well known, and the fact that Ligachev was shunted aside to head the Agriculture Commission emphasised the new line in Soviet foreign policy. Ligachev's replacement as the secretary responsible for ideology was Vadim Medvedev, who appeared to have been something of a compromise acceptable to both reformers and conservatives.

The net effect of this bureaucratic reorganization was to reduce, both symbolically and functionally, the party's role in the formation and conduct of policy toward Eastern Europe. The new head of the International Department was Valentin Falin, who had been known before the Gorbachev era for his less than orthodox views (within the ideological confines of the Brezhnev era, at least). The post of deputy chief for relations with socialist countries was in fact left vacant for some time, evidently due to difficulty in finding someone willing to take on an obviously reduced role. Rafail Fëdorov was named the first deputy chief responsible for relations with Eastern and Western

Europe in October 1988; his deputy for Eastern Europe was Georgiy Sergeyevich Ostroumov, a Liaison Department official since April 1988. The April reshuffling implied that some reorganization was in the offing. Interestingly enough, Ostroumov seemed to have taken the place of another Liaison Department official who was named an International Department deputy chief the same month, Mikhail Smirnovskiy (see *Directory of Soviet Officials*, 1986, and 1989). Little was known about any of these new people.[7]

Another important effect was that the Central Committee, instead of receiving research produced by the institutes of the Academy of Sciences for free, now was required to purchase it. This undoubtedly had the effect of reducing the quality of Central Committee work, along with the general reduction and reorganization of staff, since even the party was not immune from the continuing slowdown in the Soviet economy. Of course, the reduction of staff in general also affected the work of the *apparat*.

The departure of former deputy chief Georgiy Shakhnazarov to become a special advisor on ideological questions to Gorbachev in his capacity as Chairman of the Supreme Soviet had further reduced the prestige of the Liaison Department already by early 1988 (Directory of Soviet Officials, 1989: 3). He was one of the original members of the Liaison Department group of consultants under Burlatskiy (see Burlatskiy, 1990: 249–52), and as a specialist on socialist development for the most part wrote little which dealt directly with the concept of socialist internationalism or even Eastern Europe (see, for example, Shakhnazarov, 1985). In his most important article on international relations, he came out strongly in favor of their "de-ideologization" (Shakhnazarov, 1989). He also probed the roots of "authoritarian socialism" as developed in the Soviet Union under Stalin; as such, his article was part of the general trend in Soviet theoretical circles to come to grips with the notion of "socialism" (see Chapter 5).

Again during this period, fewer theoretical articles directly addressed the question of relations with Eastern Europe. Nonetheless, Soviet resolve to radically restructure relations with Eastern Europe was demonstrated in December 1988 when Gorbachev announced before the United Nations, in an elaborate statement of the principles of "new thinking," that the Soviet Union would unilaterally withdraw 50,000 troops from Czechoslovakia, Hungary and Poland as part of a general reduction of 500,000 in Soviet troop levels (Gorbachev, 1988d: 287). Despite the fact that a considerable number of Soviet troops would remain, such a move still called into question Soviet willingness to guarantee socialism by force in Eastern Europe. That some East Europeans recognized this was evident from the opposition of the Czechoslovaks and East Germans at the July PCC meeting.

The theoretical exercise over the concept of socialism which began at about this time reinforced the idea that the Soviet Union was no longer going to insist on adherence to its model of socialism (see Chapter 5). If the Soviets no longer could define exactly what was entailed in constructing a socialist society, how could intervention to "save social-ism" be justified? For instance, Bogomolov, director of the IEWSS, stated that "undogmatic" socialism should be the goal, and argued in favor of many Western economic practices (Bogomolov, 1989).

In light of all of this, Gorbachev's remarks and Soviet policy in the spring and summer of 1989 clearly signalled a willingness to allow events to run their course in Eastern Europe. In January 1989, the Hungarians legalized a multi-party system with nary a protest from the Soviet Union; after a visit to Moscow in March, HSWP General Secretary Károly Grósz said that the Soviets listened "with extra-ordinary calmness and objectivity" to the reasoning behind the move (Grósz, 1989a: 30). The official Soviet news program *Vremya* spoke similarly, declaring that the Soviets had taken an "understanding view," and, like Grósz, stressed that this was an "internal affair" of the Hungarians (see Grósz, 1989a, and 1989b).

The Hungarian government also began a re-examination of the events of 1956; by June they could be characterized as a "popular uprising" which had gotten out of control to develop into a "counter-revolution" ("HSWP CC Communiqué," 1989). In a display of national reconciliation, Imre Nagy, the prime minister deposed in 1956 and executed by the Soviets in 1958, was exhumed from an unmarked grave and reburied with state honors, along with four other heroes of the Hungarian rebellion and an empty coffin to symbolize the dead on both sides of the conflict. All of this was done without fear of Soviet retaliation, although Czechoslovakia, the GDR and Romania all made up for its absence with their own criticism of Hungary's "counterrevol-utionary deviation" (as quoted in Radio Free Europe Research, 1989a: 3).

In Poland, meanwhile, "round-table" talks started between Soli-darity and the government in the fall of 1988 resulted in agreement on elections to the Sejm to take place in July 1989, in which 35 percent of the seats in the lower house and all of those in the upper house would be contested. The Polish United Workers' Party (PUWP) was roundly defeated and failed in its efforts to form a government, giving the opportunity to Solidarity, in coalition with the two junior parties. A personal telephone call from Gorbachev to PUWP leader Rakowski helped secure the latter's acquiescence (Bisztyga, 1989).

Gorbachev's speech to the Council of Europe in Strasbourg, literally in the middle of these events, served to reinforce the view that on its own initiative the Soviet Union would not intervene, militarily or otherwise, to guarantee its presumed interests in Eastern Europe. He made two points which were truly revolutionary:

> Social and political orders of one country or another changed in the past and may change in the future as well. However, that is exclusively the affair of the peoples themselves ... Any interference in internal affairs of whatever kind, any attempts to limit the sovereignty of states, both of friends and allies, no matter whose it is, is impermissible. (Gorbachev, 1989b: 29)

Given that it was not Western but Eastern Europe that was experiencing growing demands for change, his first remark was clearly meant to signal that the Soviet leadership no longer viewed the "historical process" in Eastern Europe as irreversible. The second remark confirmed the object of his statements – "friends and allies."

As the previous PCC meeting had endorsed the concept of common human values, so the July 1989 meeting in Bucharest finally and officially confirmed Soviet and Pact rejection of the existence of a model of socialism. In 1988 the Pact had proceeded from the need to assert common human values; in 1989 they stated that Pact members "proceed from the fact that there does not exist any kind of universal socialist model, [and] no one possesses a monopoly on truth" ("Kommyunike," 1989: 2). Such a statement was obviously designed from the East European point of view to firmly reject domestic reform. From the Soviet point of view, however, it was just as firmly an endorsement of the unequivocal right of each party to choose its own path of development, preferably in favor of "renewing" socialism. Another sentence in the document put it even more strongly when it stated that Pact members stressed

> the necessity to develop relations between them on the basis of equality, independence [nezavisimost'] and the right of each to independently [samostoyatel'no] work out [its] own political line, strategy and tactics without interference from the outside.

There were so many strong statements of the freedom of individual countries to choose their own paths of development, however, that it almost seemed to suggest the Soviets had made attempts to convince their allies of the need for reform. There were some indications of this. In his speech to a reception for Pact leaders, Ceausescu only briefly touched on such issues as economic and scientific-technical cooperation, while Gorbachev maintained that the processes taking place in the Soviet Union and other socialist countries "could not but have an effect" on the meeting. Remarking on the interest in Soviet reforms displayed in Eastern Europe, he stated that "such a deep interest in the matters and concerns of our friends is also displayed in our country" (see their speeches in "V obstanovke," 1989).

The head of the CC International Department later revealed that

> considerable space was occupied by the question of renewing socialism as such. This process is taking place in a different way, at a different rate, and with different substance in every country. *But it is happening everywhere.* (Falin, 1989: 7, emphasis added)

When asked if consensus had been achieved at the meeting, Falin replied:

> There were shades of opinion and more than that – there were different opinions as regards international affairs and internal affairs in individual countries. But I believe this is a positive feature of the process that is under way. We must replace pseudo-unity with genuine unity. We must only tell one another the truth if we are friends. (Falin, 1989: 7)

Falin was therefore implying that a new interpretation of unity was taking shape in the Soviet Union, one in which the ugly truth of the need for reform would be told. Foreign Minister Shevardnadze was to report to the 28th CPSU Party Congress in 1990 that Soviet ambassadors reported from the East European capitals that "tragic events" could be in store unless reform was undertaken seriously (Shevardnadze, 1990). The Soviet leadership, however, was now caught in a bind. Should they stand by the principle of non-interference in internal affairs and watch inflexible (but allied) rulers be swept away, or intervene in favor of reform? They chose the former, no doubt fearing the damage that would be done to the Soviet Union's international reputation in the latter event. Economic cooperation with the West was evidently more attractive than further "integration" with the unreformed economies of the East.

Another sign that internationalism of the Soviet sort was breaking down was the increase in friction among non-Soviet Warsaw Pact members. Tension between Hungary and Romania increased dramatically in the summer of 1989 over the treatment of ethnic Hungarians by the Ceausescu regime, for example. Things deteriorated so much that the Hungarians began to consider Romania a military threat (see Radio Free Europe Research, 1989c).

Ironically, Romania's leader Ceausescu attempted to secure from his Pact allies endorsement of the interpretation of socialist international-ism which for over two decades he had vehemently rejected. He was reported to have pointed to the need to watch closely those processes taking place in countries such as Hungary and Poland, where social-ism was "threatened." What is more, with the imminent establishment of a Solidarity-led government in Poland the following month, the Romanian Communist Party called for "joint action" with other social-ist countries to defend socialism ("Polish–Romanian Documents," 1989: 39). In an exchange of late-night telegrams the Romanians claimed, in direct Brezhnev-doctrine language, that the presence of Solidarity trade union representatives in the government was "not just a Polish domestic affair, but one that concerns every socialist country" ("Polish–Romanian Documents," 1989: 40). The Poles responded by pointing out that the Romanians had pledged to respect the principles of "equality, independence, and each country's right to work out independently its own political line, strategy, tactics, without outside interference," embodied in the July 1989 PCC communique (p. 41). At least one East European country, then, made a point of holding its allies to their treaty commitments.

Statements which implied a redefinition of bloc relations were made by Gorbachev in other appearances as well, for instance, in Kiev (Gorbachev, 1989a), but these are the most significant owing to the venues in which they were made. The spirit of these remarks and declarations was reinforced in numerous articles and interviews both by Soviet officials and theoreticians throughout the late summer and fall of 1989.

In Eastern Europe, however, no major change had taken place anywhere but Hungary and Poland, and even in these countries the potential and desire for reform were inconsistent with the reality until September and October. In the other East European countries, strong statements were made denying the need for reform either of their domestic structures or of inter-socialist relations.

The August anniversary of the Warsaw Pact invasion of Czecho-slovakia provided ample opportunity for Soviet reformers to express their views on relations with Eastern Europe.[8] Among those who spoke in favor of their restructuring was Andranik Migranyan of the IEWSS, later to become known for his views on the possible need for an "iron hand" to speed up the democratization process in the Soviet Union. In the liberal newspaper *Moscow News*, he voiced an increasingly popular view among reformers that the Soviet–Finnish model of relations was, from the Soviet point of view at least, acceptable and perhaps even preferable to past practices. Writing on the twenty-first anniversary of the invasion of Czechoslovakia, he urged that Eastern Europe should "organically and painlessly join the Western world economic system," while voluntarily limiting their sovereignty "with account for the military and political interests of the Soviet Union" (Migranyan, 1989: 21). He acknowledged the impossibility of mechanically transferring experiences, but spoke favorably of the general character of Soviet relations with Finland. He also noted that the Soviet Union's *own* integration into the world economic system was impossible without "deepgoing internal changes in the economic and political spheres of the East European countries [and] a correct understanding of these processes in Moscow" (Migranyan, 1989: 21). His views suggested that Soviet elites saw little that was pejorative in the concept of Finlandization, as was sometimes the case in the West. Finlandization, from a great-power point of view, answered the needs of both countries. The security of both was guaranteed, while economic and other relations proceeded apace. That it could be demeaning to one partner in the relationship seems not to have occurred to most Soviets.

In one article criticizing such views, a Bulgarian academic adamantly rejected the ongoing redefinition of the Soviet–East European relationship taking place in the Soviet Union. Georgi Stoyanov, playing by the old rules, neglected to name "certain scholars in some socialist countries" who spoke favorably of the incorporation of Eastern Europe into the world economic system under the rubric of the "Finlandization" of Eastern Europe. He wrote scornfully of the notion that "Finlandization" would "allegedly act as a strong incentive for the economic development of the European socialist countries in particular" (Stoyanov, 1989: 11). He undoubtedly spoke for many East European conservatives when he stated the view that the West would instead "take advantage of renewal and restructuring ... for their own selfish interests" (p. 12).

The Finnish–Soviet declaration signed in October of 1989, however, implicitly endorsed "Finlandization," much as the Yugoslav–Soviet declaration the previous year had signalled recognition of different models of socialism. By signing this declaration, the Soviet Union made clear that its interests in Eastern Europe were no longer defined as the maintenance of a given political system. The document enshrined the principle that "there can be no justification for the use of force: whether by one military-political alliance against another, or within such alliances," and declared that "freedom of socio-political choice, deideologizing and humanizing relations between states, subordination of foreign-policy activity to international law, and supremacy of universal human interests and values" were the proper basis of international relations ("Soviet–Finnish Declaration," 1989).

Statements by Gorbachev's spokesman during the Finnish visit reinforced these messages. Gennadiy Gerasimov[9] reported Gorbachev as saying that change in Eastern Europe had to be allowed, and that the Soviet Union had "no moral or political right" to interfere. He went on to use an aphorism which quickly became popular in the West: "You know the Frank Sinatra song, 'I Did It My Way?' Hungary and Poland are doing it their way" (quoted in Keller, 1989). Saying that the Brezhnev Doctrine was "dead," he labelled the new Soviet policy in the region the "Sinatra Doctrine." Then, on one of his famous walks about town, Gorbachev stated that Finland was "a model of relations between states with different social systems, between neighbors" (quoted in Keller, 1990).

What made these admissions so critical for the Soviet Union was that momentous change had already taken place in two East European countries, Poland and Hungary. In Poland, the electoral defeat of the PUWP over the summer led to the establishment of the first non-communist government in Eastern Europe since the mid-1940s. In Hungary, the ruling Hungarian Socialist Workers Party had changed its name to become simply the Hungarian Socialist party, dropped Leninism as its ideology, and was aiming to transform itself into a social-democratic party instead of a Leninist vanguard. Even more significantly, on the thirty-third anniversary of the Hungarian uprising in October, Hungary officially became a republic (without the appelation "people's") in which bourgeois and socialist democracy were said to apply. In a meeting with Honecker on his visit to the GDR for the fortieth anniversary celebrations in October, Gorbachev made an attempt to convince the East German leaders of the need for reform. The "main task" for communists, he said, was "quickly to detect the currents of the time, [and] to respond to pertinent social needs and the moods of the masses" ("Druzheskaya vstrecha," 1989). Thousands of East German youths had poured out of the country through Hungary and West German embassies in Czechoslovakia and Poland since the summer, and by this time weekly demonstrations demanding change by those who stayed were beginning to strain the regime's tolerance.

By the end of October, then, the stage was set for the ultimate test of the Soviet leadership's adherence to the principles they had sought to redefine in the course of *perestroika*. After the fall of one Soviet-style government after another to peaceful protest (the GDR, Czechoslovakia, Bulgaria) in November, leaders of the Warsaw Pact met in Moscow for an "informational meeting" on the US–Soviet Malta summit. The Soviets' earlier reluctance to officially denounce the invasion of Czechoslovakia was due to concern for the pre-November leadership, in the view of many Soviets (see Ambartsumov, 1989: 28). Now, however, those leaders were gone, and the five Warsaw Pact nations which had participated in the invasion moved quickly to condemn it ("Zayavleniye," 1989a). The Polish and Hungarian parliaments had already passed resolutions in the fall denouncing the invasion. Now, alongside the Warsaw Pact declaration in *Pravda* the Soviet government declared, perhaps in an attempt to bolster what little authority the Czechoslovak Communist Party retained, that the decision to invade Czechoslovakia had been "mistaken" ("Zayavleniye," 1989b).

Thus, the concept of socialist internationalism in its worst incarnation – the Brezhnev doctrine, the doctrine of limited sovereignty, dual responsibility – had finally and officially been laid to rest after two decades. The violent Romanian revolution three weeks later and the Soviet refusal to intervene in an attempt to stop the fighting confirmed that at least at this point, the Soviet Union would stand by its declarations. Now a new stage of defining the parameters of the Soviet–East European relationship would begin.

Conclusions

Socialist internationalism in political context

Broadly, debates over the question of socialist internationalism were struggles over the character of Soviet foreign policy in general. By the beginning of the 1970s, it was becoming apparent that Soviet policy no longer served the national interests of the state; it had led to international isolation and martyrdom, and imposed burdens it could ill afford. Policy toward Eastern Europe was characteristic of this. In the 1970s, Soviet subsidies to repressive regimes which soured the image of the Soviet Union (and, more broadly, of socialism) had reached over $14 billion, by conservative estimates (Marer, 1984: 179). What is more important was that the prevailing impression among Soviet elites of Eastern Europe was one of an increasing drain on their resources for little tangible benefit.

"Finlandization," despite a pejorative connotation in the West, was to Soviet eyes a preferable arrangement. The Finns subordinated their foreign policy to the security needs of the Soviet Union, while developing a fairly robust economic arrangement which worked to the benefit of both. The problem was in developing a suitable theoretical backing for such a policy, although I would suggest that the perceived need to adopt new policies went hand in hand with theoretical elaboration.

In the course of twenty years of debate over the proper meaning of socialist internationalism, Soviet views of their hegemonistic position in Eastern Europe changed. Specifically, by the end of 1988 the Soviets no longer insisted on the universality of the Soviet model, and explicitly enshrined this principle in the July 1989 PCC documents; this implied that they had come to an official conclusion that they no longer needed to maintain control to the extent they once did in order to guarantee national security. Such a conclusion was the result of theoretical elaboration worked out earlier at the lowest levels and adopted by the leadership when the need for change arose.

This in turn suggested that the Soviet search for alternate means of security was sincere. In other words, this change in the interpretation of socialist internationalism and finally its rejection should be seen as an integral part of the development of the "new thinking" espoused by Gorbachev since 1985. A Foreign Ministry document presented to the Supreme Soviet in October 1989 is a virtual manifesto of *glasnost* which chronicles the changes in Soviet foreign policy since Gorbachev came to power, and is replete with assertions as to the Soviet pursuit of national security by economic and, above all, political means ("The Foreign Policy," 1990). New thinking, of course, emphasizes non-military means to security: economic, and certainly political. The assertion in the early 1980s that "common-democratic principles" should take their rightful place alongside internationalism represented an important widening of the parameters of the debate on which "new thinkers" could capitalize later in the decade. The rejection of the fundamental Marxist-Leninist principle of internationalism would have been much less likely had the groundwork not been prepared by scholars such as Novopashin in their attempts to redefine the concept.

In some ways, the development of the principles of "new thinking" among Soviet academics parallels similar efforts in the West to study economic means of guaranteeing national security (for example, see Rosecranz, 1986; Baldwin, 1985). This means we should place ideological debate in the Soviet Union and the adoption of "new thinking" in a broader international context. This in turn suggests that "new thinking" was not solely a product of the Gorbachev era, although he certainly facilitated its development through skilful maneuvering and the creation of a favourable political climate.

One point to bear in mind is that the debates in the early 1980s over the concept of socialist internationalism were between a conservative central party apparatus, on the one hand, and an alliance of intellectuals on the other. This comes out more clearly in the next chapter, when we see that Anatoliy Butenko of the IEWSS found an outlet for his views in the journal of the Institute of Philosophy. Novopashin, too, was able to air his views in *Voprosy Filosofii*, and it was curious that one of his more forthright criticisms of socialist internationalism was given at a conference co-sponsored by the USSR Philosophical Society.

These were not the only parties involved in ideological debates, of course. There were similar debates going on in other fields; over the nature of socialist transformation in the Third World, for example (see Light, 1988: Chapter 5), and even over the purpose of existence (see Dahm, 1985). The debates examined in this study merely represented one facet of a broader malaise felt among the *intelligentsia*, so to speak, which expressed itself in a questioning of the basic tenets of Soviet domestic and international policy.

Another point is that Eurocommunism may have had just as strong an influence on the Soviets as on the East Europeans. More often than not, Eurocommunism was seen in the West as an ideological infection which threatened Eastern Europe more than the Soviet Union, if only by virtue of cultural affinities (for example, see Hassner, 1984: 311–12). Yet, we can see a similarity of views and language between future reformers such as Novopashin and the Italians, for example (the best representatives of "new internationalism"). In many ways, it seems appropriate to characterize Soviet "new thinking" in foreign policy as "new internationalism" with a different name; many of the themes, such as the equality of communist parties and pluralism of views, were the same. It would have been politically impossible, however, for the new or aspiring general secretary to adopt the formula of "new internationalism" to characterize his plans for Soviet foreign policy in the early 1980s. By this time, the term had become almost as distasteful to the Soviet conservatives who populated the *apparat* as socialist internationalism was to the Eurocommunists. The embodiment of a "purist" segment of the *apparat* (as opposed to a corruptible, less principled (or simply conservative) segment) was Mikhail Suslov; witness his harsh criticism of the French in 1976, as discussed previously. Despite his death in early 1982, such distaste for the Eurocommunists still prevailed, perhaps exceeded only by the hatred of social-democrats. Thus, it was up to the theoreticians to develop new interpretations of the prevailing dogmas for high-level consumption.

The final aspect of the political context of these debates is that of the struggle for political power. The leadership question in the Soviet Union was almost a perennial issue, but it gained special urgency in the last years of the Brezhnev era. The invasion of Afghanistan demonstrated the kind of dangerous moves an ossified, gerontocratic leadership could undertake when it felt threatened. That this was a question of principle and not a bald struggle for power was suggested by the fact that Gorbachev did not take over his opponents' political programs, as often had been done in earlier successions. The political situation had changed, of course, and one could argue that Gorbachev's political position was never truly solidified. On the other hand, this was the key to his political maneuvering; Gorbachev's political career was one of balancing contending forces in the Soviet political establishment. He did this not by appealing to where he thought the political center lay, however, but by creating a political center through the promotion of new theoretical concepts and the re-working of the old.

Political uses of socialist internationalism

What does this analysis illustrate about the political uses of ideology? In the first place, the tendency to interpret ideological concepts innovatively was an example of explanation in that progressive Soviet scholars were using the categories and principles of Marxist-Leninism to understand the nature of relations between socialist states. In Gorbachev's case, explanation had a specific political purpose: to promote the notion of changing the basis of inter-socialist relations, and to promote reform within Eastern Europe. Statements to the effect that "unity has nothing in common with a hierarchy, with uniformity" were a fresh use of concepts which had become stale and routinized for over twenty years, if not more.

The problem with such a redefinition of socialist internationalism for inter-socialist relations was that this exposed more vividly its inherently contradictory elements. Economic decline and political "stagnation" forced a search for other ways to conceptualize the meaning of socialism on a domestic level and on the level of relations between socialist states. Therefore, the element of internationalism which suggested the appropriateness of models of socialism (and hence of reform) conflicted with that aspect which called for non-interference in internal affairs, creating an uncomfortable bind for Soviet leaders. From the East European point of view, "unity" did not mean that the Soviets had license to urge reform on conservative leaders who did not see it in their interests. These leaders, too, were in a bind: socialist internationalism meant tacit acceptance of the Soviet position in Eastern Europe, including the need to station troops and the implicit guarantee of support for their regimes. Soviet support, however, also implicitly meant Soviet domination, and the willingness to accept Soviet advice on the need for reform. Thus, within socialist internationalism contradictory elements were present: acceptance of one aspect (Soviet support) meant acceptance of the other (Soviet control).

The use of socialist internationalism to justify the invasion of Czechoslovakia after 1968, and later in the 1970s to do the same for the leading role of the Soviet Union within the bloc, robbed the concept of any usefulness. In this respect, rationalization was a source of deterioration of the term, because it came to be associated with an action which was inconsistent with certain fundamental aspects of the theory. This was especially the case when the "leading role" of the Soviet Union was known to be a euphemism for the subordination of national to international interests. In the 1970s, this subordination meant the orientation of national economies toward the Soviet Union rather than the West. Under Gorbachev, despite protestations that such subordination was no longer demanded, there was still a residual suggestion that the Soviet Union would like to see East European leaders sacrifice their interests – staying in power – in favor of Soviet interests – creating a more favorable international environment for cooperation with the West by adopting reform policies and improving the bloc's international image. Such tensions ran just beneath the surface at international convocations such as the July 1989 PCC meeting.

In addition, use of the concept of socialist internationalism to rationalize policy – whether the invasion of Czechoslovakia or the leading role of the Soviet Union – put certain constraints on how that concept could be used by others. In other words, those of a reformist bent could not use such phrases as "mutual aid," "fraternal assist ance," or other euphemisms for socialist internationalism if they wished to get their point across to like-minded elites. At the very least, they had to redefine these terms. Therefore, those who challenged the status quo were forced to devise new slogans with which to encapsulate their political program.

I would also suggest that the act of ritualistically repeating a rationalization – as in the 1970s, when loyal East European leaders proclaimed fealty at international gatherings and at home – drove changes in the perception of the concept among both listeners and speakers. In this respect, the meaning of a fundamental principle was changed through its use as a communicative device.

Ideology was used to communicate intent as well as loyalty. In the early 1980s, offering novel interpretations of dogmatized ideological concepts was a way of communicating with those of a similar bent either in other institutions or other countries. Communication here resembled the cohesion-building function of ideology which other authors have noted (see Light, 1986: 328). Reform-minded Soviets such as Bogomolov and Novopashin seem to have consciously repeated the more reformist East European interpretations of socialist internationalism; these statements in fact gave them license to do so. Later in the decade, ideology communicated Soviet encouragement of reform and a willingness to restructure relations with Eastern Europe, perhaps over the heads of East European leaders. It is doubtful that the populations of Eastern Europe carefully read PCC communiqués for hints of change, but the bureaucracy and policymaking elites certainly did. The wording of communiqués and subsequent comments by leading Soviets were attempts to call for reform in Eastern Europe without in so many words actually betraying the present leaders.

Legitimation was another important function of ideology in the Soviet–East European relationship. The concept of socialist internationalism was used in attempts to legitimate the system in a number of ways. In the first place, it provided a *raison d'être* for elites, at whatever level of the decisionmaking process. Internationalism meant that one was part of something larger, part of the historical process.

Second, that aspect of socialist internationalism which stressed the universal applicability of the Soviet model and the general laws of socialist construction served to legitimate the Soviet system. It validated the Soviet system internally and externally by demonstrating that it was not a freak of historical development. Finally, internationalism was a means of legitimating the hardships created by the construction of an immense military-industrial complex. From the official East

European perspective, internationalist duty entailed the stationing of Soviet troops. "Selfless aid" to fellow socialist countries and "unity" in the face of imperialist hostility, meanwhile, both demanded constantly growing military expenditures, in the view of Soviet leaders.

Soviet-style internationalism, once subjected to re-interpretation, was in all likelihood doomed to collapse. It was never built on a community of interest, except for a fear of Germany, and the maintenance of communist rule. These were in fact strong binding ties for a certain period, but they outlived their effectiveness when the potential benefits of interaction with the German economy came to outweigh fear in the one country which could exercise veto power, the Soviet Union. Add to this the fact that Soviet interests no longer required the maintenance of inefficient socialist regimes because of their inability to develop more efficient economies, and the entire rationale of the bloc dissolved.

5   Socialism redefined

Although it was initially a domestic issue, the question of contradictions had important theoretical implications for the conduct of Soviet policy toward Eastern Europe. The notion of contradictions is an essential element of dialectical materialism, on which the entire official Soviet worldview was based. Raising the question of the possibility of antagonistic contradictions in socialism, therefore, challenged many of the basic assumptions about Soviet domestic and foreign policy, in much the same way as did the re-interpretation of socialist internationalism.

The suggestion that contradictions could become antagonistic was a threat to the established order in a number of ways. First, it called into question the internal unity of Soviet-style systems by suggesting that the interests of various social groups within them could differ fundamentally and perhaps irreconcilably. Second, the necessary correlate was that if such could be the case *within* socialist states, then a similar non-coincidence of interests could arise *between* them as well. This, of course, threatened the unity of the bloc, which as we saw in previous chapters was a primary objective of Soviet policy.

Debates over the nature of socialist contradictions were by no means a new phenomenon. Such debates had taken place both within the Soviet theoretical community and between the Soviets and the rest of the international communist movement in the 1970s, and typically arose in response to crises in Eastern Europe which necessitated some sort of theoretical and practical response by the Soviets. The debate which developed between 1982 and 1986 was no exception, and in many ways was a conscious attempt to determine the sources and implications of the Polish crisis of 1980–1.

The crisis in Poland, of course, was not the only reason that Soviet scholars renewed the discussion of contradictions. The growing stagnation of the Soviet economy, in the first place, graphically illustrated the need for thorough reform of the economy. Combined with this economic slowdown, generational change among the Soviet leadership loosened the restrictions on ideological discourse. Significantly, the most controversial articles on contradictions appeared in late 1982, just before Brezhnev's death. With his passing, many previously unquestionable tenets became prone to re-assessment. A more immediate effect of the aging of the Soviet leadership was that with the death of long-time party secretary Mikhail Suslov in January 1982, firm control over ideological matters was relaxed.

Finally, Brezhnev had called at the 26th Party Congress in 1981 for a new edition of the 1961 Party Program. This made the proper characterization of the social development of Soviet society essential, and provided an opportunity for those of a reformist bent to influence the basic programmatic statement of the party's policy. Boris Ponomarev, chief of the Central Committee International Department, headed a commission set up after the Congress to draft a new program. Then in April 1984, it was decided that the CC Secretariat, under Mikhail Gorbachev, would direct the work of the commission. As later revealed in the party press, there were numerous opponents of a liberal rewriting of the program, and a draft finished in February 1985 required "corrections" after the selection of Gorbachev as general secretary in March ("Iz istorii sozdaniya programm," 1991: 131–2). Therefore, these articles were also part of the wider effort to influence the direction of party policy.

In addition to the Polish crisis, we may also see armed clashes between socialist states as impetus for a re-examination of the possibility of intersocialist contradictions. The 1979 war between Vietnam and China was one such example, the Soviet border conflict with China another. Despite Soviet vilification and no matter the "deformations," China was still considered a socialist state by many Soviet scholars (despite the official position that it acted "objectively" in the interests of imperialism). Some Soviet writers in fact explicitly referred to the Sino–Vietnamese conflict as an example of an intersocialist contradiction which needed to be explained. In addition, the Liaison Department for relations with socialist countries still had responsibility for relations with China within the party apparatus. Thus, a war between China and Vietnam brought up the question as to whether or not there was an objective, materialist basis for intersocialist conflicts. Soviet scholars could only return to the question of the nature of the Soviet–Chinese clash in the looser atmosphere of the 1980s.

On a more general level, continuing discord within the Council for

Mutual Economic Assistance and the Warsaw Pact over such issues as integration of national economies, the "levelling out" of development levels, burden-sharing, and out-of-area operations clearly demonstrated the difficulty of the "harmonization of national and international interests." Khrushchev's original intent for the CMEA was that it should serve as a supra-national planning agency, promoting the *"sblizheniye"* (drawing together) of the socialist countries. In the face of Romanian resistance in the early 1960s, Soviet policy became more oriented toward a less innocuous (from their point of view) integration, and attempts to coordinate economic plans (see Marer, 1984: 155–62). This approach was enshrined in the 1971 Comprehensive Program for socialist integration, although the market mechanisms for achieving integration also were given a role, at East European insistence. By the early 1980s, however, problems began to crop up in energy policy especially, as Soviet production levelled off and Soviet and East European energy inefficiency and demand continued to grow (see Hardt, 1984). These were among the different problems making themselves felt in the early 1980s.

The nature of socialist contradictions

Contradictions and crises

The debate on the possibility of antagonistic contradictions in socialism was essentially a simple one: was it possible for the nonantagonistic contradictions of socialist societies to take on the features of antagonistic contradictions? Other issues were also discussed under the rubric of contradictions, among them the degree of "integrity" of the socialist system (the question of the unity of opposites); the question of the "basic" and "chief" contradictions in socialism; and the advantages of cooperative (group) versus commonly-owned (state, all-people's) forms of ownership. Such questions had important implications for the character of any reform or change undertaken in the system. For example, those who believed that collective forms retained great potential extolled the virtues of "brigade work," in which individual labor collectives were given the right to conclude their own contracts with enterprises, providing a measure of incentive. Those who adhered to the primacy of state forms of ownership suggested the "statization" of (supposedly) cooperatively owned enterprises, such as the collective farms.

As chief editor of *Kommunist* from mid-1976, Richard Kosolapov had ample opportunity to promote such views. He had already been active in promoting the orthodox interpretations of these issues in the 1970s as an up-and-coming consultant in the Propaganda Department, and then as first deputy editor of the party newspaper *Pravda*. He came out in favor of the primacy of state forms of ownership, and championed Soviet society's increasing degree of "integrity," claiming that "the boundaries between classes have been substantially destroyed" (Kosolapov, 1973: 33–4; see also Kosolapov, 1974); he rarely spoke even of the existence of contradictions (for example, see Kosolapov, 1981).

Although the debate took place mainly between 1982 and 1984, the possibility of antagonisms in socialism had already been raised authoritatively in late 1981 by Pëtr Fedoseyev, in the journal *World Marxist Review*.[1] One of the *doyens* of the Soviet theoretical scene, Fedoseyev had been an active party philosopher since the time of Stalin (see Chapter 2), when he served as editor of the theoretical journal *Bolshevik* (later known as *Kommunist*) from 1946–1948. Fedoseyev seemed to be more willing than others to entertain novel ideas even as far back as the Stalin era (see Hahn, 1982: 30–1), when he had been criticized by Suslov for "subjectivism" and misinterpretation of Stalin's *Economic Problems of Socialism in the USSR* (see Hahn, 1982; Petroff, 1988: 65–6). By 1981 he was a vice president of the Academy of Sciences and the head of its philosophy and law department. A number of important institutes were subordinate to this department, including the Institute of the International Workers' Movement and the Institute of Philosophy. The former institution published the journal *Rabochiy Klass i Sovremennyy Mir*, in which Novopashin's important 1985 article appeared; the latter published *Voprosy Filosofii*, where many of the important articles on contradictions were printed. He was also a full member of the Central Committee, and later became the head of the Academy's Social Sciences Section (see Appendix).

Discussing the role of contradictions in the development of socialism, Fedoseyev claimed that in the Soviet Union there was a "lag" of certain forms of management and distribution behind productive forces; in other words, a contradiction, albeit partial (Fedoseyev, 1981a: 26). He also noted an "imbalance" in the development of heavy and light (consumer goods) industries, and used this to urge more investment in the latter. Then, discussing the development of the socialist world and with an obvious nod to those countries in which "crisis situations" had developed (such as Poland), he declared:

> it would be an oversimplification to think that all contradictions in a
> society following the socialist road are always and under any circum-
> stances bound to be nonantagonistic ... Historical experience show
> that in certain conditions ... nonantagonistic contradictions could
> acquire the features of antagonistic ones. (p. 27)

This was a carefully worded view which differed markedly from that
of other leading Soviet ideologists. (Curiously, in a statement which
could be aimed at his fellow Soviets as much as at the West, he also
criticized "metaphysically minded people" who could not reconcile
peaceful coexistence with class struggle: "[T]hose who use the concrete truths of yesterday are always in danger of sliding into dogmatism" (p. 29).)

That this article may have sent the wrong signal was evident by the
fact that Fedoseyev partially retracted this view in an article in Kosolapov's *Kommunist* in November. Much of this article was taken from
that which appeared in *World Marxist Review*, but the possibility of
antagonistic contradictions was notably absent (compare Fedoseyev,
1981a: 27 and 1981b). Instead, the article included an extensive discussion to the "homogeneity" and "integrity" of Soviet society. In fact, this
article was striking in that it virtually never used the word contradictions and referred instead to "differences" (*razlichiya*) (see
especially p. 47).

Whether this was Fedoseyev's doing or otherwise is impossible to
say. His article, however, did appear in the same issue as a speech by
Suslov to a union-wide conference of leading figures in the social
sciences (Suslov, 1981). Suslov's speech also did not mention contradictions at all, an omission made even more glaring by the fact that he
urged analysis of the problems of the materialist dialectic – "the living
soul of Marxism" (p. 7). Suslov also pointed to "imperialist" efforts at
undermining the "foundations" of socialism in Poland as the main
cause of the crisis (p. 5–6). This suggested that Fedoseyev's article in
Kommunist was edited to present a more conformist line.

The *World Marxist Review* article by Fedoseyev, however, gave
license to other Soviet scholars to open the debate on contradictions,
and articles by Vadim Semënov and Anatoliy Butenko in *Voprosy
Filosofii* in 1982 brought the debate to a broader audience (Semënov,
1982a, 1982b; Butenko, 1982b). In a two-part article published in the
July and September issues of his own journal, Semënov wrote favorably of the 1965 Liberman reforms (1982a: 30), noting that they had
served to temporarily overcome the growing contradictions of Soviet
society. High growth rates, on the one hand, and the incomplete

nature of the reforms, on the other, however, had allowed new contradictions to develop in the 1970s, Semënov wrote. In the second part of his article, Semënov took Fedoseyev's views on contradictions further, developing in detail the proposition that contradictions could become antagonistic and lead to crises in socialist societies (Semënov, 1982b: 9–16). He qualified it, however, with the assertion that the disruptive activities of imperialism were essential in this process. Nonetheless, his list of the five factors which facilitated the growing over of nonantagonistic contradictions into antagonistic contained four internal and one external, thus emphasizing the former (Semënov, 1982b: 14–15).

Butenko, however, paid but scant attention to external factors in the development of antagonistic contradictions. He, too, quoted Fedoseyev's "well-known" article, and put forward the view which was to earn him the honor of vitriolic attack by the party *apparat*; namely, that the basic contradiction of socialism was in "the interaction of productive forces and production relations" (Butenko, 1982b: 20). The question was whether or not there was a real contradiction between them, or simply a lag. Fedoseyev's position was slightly more conservative in that he saw it mainly as a lag, and therefore a "partial" contradiction. Butenko was much more forthright, saying

> the *basic contradiction of socialism* is a contradiction of the socialist means of production, namely: the contradiction between the growing productive forces of society and the existing real system of socialist production relations in society ... The basic contradiction of socialism, although it is included in the means of production, nonetheless is connected not only with the entire economic system, but also with the political organization of society. (Butenko, 1982b: 22, original emphasis)

Although this differed slightly from Semënov's position, the point is that both proposed that periodic crises in Eastern Europe more often than not were mainly caused by internal factors.

Imperialist interference, while an important factor for Butenko, still was seen largely as a catalyst which aided in the development of antagonisms. In a less outspoken article, Butenko (1982a) urged the adoption of measures similar to the New Economic Policy of the 1920s in order to avoid "deformations" of socialism. The Soviet NEP was a period in which many market mechanisms were re-introduced after the draconian measures of War Communism, such as the requisitioning of food for the cities. The Bolsheviks retained what were known as the "commanding heights" of industry – transportation, heavy industry – while consumer industries were left largely in the hands of small-scale entrepreneurs. In other words, Butenko and others were suggesting the appropriateness of some kind of market mechanisms which would better answer the needs of Soviet consumers.

Such views differed enormously from that which prevailed in the stagnant ideological atmosphere of the Brezhnev era, however. Kosolapov came to the defense of the party's position, this time in the pages of *Pravda*. In a March 1983 article, he stressed the "integrity" (*tselostnost'*, as in an integral whole) of Soviet society. He spoke of two general trends of socialist progress, epitomized in the Soviet experience: the continuous industrialization of all branches of the economy (especially agriculture), and the "consistent bringing together" (*sblizheniye*) of the two forms of socialist ownership, cooperative and all-people's (*obshchenarodnoye*). Such general trends, he claimed, allowed one to speak of the elimination of class differences, and hence antagonisms, between the workers, peasantry and *intelligentsia* (Kosolapov, 1983).

Kosolapov noted the attempts, "in certain publications," to portray the events in Poland as proof of the possibility of antagonistic contradictions in socialism. His response was to assert that in Poland, "it is impossible to consider the tasks of the transitional period finally decided; Polish society is [still] coping with the task of the full construction of socialism." In other words, the experience of crises in Eastern Europe was of little relevance for the Soviet Union, where it had been claimed since the 1930s that socialism had been built. Any "differences" (*raskhozhdeniya*) which did arise in socialist societies were explicable, in this view, as differences between individuals, or between "egoistic" individual and group interests, and were more often than not "remnants" of the pre-socialist past. Kosolapov made no mention of contradictions other than to refute the possibility of antagonism.

The debate at this stage was limited more or less to the domestic Soviet repercussions of the Polish crisis. Soviet authors who analyzed it undogmatically but still within the framework of dialectical materialism were led to the conclusion that an objective basis for the growth of nonantagonistic contradictions into antagonisms did exist in socialism. Kosolapov's response bore the stamp of official approval in several respects, including its venue (the party newspaper *Pravda*) and author (the chief editor of the party theoretical journal). What is more, it betrayed a fear on the part of the party that talk of antagonisms within socialist society could provide a basis for the expression of basically irreconcilable group interests, including ethnic. Kosolapov's article contained several assertions that the elimination of class differences had proceeded hand in hand with the elimination of national differences in the Soviet Union.

As we have seen, one of the elements of socialist internationalism was Soviet emphasis on the "general laws" of socialist development. Analyses such as those of Butenko, Semënov and to a lesser degree Fedoseyev which asserted the possibility of antagonisms and conflicts within socialist societies implied that such could be the case within the Soviet Union – the paradigm for socialist development. At issue here was the definition of those general laws, and thus what was acceptable within socialist societies. More basically, the debate over contradictions was also a debate over the model of socialism to which the rest of the bloc was to adhere.

What is more, one's characterization of the causes of crises in socialist countries determined one's response to those crises. If primarily internal factors were to blame, then the suggestion was that reform of the system from within was appropriate. If, on the other hand, one identified the causes of instability in the actions of imperialism and "remnants" of bourgeois consciousness in individuals, then a response which stressed strict discipline and increased "educational" work was appropriate. In addition, a position such as Kosolapov's which held that a "general trend" in socialist development was the fusion of two forms of socialist ownership allowed little scope for market reform, suggesting instead increasing centralization and discipline.

The reform-oriented position did, in fact, receive limited backing from the new general secretary, Yuriy Andropov, in his February 1983 article on "The Teaching of Karl Marx and Certain Questions of Socialist Construction in the USSR." Andropov's article repeated the Leninist tenet that "antagonisms and contradictions are not one and the same. The first disappears, the second remains under socialism." However, he went on to admit that "inattention" to contradictions could produce "serious collisions" in socialist societies (Andropov, 1983: 15). In what became a signal to the theoretical community (and gist for the title of innumerable articles), Andropov called for the "correct use of the contradiction of socialism as a source and stimulus of its progressive development" (p. 15). Andropov also sent a signal to the Soviet theoretical community by stating that the Soviet Union was still in the *beginning* of a "long historical stage" of the construction of developed socialism; not, as Soviet theoreticians had been wont to declare for many years, well along the way (p. 14). We shall see later in this chapter that Gorbachev, often considered Andropov's protégé, in fact gave a more definite, but still qualified, endorsement of the reform position in December 1984.

The absence of any reference to antagonistic contradictions should not lead us to place Andropov in a camp which denied the need for reform. There are three points to consider. In the first place, even Gorbachev never clearly came out and spoke in favor of the view that contradictions could become antagonistic, indicating that even among reformers it took a great deal to overcome old modes of thinking. Secondly, Andropov would have been constrained simply by what was possible. Even the general secretary had to acknowledge certain realities and interests in the society, and no Soviet leader could openly deny such a basic Leninist tenet as the nonantagonistic nature of socialist contradictions. However, it was possible to identify the non-correlation of production relations with productive forces as a contradiction in need of resolution, and Andropov's reference to "serious collisions" seemed to have been an acceptable euphemism.

Finally, it may be the case that the article was slightly edited. Fëdor Burlatskiy claims he participated in the collection of materials for the article, and asserts it was more oriented to reform along the lines of NEP in its original form. However, it "fell into the hands of the ideologues from the journal *Kommunist*," he writes, and was given a different cast, one emphasizing discipline and state control of the economy (Burlatskiy, 1990: 359). The article was published first in that journal, which of course was edited by Kosolapov at the time.

This would not seem to be something that Kosolapov could have accomplished on his own, however. It surely would have required the agreement of the general secretary, albeit perhaps under pressure from other leaders; Burlatskiy has described a process under Brezhnev in which all members of the Politburo and Secretariat had the right to comment on articles and speeches reflecting the party line (p. 291). We saw in the last chapter as well that as late as November 1987, the Politburo could influence the tone of a speech, as in Gorbachev's speech for the 70th anniversary of the October Revolution.

In the early 1980s there seemed to be three main views on social development, contradictions and similar questions: the *purist, conservative,* and *reformist* views. Some authors have adhered to a bipolar scheme: Suslov reportedly viewed the main cause of the Polish crisis in the lack of discipline within the Polish United Workers' Party (PUWP), while Konstantin Chernenko saw the problem not so much in a lack of discipline, but rather in the fact that the PUWP had lost contact with the "masses" (see Brahm, 1985; a similar view is given in Dahm, 1985b).

Fedoseyev reflected the latter view in a speech to the Academy of Sciences in March 1983 (Fedoseyev, 1983). Elizabeth Teague, meanwhile, has suggested a similarity between the views of Fedoseyev and Kosolapov (Teague, 1988: 299). While her description of Kosolapov as a "purist" is accurate, Fedoseyev seems to have been more willing to entertain novel interpretations of theoretical concepts such as contradictions. His September 1981 article clearly set him apart from Kosolapov in his willingness to accept the possibility of antagonisms, but in November he was considerably less innovative in an article in Kosolapov's journal. (There has been some indication (Ploss, 1986: 151) that Soviet intent *vis-à-vis* the Polish crisis changed in September; this may suggest why Fedoseyev, as an official party philosopher, changed his line after that time.) Then, after Andropov's comments in February 1983, he once again had license to discuss contradictions. Writing in *Voprosy Filosofii* (a definitely more friendly journal than *Kommunist*), Fedoseyev discussed the (nonantagonistic) contradiction between productive forces and production relations, a concept missing from his articles of late 1982 (see Fedoseyev, 1983). He did not repeat his assertion of the possibility of antagonisms, but still went farther than "purists" such as Kosolapov.

It seems logical to see Fedoseyev as belonging to a "conservative" wing of the party which favored limited reform; this is the line which prevailed during 1983 and would explain his views that spring. It would also explain any similarity between the two, since Kosolapov as editor of the party theoretical journal had to reflect the current line to some degree as well. The conservative position was defined in the maneuvering for power in Brezhnev's last months, when Chernenko published article in which he reiterated the possibility of nonantagonistic contradictions, thus presenting himself as recognizing the need for limited reform of the system. He wrote that contradictions were inherent in socialism, and that they differed from the antagonisms of capitalism, of course. But, he noted, not all the contradictions of socialism were due to "remnants" of the past (Chernenko, 1982: 30). In this he seemed to go beyond an orthodox view, while still adhering to the distinctive and non-conflictual nature of socialist contradictions.

The purists, meanwhile, were those such as Kosolapov and Suslov who stressed the homogeneity of Soviet society and the unity of opposites to deny the existence of contradictions. In his 1977 speech to a scientific conference dedicated to the October Revolution, Suslov stated that the "major theoretical problems are those connected with progress towards homogeneity of the social structure of our society, its increasing unity, and ever greater cohesion" of Soviet nationalities (Suslov, 1977: 2). It was only when challenged by a third group, the reformists who asserted that there were indeed serious (and possibly antagonistic) contradictions in socialist societies, that purists and conservatives turned to the Leninist distinction between antagonisms and contradictions.

Contradictions and the socialist community

If the early 1980s witnessed initiation of a debate over the question of contradictions within socialism, it also saw a broadening of the debate to include the question of contradictions between socialist countries. If it was hard for reformist theorists to gain acceptance of the notion of antagonisms within socialist states, however, it proved considerably harder to win approval for the assertion of even nonantagonistic contradictions between them.

As we saw in Chapter 4, Yuriy Novopashin of the Institute of the Economics of the World Socialist System (IEWSS) had contributed to the debate over the concept of socialist internationalism with a 1983 article in *Nauchnyy Kommunizm* (Scientific Communism). Novopashin's article was the first serious treatment not only of the question of the relationship of international and common-democratic principles within the concept of internationalism, but also of the possibility of contradictions between socialist countries. It was based on a "round-table" conference given by the editorial staff of the journal together with the IEWSS and the Moscow section of the USSR Philosophical Society ("Sotsialisticheskiye," 1983: 125).

Among the participants in the conference was Butenko, who, as a social scientist of some repute, gave the first remarks on Novopashin's presentation. But it was not so much what was said as the fact that the possibility of contradictions not only within but between socialist countries, raised earlier in the 1970s, was again being discussed. This time, however, taking part in the discussion was a leading proponent of the view that contradictions could become antagonistic, and one of his colleagues at the IEWSS, who urged a re-interpretation of socialist internationalism.

Novopashin's article, which was edited and expanded between its presentation in March and its publication in *Nauchnyy Kommunizm* six months later (it contained references to the June 1983 Central Committee plenum), also spoke of contradictions between socialist countries. He noted three main causes:

the socialist countries' transition to intensive economic development and the non-coincidence of these states' interests in some respects;

the differences in approach to certain questions of world politics; and

the consequences of the effects on social life within certain socialist countries of "class-hostile" forces. (Novopashin, 1983: 75)

This was a frank assessment of Soviet differences with the rest of the "socialist world." Novopashin was to become even more outspoken in 1985, however, as we saw in the last chapter, when he questioned the hierarchical aspects of the principle of socialist internationalism.

Although views such as these were dangerous even while confined to one or two institutes, they undoubtedly took on a greater threat to prevailing ideological dogmas when shared more widely within the theoretical community as a whole. For instance, the famous "Novosibirsk report," given by the sociologist Tatyana Zaslavskaya in April 1983 to a closed seminar organized by the Academy of Sciences, the Central Committee and the state planning agency Gosplan, demonstrated directly to the *apparat* that the notion of antagonistic contradictions was an attractive ideological explanation for many Soviet scholars. Describing the main elements of the system of economic administration in the Soviet Union, Zaslavskaya pointed to the tenet which held to the "absence under socialism of deep, and all the more, antagonistic, contradictions between personal, group and social interests, just as between the interests of various classes and social groups." In a footnote, she stated: "A quite convincing criticism of these positions was given by A. P. Butenko in the article 'Contradictions of the development of socialism as a social structure' in the journal *Voprosy Filosofii*" (Zaslavskaya, 1983: 5). One of the major conclusions of this report was that any meaningful reform would necessarily engender significant social tensions; in other words, contradictions. She also noted the representation of *bona fide* interests by definite social groups such as managers, workers, and the bureaucracy. This was another rejection of the unity of Soviet society, inasmuch as the party had always been portrayed as the true representative of societal interests. Her conclusion was that this would complicate any reform by impinging on the interests of certain groups, the bureaucracy in particular (Zaslavskaya, 1983: 18).

A purist counterattack

Kosolapov's firm rebuff in *Pravda* to those who held to the possibility of antagonistic contradictions had evidently fallen on deaf ears. Accordingly, more criticisms of dialectically unsound (from the party point of view) theoretical works appeared throughout the summer of 1983. One such criticism appeared in *Kommunist* under the harsh title of "Is this a development of the Marxist-Leninist teaching on contradiction?" (Dudel', 1983). Written by a prominent party philosopher, the article scored a number of methodological points in criticizing a book written by V. V. Borodkin. Noting that Borodkin worked in the Institute of Philosophy's Materialist Dialectic section, the author asked menacingly: "Is the position of the author the position of the sector of the Institute of Philosophy? This question awaits an answer" (Dudel', 1983: 115). Although Borodkin's book did not deal directly with the question of antagonistic contradictions, this is representative of widespread criticism aimed at the Institute of Philosophy in the summer of 1983.

Another critical article was published by a member of the Institute of Philosophy itself, Tsolak Stepanyan. He noted that the debate over contradictions in *Voprosy Filosofii* was "positive," but criticized Butenko's position on antagonistic contradictions. Stepanyan wrote:

> In this case social class antagonisms are obviously being confused with the vestiges of capitalism [and] the transitional period ... is simply being identified with the socialist phase. (Stepanyan, 1983: 24)

With statements such as these, Stepanyan seemed to be disassociating himself from his colleagues at *Voprosy Filosofii*.

Such distancing seemed appropriate in light of the June 1983 party plenum which strongly denied the possibility of antagonistic contradictions. At this meeting Chernenko assumed the mantle of party ideologist, and in his speech on ideological work reaffirmed the inadmissibility of antagonistic contradictions. The plenum as a whole took something of a middle position, however, when it adopted Chernenko's position urging more "educational work," while in the very same sentence claiming that not all the inadequacies of socialism could be traced to "remnants of the past in the consciousness of the people" (as quoted in Butenko, 1984).

These remarks pointed to the fact that Butenko's and Semënov's articles had attracted a great deal of attention; what is more, they were the subject of discussions "in various scientific and educational institutions" throughout 1978 ("Diskussiya," 1984). Kosolapov[2] restated his views in a long interview in the intellectuals' newspaper, *Literaturnaya Gazeta*, at the beginning of February 1984 (Kosolapov, 1984a). Butenko and Semënov were subjected to criticism in the "discussion" mentioned above published later that month in Semënov's journal. Interestingly, some of these criticisms were taken from a conference held at the Moscow State Institute of International Relations (MGIMO), an institute for training cadres associated with the Ministry of Foreign Affairs. This implies that there was a need to address such views even within the Foreign Ministry.

This indicates that a rather sharp struggle was taking place behind the scenes in the Soviet political establishment throughout 1983. Two important political changes took place: the selection of Vadim Medvedev in August to become chief of the Central Committee Science and Educational Institutions Department, and the return of Aleksandr Yakovlev from Canada to head the Institute of World Economics and International Relations (IMEMO). Curiously, August also saw the replacement of Boris Ukraintsev as director of the Institute of Philosophy and his replacement by Georgiy Smirnov. All three – Yakovlev, Medvedev, and Smirnov – had worked together in the Propaganda Department in the early 1970s. Smirnov alone had remained there, in the capacity of first deputy chief. Yakovlev was made ambassador to Canada after his attack on Russian nationalists in the early 1970s, and Medvedev became director of the Academy of Social Sciences, one of the most authoritative ideological outlets, in 1978.

All three appointments were clearly promotions, and seemed calculated to take control of the three institutions which would prove crucial in developing a theoretical backing for reform. The Science Department exercised control over institutes of the Academy of Sciences, and one must admit the philosophical content to Gorbachev's "new thinking" in foreign policy (see the article by Yakovlev's successor as head of IMEMO, Yevgeniy Primakov, 1987). Yakovlev and Medvedev fared better in the Gorbachev period than did Smirnov; they went on to become secretaries and members of the Politburo, while Smirnov became an advisor to Gorbachev in 1985. He then seemed to fall from grace, becoming head of the Institute of Marxism-Leninism. In any case, it seemed that Gorbachev, as the secretary in charge of personnel at this time, was consolidating control of an important segment of the scientific establishment.

In early 1984, Butenko and Semënov published self-criticisms in *Voprosy Filosofii*. Semënov's was certainly more far-reaching than that of Butenko, who in fact criticized some of his fellow's views. In his self-criticism, however, Butenko gave a strident defense of his positions and an attack on those of Kosolapov. The latter had stated in *Literaturnaya Gazeta* that the basic contradiction in socialism was between "the old and the new;" in other words, between the new socialist nature of social relations and the remnants of pre–socialist tendencies in the consciousness of individuals. Relying once again on the example of Poland, Butenko asked why similar crises had not occurred in countries where the same objective factors existed. He went even farther, claiming that the PUWP had not been able to resolve contradictions in time because it did not have a "scientific conception of the solution of contradictions" (Butenko, 1984: 127). Just as Kosolapov could rely on the directives of the June 1983 plenum to deny the possibility of antagonistic contradictions, so did Butenko, in this case to remind his readers that the plenum had criticized those who primarily blamed "remnants of capitalism" for crises in socialism.

Several things are interesting about the Butenko–Kosolapov debate from the point of view of Soviet–East European relations. As mentioned above, it was essentially a debate about not only the nature of crises and contradictions, but how to resolve them. As such, disagreements about how to resolve crises were debates over how much leeway to allow the East European regimes to do so. This depended, in large measure, on the initial conception of socialism with which one started. Butenko, Semënov and Ambartsumov (see below) all spoke quite favorably of the New Economic Policy (NEP) of the 1920s, implying that one acceptable response to crisis, as far as they were concerned, was the implementation of some kind of limited market reform and the restoration of the *smychka* (link) between the peasantry and the working class (rather than the former's destruction, as under Stalin). Kosolapov, meanwhile, presented a vision of socialism – communicated as the prevailing view through its prominent display in the pages of the central press – which left no room for types of ownership other than cooperative and state, similarly limiting the East Europeans through the notion of the universality of the general laws of socialist development.

Challenge to the party

The repeated endorsement of the orthodox position in party forums, combined with criticisms and self-criticisms appearing in the original journal of dissemination, sent a clear signal to the East Europeans. Despite the hopes raised by Andropov's brief tenure, by the spring of 1984 there was little prospect of meaningful reform in the Soviet Union, and even less chance that the East Europeans would be allowed to experiment on their own.

Thus, the publication of yet another article, in April 1984, which suggested the applicability and appropriateness of NEP must have pleasantly surprised reform-minded East Europeans. Yevgeniy Ambartsumov's article in *Voprosy Istorii* was taken as a broadening of the debate and a sign of the strength of reformist views in Moscow, coming as it did in the normally staid history journal, previously uninvolved in the discussions.

Ambartsumov's article raised many hackles in the party and earned harsh criticism in *Kommunist* (see below, p. 149). It is easy to see why, because it was the most strident attack on the Party's positions – figuratively and literally – seen in an official publication in years. It is worth quoting at length, not least because it faithfully reflected many of the views expressed by others in less direct fashion.

As a means of combatting "bureaucratic perversions," Ambartsumov quoted Lenin to call for more non-party participants in the government (Ambartsumov, 1984: 26–7). As for party privilege, he quoted the 10th Party Congress document titled "General Measures for the Revitalization of the Party," which called for "a decisive struggle with the misuse on the part of Party members by means of the position for material advantage" (p. 28). Worse, from the party's point of view, even its leading role was subject to scrutiny. "In the opinion of Lenin, strengthening the leading role of the party should not mean substitutions of government organs by the party leadership, *since this breeds irresponsibility*" (p. 28, emphasis added).

As for the Soviet Union's own crisis experience, he described the Kronstadt rebellion of 1921 mainly as an internal socio-political crisis, rather than laying the blame on counter-revolutionaries. Ambartsumov put it in even stronger terms when he stated that it was a "conflict within the system, between the regime and a part of its social base" (p. 17). The most attention he gave to counter-revolutionaries was to say that they feed on mistakes made by socialist governments; mistakes which first of all had internal sources. It was certainly not accidental, of course, that these views were so similar to those of Butenko since both were section heads at the same institute, the IEWSS. Butenko and Bogomolov had been active since the early 1970s in bringing reform-minded scholars to the IEWSS and creating an atmosphere conducive to progressive thought.

In the conclusion of the article, NEP is described as "beginning as an anti-crisis measure, which grew into the optimal strategy of the transition to socialism" (p. 29). Ambartsumov stated that the socialist countries, in analyzing the causes of their internal crises, turned to the Leninist experience for solutions to their crises. "The success of NEP," he wrote, was its "clear orientation toward the stimulating role of individual, above all economic, interests" (p. 25). And not only among the peasantry, but among government enterprises as well. Such lessons, he claimed, were useful and meaningful "even today."

Interestingly, Ambartsumov had served as co-editor of a book on "Politics and Socialism" published by the IEWSS jointly with the PUWP Higher Party School in 1982. His views and those of his most prominent colleagues at the IEWSS, whose articles appeared in the book as well, therefore must have been quite well known to Polish political scientists (see the review in *Voprosy Filosofii*, no. 3, 1984).

One of the first responses to this attempted re-interpretation of a key event of Soviet history was a review article in *Kommunist* which roundly criticized Butenko and Semënov by name. The author equated the "organizers and participants" of such debates with "revisionists" such as Bernstein and Kautsky (Kuzmen'ko, 1984: 114). He also criticized Butenko in particular for suggesting that the notion of nonantagonism was aimed at the "theoretical justification" of the chronic shortage of consumer goods in the Soviet Union (p. 113).

Kosolapov and one of his first deputy editors responded to this latest heresy as well. Kosolapov published an article in July 1984 in *Pravda*, as the year before, in which he went into an even greater and more forceful defense of the orthodox position that antagonisms had nothing in common with socialist contradictions. He admitted that "local conflicts" could arise, but stated bluntly that any attempt to present conclusions about the possibility of antagonistic contradictions "is taken as a strange movement of thought backward" (Kosolapov, 1984b). More concretely, he rejected the suggestion that socialism's basic contradiction was between production relations and productive forces as any kind of "innovation" or "find." He also stressed the Leninist tenet of the unity of opposites to explain why contradictions could not be antagonistic. This was a favorite conservative view which stressed the unity of dialectical opposites, much as socialist internationalism stressed the international over the national. "Unity of opposites" tended to downplay the importance of contradictions simply by asserting that unity was more important than any tension in a relationship.

Yevgeniy Bugayev's criticism of Ambartsumov, meanwhile, appeared in the September issue of *Kommunist* (Bugayev, 1984). Unlike most other participants in these debates, Ambartsumov was directly singled out for criticism. Bugayev repeated most of the orthodox positions, and stressed especially the role of imperialism in the development of crises. Bugayev accused Ambartsumov of lumping all crises in Eastern Europe and the Soviet Union together, and of viewing countries in the transitional period as "finished socialism" (p. 120). Most telling was Bugayev's description of Lenin's warnings of the dangers inherent in NEP; Ambartsumov's characterization of it as the "optimal strategy" for the transition to socialism was labelled "unproved and incorrect" (p. 123).

Retractions, self-criticisms, and a message from Gorbachev

At this point, another section of the central *apparat* became involved in the controversy. An article by Vadim Medvedev in the August issue of *Voprosy Filosofii* was significant for a number of reasons. As mentioned earlier, in August 1983 Medvedev was moved to the CC Science Department, which was generally responsible for institutions of higher education. It also participated in the task of controlling the media, although the Propaganda Department had primary responsibility (Dzirkals, 1982: 25–6).

Medvedev's article appeared in the midst of this vociferous debate over the nature of contradictions and addressed it directly (Medvedev, 1984). The article was noteworthy both for its author's position and for the fact that he took a view somewhat at odds with the prevailing conservative sentiment which had been expressed by the likes of Kosolapov and others in the official party press. Medvedev spoke, as had Butenko, of contradictions which were intrinsic (*immanentniye*) to socialism, and noted that this meant the "inadmissibility" of attempts to identify contradictions only with subjective mistakes (Medvedev, 1984: 7).

While criticizing the conservatives' thesis of the unity of opposites, however (p. 4), he just as harshly criticized the notion that nonantagonistic contradictions could become antagonistic (p. 9). With such an approach, Medvedev seemed to be taking a middle position in the debate; that is, between the reformist and purist positions. We see this as well with his refusal to state clearly his view of the "basic contradiction," saying only that the problem needed more "concretization" (p. 8).

Even though he criticized the liberals, Medvedev still refrained from direct rejection of the notion that the basic contradiction of socialism was between production relations and productive forces. In fact, he came out guardedly in favor of reform with his view that "the treatment of the basic contradiction as contradictions between the directly social character of production and commodity-money relations is quite attractive" (Medvedev, 1984: 8). In other words, Medvedev did not view the contradictions of socialist society mainly in the remnants of bourgeois consciousness or in a struggle of the old and new (as did orthodox theorists), but in the nature of socialism itself. In the early 1980s, the term "commodity-money relations" was the euphemism for broaching the subject of market reform. In other words, then, Medvedev was suggesting that pricing mechanisms were perhaps a source of socialist contradictions.

The criticisms voiced by the *apparat* and Medvedev's less than wholehearted endorsement of reform produced a broad retreat all along the reformist front. *Voprosy Istorii* quickly recanted, with a letter from its editor Trukhanovskiy to *Kommunist*, and a self-criticism conference with the participation of the leadership of the History Department of the Academy of Sciences (see "Posle vystupleniya 'Kommunista'," 1984, and "Ot redaktsionnoy kollegii," 1984).

Voprosy Filosofii's self-abnegation consisted of a long editorial in October acknowledging its mistakes, as well as a theoretical conference the following month. The editorial ("Marksistsko-leninskaya filosofiya," 1984) described a meeting of the scientific council of the Institute of Philosophy in June 1984, which had discussed the work of the journal "for the last two years" – in other words, since the publication of Semënov's first article. It stated that both "shortcomings" and "serious mistakes" had been made, singling out especially Butenko's article of February 1984 and quoting Kosolapov's July *Pravda* article approvingly (if ritualistically). The November theoretical conference, interestingly enough, was arranged by the Historical Materialism section of the Moscow section of the USSR Philosophical Society, among other institutions ("Rol' protivorechiy v razvitii obshchestva," 1985: 150). The Philosophical Society had also been one of the sponsors of the conference on "Socialist international relations" two years earlier, at which Novopashin and Butenko had spoken about contradictions between socialist states. In other words, one of the sponsors of the conference at which Novopashin had aired his views was forced to arrange its own execution, so to speak.

But a pardon from the governor was on the way. In this case,

however, it is more appropriate to speak of the future governor –
Mikhail Gorbachev. At a union-wide "scientific-practical" conference
in the Kremlin devoted to party ideological work, the future general
secretary was the keynote speaker. Listed among the participants were
Fedoseyev; Medvedev; Boris Yel'tsin, then Sverdlovsk *obkom* first
secretary; Aleksandr Kapto, at the time a secretary of the Ukrainian
party organization and later chief of the CC Ideology Department; and
Richard Kosolapov among others (see "Sovershenstvovaniye razvitogo sotsializma," 1984). All became prominent figures in the Gorbachev leadership, with the exception of Kosolapov. In addition, many
other Soviet leaders were there, including Mikhail Zimyanin, the
secretary for ideology and culture; Konstantin Rusakov, the secretary
for bloc relations; and Boris Ponomarev, secretary and candidate
member of the Politburo and head of the International Department.

As others have noted (Remington, 1988: 21; White, 1988: 17), Gorbachev's speech can be seen as something of an election statement,
in which he put before the country's political elite a political slogan
to characterize his agenda.[3] Later, in February 1985 in his Supreme
Soviet election speech, he spoke of Europe as "our common home"
(Gorbachev, 1985a). If such a phrase came to figure prominently in Gorbachev's foreign policy, the same was true for domestic policy of the
phrase "the living creativity of the people." This was the title of
Gorbachev's speech and seemed to encapsulate his reform agenda.[4]
This turn to the "creativity" of the masses was a catch-phrase among
reformists at the time; after Andropov had introduced it at the official
level in his speech on Lenin's birthday in 1982, Butenko and others
used it. Gorbachev's speech was also issued in booklet form in a much
more complete form, in a press run of 100,000 copies, signed to the
press within three days of the conference. The conference proceedings
as a whole were published after three months ("Sovershenstvovaniye
razvitogo sotsializma," 1985).

In discussing the work of the country's scientific and research
organizations, Gorbachev first noted that "certain scientists at times
cannot part with outdated conceptions and stereotypes" (Gorbachev,
1984: 11). Immediately following this and no doubt purposefully,
Gorbachev turned his attention to "such a vital and topical problem, as
the interaction of contemporary productive forces and socialist production relations" (p. 12). "Dogmatic conceptions," he noted, still had
not been completely overcome in this regard, especially the "well-
known thesis about the correspondence of production relations to
productive forces under socialism." Such a thesis had been used since

the time of Stalin to suggest that socialist production relations natur-
ally corresponded to the level of productive forces, so theoretically
there could be no contradiction between them.

Assessing the causes of the slowdown in economic growth, meanwhile, he noted the influence of external factors, but stated that at the
same time, "the necessity of changes of certain aspects of production
relations was not recognized." Finally, Gorbachev discussed contradictions, and gave a very frank characterization of the Soviet Union's
situation:

> Under socialism, of course, they are nonantagonistic. But with the
> stagnant retention of outdated elements of production relations, a
> worsening of the economic and social situation can set in. (Gorba-
> chev, 1984: 13)

To this he added a condemnation of inertia and "conservatism of
thought" for their role in preventing the overcoming of contradictions.

There were telling differences between the texts published in *Pravda*
and in booklet form (see Remington, 1988: 21–3), suggesting that the
former's version was edited to present a less radical line – references to
money-commodity relations and the need for changes in production
relations were deleted.[5] Remington has noted that Boris Stukalin, head
of the Propaganda Department which would handle such matters,
was considered a protégé of Zimyanin, the conservative ideology
secretary with overall responsibility for the press (p. 215, n. 50). Stukalin was an early casualty of Gorbachev's consolidation of power in July
1985, and was replaced by Aleksandr Yakovlev.

We should also note that Richard Kosolapov had connections to
Zimyanin; between 1974 and 1976, Kosolapov worked as a deputy
editor under Zimyanin at *Pravda*. When Zimyanin was promoted to
secretary in 1976 and left the party newspaper, Kosolapov also left,
being promoted to editor of *Kommunist*. Kosalapov recently suggested
that good relations with Zimyanin continued into the 1980s (Kosolapov, 1991), and also that he had good relations with *Pravda*, which he
stated was why he was able to publish his articles on contradictions
there. Another indication of his connection with Zimyanin is that he
claims that neither Brezhnev nor Suslov paid much attention to his
work as editor of *Kommunist* (Kosolapov, 1991); by default, then, the
one secretary who would have had responsibility for ideology and the
press was Zimyanin.[6]

Zimyanin, too, spoke at this conference. As might be expected, his
speech contained no reformist statements, and he even claimed that
a speech given by Chernenko to the Politburo on the economy the

month before was "a party document of strategic significance." Zimyanin described Gorbachev's comments, meanwhile, only as "important" (see "Sovershenstvovaniye razvitogo sotsializma," 1984: 2).

With this speech and his accession to the post of general secretary three months later, Gorbachev clearly tipped the balance in favor of the reformist view of contradictions, although it remained politically impossible to admit that socialist societies could give birth to antagonistic contradictions. The Soviets never officially and explicitly admitted this possibility, even though outbursts of ethnic violence would seem to confirm it; they would admit to conflicts, but not "antagonisms" (see, for instance, "Protivorechiya i dvizhushchiye sily," 1989). This was certainly a manifestation of the ideological thinking which limited the capacity for successful reform.

Kosolapov published an article that summer which did not directly mention the debate of the previous two and a half years. What is more, this article was based on the speech Kosolapov gave to the same scientific-practical conference at which Gorbachev had given his criticisms of the orthodox position. Kosolapov had attempted to defend his position at the December conference, unsuccessfully as it turned out. He noted that in his capacity as editor, he came across

> many articles in which the all-around development of commodity-money relations, as before, is declared the panacea of all the disorder in the economy. But at the stage of developed socialism we have already outgrown such a one-sided approach. (Kosolapov, 1985: 17)

With this, Kosolapov clearly set himself against even moderate reform.

An article by Bogomolov in *Kommunist* on the "economic interests" of socialism suggested that Kosolapov had lost much of his influence by this time (Bogomolov, 1985). This was a clearly reformist article, speaking of the possible non-coincidence and even clash of interests among different groups in socialist societies (p. 84). He also came out in favor of the view that an objective contradiction existed between the centralization of power and "the demand for broadening the independence and initiative" of lower economic units, and noted that a "strengthening of the democratic bases of administration" was necessary for unleashing the "creativity" of the masses (p. 86).

In addition to discussing the expression of interests within socialist societies, he also touched on inter-socialist relations. In an echo of the Polish leader Jaruzelski's comment at the Warsaw Pact meeting two months before, in May, Bogomolov seconded the reformist East European view by stating:

> every socialist country, pursuing its own national-state interests ...
> thereby achieves the realization both of its own general interests and
> those of other socialist countries, and also of specific interests which
> are characteristic only for the given country, and accordingly, may
> not coincide with the interests of other countries. (p. 90)

This was very similar to what Jaruzelski had stated. It meant that on
the theoretical level, some scholars were beginning to understand that
the Soviet Union had an interest not so much in guaranteeing socialism in Eastern Europe, but in guaranteeing *stable* socialist societies.
They saw that stable regimes in Eastern Europe would benefit the
world socialist system and "international" (Soviet) interests by providing healthy economic partners and also by improving the international
image of the Soviet Union and socialism.

These views were clearly at odds with the conservative position.
This article was published in July of 1985, and it is certainly not
coincidental that this would have been one of the first issues of
Kommunist to come out with Yakovlev at the head of the Propaganda
Department.

As mentioned in the last chapter, Kosolapov was removed as editor-
in-chief of *Kommunist* by the time of the 27th Party Congress in early
1986. The whole debate on contradictions, in fact, largely subsided
after the congress. Gorbachev's speech there added more weight to the
reformist position that the "interaction" of productive forces and
production relations was the main aspect of Soviet economic practice
in need of reform (Gorbachev, 1986: 43). What is more, the new edition
of the party program stated that "objective contradictions in socialist
society" – not subjective, as in the shortcomings or mistakes of individuals – should be studied and resolved ("Program," 1986a: 199).
While not going as far as the Polish United Workers Party new
program, which acknowledged the existence of "social contradictions
based on classes" in Polish society ("Program," 1986b), it was at least an
admission of the need to go farther.

In two articles in early 1987, Butenko examined "the dialectics of
productive forces and production relations" (Butenko, 1987a), and the
"socio-economic nature of socialism" (Butenko, 1987b). In the first, a
co-authored article, Butenko referred approvingly to the 27th Congress documents, and noted that "the debate on the contradictions of
socialism is no longer something that a given journal may open on its
own initiative" (Butenko, 1987a: 41). This article also criticized the
views which Kosolapov had put forward in his 1985 article, although
not mentioning him directly. In the second, Butenko again noted the

acceptance of his views by the 27th Party Congress, and also took the opportunity to level a personal attack on Kosolapov, this time for his supposition that the further "statization" of collective farms was the next necessary step in Soviet economic development (1987b: 23).

Kosolapov responded with a long letter to the editors of *Voprosy Filosofii* in which he pointed out that Butenko had been a "pioneer" in the development of the term "developed socialism," quoting long passages from his less recent works to accuse Butenko of hypocrisy (Kosolapov, 1987).[7] Butenko, for his part, responded with a letter of his own in which he pointed out that while "developed socialism" was indeed a stage through which all socialist countries must pass, the Soviet Union itself by no means fulfilled all the criteria (Butenko, 1987b: 146).[8]

This final installment in the contradictions debate illustrated, more importantly, that by 1987 the important issue for Soviet theoreticians was not the question of contradictions within socialism, but the very nature of socialism itself. Much as the debate over socialist internationalism grew into a larger debate over "class" and "human" values in foreign policy, so too did the debate over contradictions in socialism become something larger, in this case a search for what was meant by the term "socialism." The debate over socialist internationalism also gave impetus to this theoretical exercise, as the growing willingness among Soviet authors to accept different models called into question exactly what criteria were to be used in deciding the socialist character of a political system.

Redefining socialism

On the concept of socialism

The attempt to develop a new "concept of socialism" was not so much a debate as an ongoing attempt to redefine what was meant by the term "socialism." We can identify the beginnings of this exercise in late 1987, and it certainly was well underway by mid-1988.

In his speech marking the 70th anniversary of the October Revolution, Gorbachev declared that the objective of *perestroika* was "to fully restore, both theoretically and practically, the Leninist conception of socialism" (Gorbachev, 1987: 49). Gorbachev's understanding of the "Leninist conception" of socialism, at least in 1986, was one in which "undisputed priority" was given to "communist values" in economic, social and political life. He also made clear, however, that in his view democratization and radical economic reform were also part of this concept.

Gorbachev presented his understanding of the concept of socialism in the conclusion to his speech to the 19th Party Conference in June 1988. Regarding international relations, Gorbachev said that socialism entailed the

> establishment of normal civilized relations between all peoples and states on the basis of democratic principles, equality of rights, noninterference in each other's affairs, and recognition of the sovereign right of all peoples to determine their own fate themselves. We have in mind precisely this kind of democratic, human face of socialism when talking about the qualitatively new situation in our society ... (Gorbachev, 1987: 35)

As we saw in Chapter 4, the party conference came in the midst of a debate within the Soviet Union as to the proper basis of Soviet foreign policy, and Gorbachev s statement was an important endorsement of the priority of democratic principles and "common human values." The fact that he followed such an endorsement with a reference to the "human face of socialism" also sent an important signal to Eastern Europe; by using the term associated with Czechoslovakia's Prague Spring, he thereby removed the taboo formerly associated with it.

It is true that a "return to Leninist principles" had been a feature of every Soviet general secretary's attempts to consolidate power. Stalin's claim to the Leninist theoretical mantle was put forward in a series of lectures entitled "Questions of Leninism;" these, in fact, provided many of the fundamental principles of Soviet ideology until the Gorbachev era, despite limited de-Stalinization. Both Khrushchev and Brezhnev claimed to restore Leninist principles of "collective leadership" to the Soviet system after their predecessors' excesses. Gorbachev's call for a return to the true meaning of Leninism, then, could be seen in one respect as one more Soviet leader's attempt to legitimize his rule.

At the same time, similar attempts in the past had relied on declarations from above to define "Leninism." Gorbachev's remarks, however, combined with *glasnost* (openness), initiated a broad and open debate on the concept of socialism. It seemed to accompany the reorganization of the Central Committee *apparat* in October 1988, which resulted in the creation of six commissions endowed with responsibility for different areas, including ideology and international relations (see *Izvestiya TsK KPSS*, no. 1, 1989). Vadim Medvedev, former head of the Liaison Department, was appointed to head the Ideological Commission, and it was under his aegis that the concept of socialism exercise developed in earnest.

The exercise in developing a new concept of socialism also sent a number of signals. For example, here was Medvedev, the party official formerly responsible for relations with Eastern Europe declaring in *Kommunist* that the time was past when a variety of approaches in socialist countries "was looked at with dogmatic and sectarian suspicion, considering it almost a retreat from Marxism-Leninism and socialist internationalism" (Medvedev, 1988b: 7).

At the same time, Butenko, his cohorts from the IEWSS and others were by no means idle. They took part in a discussion on "problems of working out a conception of contemporary socialism," which appeared in *Voprosy Filosofii* in late 1988 ("Problemy," 1988). The article which appeared was based on a discussion of a paper by Fëdor Burlatskiy held in April 1988,[9] and was more wide-ranging and frank in its assessments than a similar discussion which appeared in *Pravda* in the summer of 1989 ("K sovremennoy kontseptsii sotsializma," 1989). A third important article in this exercise appeared in *Kommunist* in the fall of 1989, and attempted to sum up the discussion to that point ("K novomu obliku," 1989).

In the *Voprosy Filosofii* article, we can see evidence of a growing recognition of the need to deal with the Soviet Union's past in order to overcome its present. Butenko, Burlatskiy, and many others pointed to the Stalinist roots of the "administrative-command" system, noting that this was the predominant image of the proper form of socialism in the Soviet people's consciousness. The *Pravda* article, meanwhile, emphatically stressed that the concept of socialism "presupposes the existence of a number of 'models' [variants] of development." It is noteworthy that this appeared within days of the July 1989 Warsaw Pact Political Consultative Committee meeting which had adopted a communiqué asserting exactly the same (see Chapter 4).

It is also interesting to note for our purposes that in each of these articles considerable attention was devoted to the ways in which ideology had been used to rationalize, for instance, the differences between official declarations and social reality. The discussion in *Kommunist* even went so far as to ask if working-class interests truly had been represented by Soviet ideologues, and answered:

> Hardly. The real situation of the worker in the system of production relations was hidden not only by ideology, but also by the ideological social institutions – official social science: political economy,

social philosophy, sociology, jurisprudence ... ("K novomu obliku,"
1989: 22)

In other words, ideology and its official disseminators had played a
negative ideological role, hiding the contradictions of the social system,
and serving to justify the discrepancies between official promises and
reality.

An article by Kosolapov which appeared in late 1989, meanwhile,
demonstrated that conservatives had not lost every outlet for their
views. Writing in the journal *Politicheskoye Obrazovaniye* (Political Education, formerly Political Self-Education), the former *Kommunist* editor
gave his interpretation of the Leninist concept of socialism. Kosolapov's Lenin, even during the period of the New Economic Policy, was
an advocate of subsidizing heavy industry (Kosolapov, 1989: 40). In this
purist's worldview, Lenin was primarily "the great industrializer and
electrifier of Russia," rather than the initiator of NEP (Kosolapov, 1989:
47). It was a false "modernization" of Lenin to portray him as a liberal
or an advocate of a mixed economy, and to prove his point – a political
point – Kosolapov roundly condemned the views of Nikolay Bukharin,
the architect of NEP.

1989: the socialist idea and Eastern Europe

This theoretical exercise served several political functions, all
of which were well illustrated in Gorbachev's landmark article of
November 1989 on "The Socialist Idea and Revolutionary Restructuring." In the first place, it served to promote and legitimate *perestroika* by
re-assessing the Stalinist notion of socialism which still prevailed in the
Soviet Union. Gorbachev repeatedly condemned the Stalinist model of
socialism as a "command-administrative" system, and rejected "barracks" (*kazarmennyy*) communism, with its "crude" notions of egalita-
rianism and "levelling" (Gorbachev, 1989c: 5). This use of the term
"barracks" communism, in fact, was an interesting example of symbolic
communication. The term is used today for a military barracks, and was
used in tsarist times to describe workers' dormitories. The term thus
carried with it a number of negative meanings.

In the second place, the concept of socialism debate communicated a
willingness to accept change in other socialist countries, by accepting
the notion of a multiplicity of models of socialism. Restating his slogan
of December 1984, Gorbachev declared that "socialism is just as varied
in its manifestations as life itself, since it is the living creativity of the
multi-millioned masses" (p. 6).

This was also an attempt to broaden the notion of socialism so as to legitimize the acceptability of social democracy as a valid contribution to socialist thought, in effect making it an acceptable form of socialism. Given that this article appeared during the continuing upheaval in Eastern Europe, it may have been an attempt to legitimize social-democracy and multi-party political systems in an attempt to salvage the best of the situation. At the same time, there was a conscious effort on the part of the Gorbachev leadership to cultivate ties with social democrats and other left-wing forces. A CPSU delegation headed by the first deputy chief of the new International Department, Karen Brutents, attended the Stockholm congress of the Socialist International in July 1989, marking the first appearance of a Soviet party delegation at such a gathering (Brutents, 1989).

Like the pro-reform theorists, Gorbachev also condemned the fact that under Stalin, and by implication more recently,

> theory had to carry out the distorted ideological function ... of justifying practice, creating in the social conscience a finished model of socialism, supposedly corresponding to the principles of Marxism-Leninism. (Gorbachev, 1989c: 9)

This was a frank recognition of the political uses which had been made of ideology in the interests of the ruling bureaucracy.

Finally, a return to Leninism for Gorbachev and those Soviets in favor of reform did not mean a mechanical repetition of the basic tenets, as so often in the past. Instead, it entailed, in their view, a return to the method of Lenin and a willingness to be guided by practice: "To act in a Leninist fashion means to examine how the future grows out of the present reality, and in accordance with this to draw up one's plans" (p. 4). In other words, the concept of socialism debate appeared to be a development of ideology in the positive sense, in terms of using ideology to explain and change the world. The problem was getting the more conservative segments of the party to accept this shift in worldview.

Political functions in the contradictions debate

Legitimation of the social system was an important political function of this debate over a theoretical concept. In this case, at issue was whether or not unrest in a socialist society could be considered as the legitimate expression of the interests of certain social groups. The concept of contradictions was threatening from the official point of view because not only would the acceptance of social unrest in Eastern Europe invalidate the Soviet model of socialism, but it would also suggest that such unrest could occur within the Soviet Union.

This ideological debate was also a mode of communication within the Soviet elite and to Eastern Europe. Reformers, such as Butenko, Bogomolov, Novopashin, and others could identify themselves with leaders such as Gorbachev by using the same concepts: the "living creativity of the masses," for example. Conservative and orthodox party members, meanwhile, identified with each other by not mentioning even the nonantagonistic contradictions of Soviet society, promoting its "integrity" and "homogeneity" instead.

The orthodox position, when defended by those in office, was an example of a negative use of ideology, as in the concealment of contradictions in the interests of preserving a social structure. It is striking that those who defended the status quo most stridently were those who stood to benefit from its preservation. As in the case of socialist internationalism, for the most part these were members of the party apparatus. In the case of contradictions, it is embarrassingly obvious (at least to a Western observer) that they were attempting to conceal the social system's contradictions in order to defend the existing order in the interests of a ruling elite – the party *apparat*. This is why Ambartsumov's article was so important and why it was attacked so harshly. His views on contradictions were shared by others and had been aired throughout the previous year, albeit perhaps less graphically. What was most disturbing about his article to conservatives were his attacks on party privilege and the abuse of power, not so much the proposition that contradictions could become antagonistic. At the same time, only in some cases were the attempts to explain away contradictions cynical. In Kosolapov's case, while he pictured himself as a defender of the party's interests, he was a true believer, and remains active to this day in orthodox communist movements in the former Soviet Union.

For the most part, it is best to characterize the views of the opponents of orthodoxy as positive. Butenko's views were clearly widely shared within Soviet theoretical circles, as we saw in Zaslavskaya's approving comments before the Central Committee. These scholars were attempting to utilize the concepts of Marxism-Leninism not only to attack the sources of conservatism and stagnation in the Soviet Union, but also to explain social phenomena. From the point of view of political expediency, it would have been easier to pin the blame for shortcomings in Soviet society on individual leaders, which would not have necessitated a search for materialist explanations for the obvious decline in Soviet economic growth. This argues against the view that ideology was merely a mask for the self-serving attempts of one social group to deprive another of political power.

Finally, if we recall that in the positive view of ideology it is the expression of the worldview of a social class (in Lenin's view, an ascendant class), this does in fact seem to describe what was taking place in the Soviet Union in the early 1980s. Gorbachev has been characterized in the West as the intellectuals' general secretary, in that he represented and answered their aspirations for greater freedom to travel, of information, Western standards of living and so on. What is interesting is that most of those who put forward views at odds with those of party conservatives tended to come from the ranks of the intellectuals; more often than not, from within the Academy of Sciences. Medvedev's appointment to head the Central Committee Science and Educational Institutions Department was therefore especially important, because this department was responsible not only for educational policy for institutions of higher education, but also for the Academy of Sciences.

Conclusions

Soviet theoretical debates over contradictions, then, were significant for a number of reasons.

In the first place, it was important because those who took the most radical views were members of the Soviet Union's most important institute for the study of the world socialist system. All of these scholars were therefore well known to their colleagues in Eastern Europe, and the publication of such views sent implicit signals that a basic change in Soviet policy toward the region was perhaps in the offing. The early 1980s was a time of increasing friction over various issues within the alliance, and the assertion by some of those who studied the world socialist system that contradictions could become aggravated within and between socialist states must have been taken in Eastern Europe as an important sign of growing recognition by the Soviets that East European interests had to be taken into account.

Gorbachev's public statements after his accession to the post of general secretary reinforced this view, despite the pre-occupation with domestic issues and relations with the United States. In his acceptance speech after his election to the post of general secretary, he stated that the "first commandment" of his administration would be the improvement of relations with Eastern Europe (Gorbachev, 1985). As we saw in the last chapter, the fact that he did not offer any concrete elaboration of socialist internationalism at the Warsaw Pact renewal ceremonies the next month left the direction of Soviet policy toward Eastern Europe uncertain.

A second important point is that a debate over the nature of socialist contradictions was also a debate over crises in Eastern Europe, how to resolve them, and also how to avoid them. Crises in Eastern Europe affected the Soviet Union in a number of ways. A Soviet response, whether in the form of direct invasion or silent complicity in the imposition of martial law, raised international tension and contributed to superpower competition, diverting yet more resources from meeting the needs of Soviet consumers. Second, such a response also tarnished the international image of the Soviet Union (not least in Eastern Europe), complicating efforts at international cooperation. Finally, crises and unrest in Eastern Europe brought home to Soviet conservatives the dangers of any relaxation of control, which made domestic reform that much less likely.

Those who argued that subjective factors such as remnants of the past in peoples' consciousness were to blame, as did Kosolapov, were suggesting that crises could be averted by increasing party discipline and "educational" work. Scholars such as Butenko and his colleagues from the IEWSS, on the other hand, argued that there were basic shortcomings in socialist societies which needed to be addressed. Hence, basic reform – "radical reform," as Gorbachev was to say at the 27th Party Congress – was necessary (Gorbachev, 1986: 113). Debate over both of these concepts, then, should also be seen in the wider context of the political struggle over the basic direction of Soviet domestic and foreign policy.

The third point is that through debates over the notion of contra-dictions and the concept of socialism, Soviet elites came to accept that in socialist systems, pluralism and an attendant non-coincidence of interests was possible, and perhaps even preferable in terms of effi-cient economic development. The acceptance of the notion that differ-ent social groups (or different countries) could have different interests meant, however, that the communist party was no longer the sole guarantor of those interests. The question then became the proper representation of interests in the political systems of socialism, a question for which Marxism-Leninism had few answers other than the unifying role of the communist party.

6   Ideological debates and Eastern Europe

What role, then, did ideological debates over socialist internationalism, the nature of contradictions, and the concept of socialism play in the events of the fall of 1989 in Eastern Europe? In the immediate sense, none. The social pressures which drove thousands of East Europeans into the streets to demand responsive and open political systems had, of course, been building up for years, and to point to any one Soviet statement or political debate as the cause of these events would be absurd.

What these debates did was develop the theoretical basis for the acceptance of change among Soviet elites. Without rethinking the traditional ideological interpretations on which Soviet power was based, there would have been little reason not to intervene in Eastern Europe. Ideological debates also communicated an unwillingness to maintain the traditional Soviet–East European relationship, by force or otherwise. In other words, through ideological debate, reform-minded Soviet intellectuals attempted to change the fundamental principles of Marxism-Leninism so as to accommodate change and communicate the willingness to accept it. Ideological debates over the concept of socialist internationalism in the early 1980s were an expression of the recognition by some within the Soviet establishment of the need to rethink the basis of bloc relations and the prerogative of the Soviet Union to intervene in Eastern Europe. Debates over the nature of contradictions, meanwhile, were efforts to provide autonomy to Eastern Europe in finding solutions to periodic crises. To be able to grant such autonomy, however, Soviet reformers had to earn it for themselves by breaking the power of a largely conservative bureaucracy which had for years denied the need for thorough-going reform by asserting the unity of Soviet society.

Ideological debates combined with political change did not cause the collapse of socialism in Eastern Europe, but they did mean the

Soviets could not intervene to save it. In domestic terms such intervention would have meant the triumph of conservative forces, as in the case of the intervention in Czechoslovakia in 1968. It would have meant the unacceptability of reforms the Soviet Union itself was carrying out, or at least had not raised serious objections to. Even by the time of the April 1987 Gorbachev visit to Czechoslovakia, planned Soviet political reforms had gone beyond those of that country's Prague Spring.

In the international sphere, any intervention in Eastern Europe would have destroyed the legitimacy the Soviet Union had in the eyes of the West, of the East Europeans, and of their own people. It would have exposed "new thinking" as a sham by demonstrating to the West that it was simply one more Soviet attempt at duplicity. All the credibility that Gorbachev had painstakingly rebuilt for the Soviet Union over four years would have been lost. Previous Soviet leaders had not been swayed by such concerns, but the Gorbachev leadership had staked the success of its reform effort on integration into the world economy in an attempt to make the Soviet more responsive and rational. The few Soviet leaders opposed to the invasion of Czechoslovakia, for example – Suslov, Ponomarev, Andropov – cared most about the effect it would have on Soviet relations with the rest of the world communist movement.

But by 1989 even the world communist movement was no longer seen as an essential component of Soviet foreign policy, in terms of its value to what were now defined as Soviet interests. This was partly a result of the major communist parties' unwillingness to sacrifice their interests to those of the Soviet Union, as seen in the debate in the 1970s with the Eurocommunists. These parties had lost most of their faith in the Soviet system after the invasion of Czechoslovakia. It was also a result of Soviet efforts to create a more favorable international climate for reform in the mid-1980s by abandoning the class-based approach to foreign policy which had produced international tension.

In the process of re-interpreting the basic principles of the relationship with Eastern Europe, however, Soviet theorists exposed Marxism-Leninism as unable to answer many of the needs of the system, internally and externally. The Stalinist legacy in many ways was simply too great, in the sense that it remained the prevailing conception in the minds of many as to what socialist practice was and should be. More importantly, orthodox interpretations of Marxism-Leninism obstructed reform by prohibiting the legitimate expression of group interests outside of the framework of the party. For their part, reformers were unable to develop any acceptable alternative outside of Stalinist rigidity but yet within Marxism-Leninism. A similar problem arose within the world socialist system as a whole: when change led to the demise of Marxist-Leninist one-party states (as in Hungary and Poland by October 1989), Marxist-Leninist ideology disappeared as a binding mechanism among bloc members. But in order for common economic interests to quickly supplant it, healthy economies needed to be in place in which those interests could be expressed through other than administrative mechanisms.

I also have attempted to place ideological debates within their political context; in the early 1980s, the appropriate political context was that of succession struggles. Debates over other concepts throughout Soviet history can also be seen in this context, but sometimes an equally important function was the articulation of institutional and bureaucratic interests. We see this for instance especially vividly in debates over military doctrine, be it "reasonable sufficiency" in the late 1980s or détente in the 1970s. The defense of party privilege can be seen both as the articulation of an institutional interest and as part of the succession struggle, which illustrates that in most cases there was some degree of overlap.

It is interesting to note that innovative theoretical articles tended to appear during times of uncertainty associated with impending political succession. In this regard, ideology thus served as a form of communication between disfranchised elites at the lower reaches of the power pyramid and those within the leadership who aspired to higher position. It is undoubtedly the case, however, that the uncertainties of political succession themselves also served to loosen ideological strictures. The simple fact of turnover in the personnel responsible for enforcing orthodoxy was a structural source of ideological relaxation. With the loosening of ideological strictures, the search for solutions to pressing problems could become that much more far-ranging.

With these remarks in mind, let us review the general development of the ideological concepts examined in this study.

Socialist internationalism

The rise and decline, so to speak, of socialist internationalism was marked by use of the concept to perform four main political functions. The fact that the concept was used to rationalize and defend the invasion of Czechoslovakia meant that the term became laden with meaning and symbolic of the worst features of the Soviet–East European relationship, at least to those of a non-orthodox bent.

After the invasion of Czechoslovakia, the aspects of socialist internationalism which stressed "defense of the gains of the revolution" and the leadership of the party came to the fore. The concept was used as a rationalization to justify the invasion; to the world, to other communists, to a domestic audience. This was an example of a negative use of ideology, as described in the Introduction; ideology was used to conceal contradictions in the Soviet bloc by stressing its unity. The interpretation used to justify the invasion – the right and duty of socialist states to defend socialism collectively – came to be repeated ritualistically by Soviet and East European leaders for the next twenty years. It was an affirmation of loyalty to the primacy of Soviet interests. In the 1970s, the concept therefore came to be used as symbolic communication. Its appearance in a document was a measure of East European willingness to subordinate their interests to those of the Soviet Union. At the same time, the concept was still used negatively, to deny contradictions of interest within the bloc by asserting that the "regularities" of socialist construction bound the East European regimes to a Soviet model.

Given the meanings associated with socialist internationalism, when the Eurocommunist parties wished to assert their independence, they had to do so by devising a new term – "new internationalism." Soviet scholars, however, had no such option available to them, and in the early 1980s intensified their own efforts to re-assess the meaning of socialist internationalism. Scholars such as Yuriy Novopashin and Anatoliy Butenko of the Institute of the Economics of the World Socialist System (IEWSS) were foremost in discussing the relationship of "internationalist" and "common democratic" principles within socialist internationalism. This was a way to promote a more equitable relationship between the national and international interests of socialist countries within the bloc. At the same time, the attempt to emphasize common democratic principles was a precursor of the debate over "class" versus "common human" values as the general basis of Soviet foreign policy in mid-1988. Suggestions that there were different models of socialism were attempts to broaden the notion of what was legitimately socialist, and also to redefine Soviet interests by suggesting they would not be threatened by reform communism in Eastern Europe.

The debate over socialist internationalism was only partially resolved with the election of Mikhail Gorbachev to the post of general secretary. It still took over four years for re-interpretations of the term to be accepted among the bureaucracy and by bloc leaders. When the system of Soviet control began to collapse in the fall of 1989, there was little doubt that barring its overthrow, the Soviet leadership was willing to let events run their course and refrain from intervention to save socialism as they knew it in Eastern Europe.

Socialist contradictions

Debate over the possibility of antagonistic contradictions in socialism began in the early 1980s as attempts by some Soviets to determine the internal causes for periodic crises in Eastern Europe (as opposed to external causes; in other words, "imperialist interference"). Such efforts led some to the conclusion that socialist, "nonantagonistic" contradictions could become antagonistic, and thus a source of social unrest and revolutionary situations.

In proposing the view that contradictions could become antagonistic, these scholars were promoting a positive concept of ideology; one in which theoretical concepts were used to explain and understand reality and to reveal the contradictions of a society. Party theoreticians, meanwhile, in denying this possibility promoted a negative conception of ideology; concealing contradictions to maintain a social system in the interests of a ruling elite. The collapse of these systems testified to the fact of contradictions and irreconcilable antagonisms within them.

If reformists could win acceptance for the view that nonantagonistic contradictions could develop into antagonisms, then the next logical step was to promote reform strategies in order to resolve such contradictions. Conservatives, on the other hand, denied the need for major reform by promoting the view that the only antagonisms left in socialist systems were those inherited from the past, in peoples' subjective consciousness, or manifestations of interference from the outside.

Debate over the concept of antagonistic contradictions served the function of communication in that it signalled to the East Europeans that there was some sentiment within Soviet circles for a rethinking of the principles underlying intersocialist relationships. It was one thing if such signals came from Novosibirsk or Vladivostok. The authors of these views, however, worked in the leading Soviet institute devoted to the study of world socialism, which implied that they enjoyed some kind of political protection and that these views were shared at the highest levels. By sending such signals, however, the Gorbachev leadership ran into the dilemma of wanting to promote reform but swearing non-interference.

We should therefore see the political context of these debates essentially in a struggle over the general direction of Soviet domestic and foreign policy. By the early 1980s, the need for reform was obvious to most outside of party establishment, and to many within it as well. Mikhail Gorbachev did not spring full-grown, Venus-like, from the head of the party bureaucracy. His values and worldview were representative of a much broader stratum within the Soviet elite, and he was in many respects the intellectuals' general secretary until losing their confidence, probably sometime in 1990. Gorbachev did not create the pent-up desire for change; he merely created conditions which allowed it to be expressed. The debates over the ideological concepts examined in this study demonstrated how such reform inclinations developed and were voiced in the Soviet Union in the early part of the 1980s. They demonstrated the use of ideology as a code of communication among like-minded actors in a closed political system to build informal alliances.

The institutional setting

The debate over contradictions began at roughly the same time as that over socialist internationalism, which suggested that they were part of a more general dissatisfaction with Brezhnev's rule among the Soviet *intelligentsia*. It is appropriate to examine the institutional links between participants in these debates in order to identify sources of support for reform before and after the ascent of Mikhail Gorbachev to the post of general secretary. It is striking that many of those who re-interpreted the basic concepts of Marxism-Leninism later came to hold prominent posts in the Gorbachev administration, and constituted something of an informal reform alliance in the first half of the 1980s.

The most important CPSU Central Committee department responsible for control of the press was the Propaganda Department (see Dzirkals, 1982). Studies done on party control of the media suggest that during the Brezhnev era the expression of different views in the press was for the most part kept in check. It is interesting to note, however, that the Propaganda Department "journals sector" chief in the early 1980s (since 1973; see Directory of Soviet Officials, 1979: 29) was Naily Bikkenin, a noted author on ideology. Under Gorbachev he was to become deputy chief of the Propaganda Department (Directory of Soviet Officials, 1987: 18), and later was named editor-in-chief of *Kommunist* (see no. 9, 1987). That he came to hold a notable position in the Gorbachev administration suggests that he was not unsympathetic to views such as those examined in this study. Unfortunately, we do not know enough about the workings of the *apparat* to ascertain the level of autonomy of sector chiefs; it was unlikely to be great during the Brezhnev era. What we do know is that the first deputy chief of the Propaganda Department until September 1983 was Georgiy Lukich Smirnov, who then became head of the Institute of Philosophy, and in December 1985 an advisor to Gorbachev (Director of Soviet Officials, 1986: 4). (Most recently he was director of the Institute of Marxism-Leninism.) In other words, some of those with responsibility for control of the press later came to hold fairly important positions.

In addition, Aleksandr Yakovlev and Vadim Medvedev, two prominent members of Gorbachev's reform team, worked together in the Propaganda Department in the early 1970s along with Smirnov. This suggests that a connection between those of reformist views was formed already in this time.

After his tenure as head of the Academy of Social Sciences, Medvedev from 1983 to 1986 headed the Central Committee Science and Educational Institutions Department, which oversaw the Academy of Sciences, its institutes, and the education ministries. Interviews in Moscow[1] confirmed that under Sergey Trapeznikov, the previous Science Department chief, control of the Academy of Science institutes was much more harsh (see also Hahn, 1982: 175). His removal in 1983, then, was an important watershed in the broadening of the limits of acceptable speech. What is more, Novopashin pointed out that even before Trapeznikov's removal, it was possible to play one department off against another, since both the Science Department and the Liaison Department directed the work of the IEWSS. In addition, the Propaganda Department also had a say in the activities of the scientific institutes, inasmuch as it had ultimate oversight in the field of publishing.

Therefore, it seems that the party's efforts to control Soviet scientific life may have worked *against* that control. For example, when Butenko published a controversial article, it fell under the jurisdiction of three different departments: (1) The Liaison Department, in its capacity as overseer of an institute dealing with the socialist countries; (2) the Science Department, since it was written by a member of an institute of the Academy of Sciences; and (3) the Propaganda Department, since it appeared in a Soviet publication subject to censorship.

Who were the officials responsible in each department? Olimp Chukanov, a deputy chief of the Liaison Department, had responsibility for economics (and therefore the IEWSS) from 1967 until the reorganization of the apparatus in 1988 (Directory of Soviet Officials, 1989: 11). The IEWSS belonged to the sector of Economic Sciences in the Science Department, which was headed for many years by Mikhail Ivanovich Volkov (from at least 1972; see Directory of Soviet Officials, 1979: 31). "You might say he was the right hand of Trapeznikov, the head of the department," Novopashin said in an interview. It seems that neither Volkov nor Chukanov were well disposed to novel ideas. Within the sector for Economic Sciences, there was a worker responsible for each institute, who would approve its scientific plan for a given period. Finally, the Central Committee had control in terms of hiring directors, deputy directors, and senior researchers at the institutes, who had to be approved by the corresponding sector in the Science Department. In the Propaganda Department, the responsible official would be the appropriate sector chief, be it for journals, newspapers, or even television and radio. This is where the IEWSS seems to have enjoyed its greatest support; perhaps through Naily Bikkenin (another, like Smirnov, who worked with Butenko at *Kommunist* in the early 1960s), although his name came up less frequently than others; certainly through Smirnov.

The article by Medvedev which appeared in *Voprosy Filosofii*, in August of 1984 (see Chapter 5) was based on a presentation made at the Academy of Social Sciences. Medvedev, however, by this time was no longer head of the Academy, working instead in the Central Committee *apparat*. Thus, it seems significant that the article in which he gave qualified endorsement to the reformist position was (a) given in his former domain, which seemed to have harbored reform sentiment; and (b) printed in *Voprosy Filosofii*. Dialectics and contradictions, of course, were within the purview of this journal, so it would have been only natural that the article would be published there. On the other hand, it could have been published in any number of places, for instance in *Kommunist* (especially given Medvedev's position in the *apparat*), or in the journal *Sotsiologicheskiye Issledovaniya* (Sociological Research), which served as a forum for conservative views.

This is not to suggest that these were the only such alliances which developed among Soviet intellectuals in this period; further study would undoubtedly reveal similar cooperation in other areas. The point is that there seems to have been an identifiable coincidence of reform sentiment among the IEWSS, the Institute of Philosophy, and the Academy of Social Sciences. Of course, while their members may have harbored reform sentiments, we should keep in mind that each was an enormous institution whose workers held diverse views. The IEWSS, for example, employed close to 250 researchers in the early 1980s (Directory of Soviet Research Officials, 1986). As we saw in Chapter 5, some of the most scathing criticism of the progressive position on contradictions came from within the Institute of Philosophy itself.

Another point is that Bogomolov's institute (the IEWSS) was already a thorn in the party's side as early as 1980, when it sent a *zapiska* (memorandum) to the Politburo protesting the invasion of Afghanistan (see Bogomolov, 1988). In other words, by the time Butenko and Novopashin started vociferously to question Soviet policy toward Eastern Europe in 1983, the IEWSS had been unorthodox and critical of leadership decisions for three years, and in areas outside their competence, no less. Butenko confirmed what Bogomolov had written in 1990, that the IEWSS had written numerous *zapiski* and other reports to the Central Committee and Soviet leaders since the mid-1970s in attempts to give them a more realistic appraisal of the situation in Eastern Europe and other parts of the world (Bogomolov, 1990). Novopashin in particular described one *zapiska* written shortly after the unrest in Poland in 1976; it got no farther than a discussion between Bogomolov and the head of the Polish sector in the Liaison Department. Nonetheless, when the events in Poland did come to a head, Bogomolov's institute was safe from criticism of the kind levelled in the late 1960s, when (under a different director) it gave no hint of what was to unfold in Czechoslovakia. The *zapiska*, like all others sent to the Central Committee by Academy of Sciences institutes (see Schneider, 1988: 151) had been returned to the institute and retained.

There remains the question of why Butenko and others at the IEWSS were able to go farther than most in proposing novel interpretations of ideological principles with few ill effects. One of the most likely protectors was Pëtr N. Fedoseyev, a vice president of the Soviet Academy of Sciences. Fedoseyev was among the first and most important of Soviet theoreticians to broach the notion that nonantagonistic contradictions could become antagonistic, as early as 1981 in the *World Marxist Review* (see Chapter 5). In interviews in Moscow in 1991, Butenko mentioned Fedoseyev repeatedly in this regard, and stated that while he was indeed a very "semi-official" (*ofitsioznyy*) philosopher (that is, he reflected the party line), he "looked after" the Academy of Sciences. Novopashin seconded this, and said it was his impression that Butenko and Fedoseyev were quite close. Kosolapov also described him as *ofitsioznyy*, and claimed that after the 1983 article refuting the notion of antagonistic contradictions, Fedoseyev wrote two letters to the Central Committee criticizing his position. Kosolapov, however, said that since both were Central Committee members, the criticism had little effect.

That Butenko did not mention the letters in our conversations implies only that political protection in the Soviet system was not necessarily overt or acknowledged; in other words, he may not even have known that Fedoseyev wrote letters on his behalf. The point, too, is that protection, like so much else in the Soviet system, was very much a function of personalistic relationships; Butenko was simply better received than others, even Bogomolov, by influential figures such as Fedoseyev. Butenko himself at one point stated that he could take more controversial positions because "My spine was a little more firm; after all, I have friends in the CC."[2] Kosolapov, who worked for Butenko in the mid-1960s at the IEWSS, confirmed this in an article in a conservative newspaper in early 1991:

> My new boss, in his own words always trying to rush "ahead of progress," had wide contacts in party and academic circles (and loved to refer to this). More often than [any] others turned up the names of A. Ye. Bovin, F. M. Burlatskiy, and [Georgiy] Arbatov, known to me only for Kuusinen's "Basics of Marxism-Leninism." (Kosolapov, 1991)

Another clue to the question of political protection may lie in the fact that Bogomolov, director of the IEWSS, worked in the Liaison Department in the 1960s under future general secretary Yuriy Andropov; this would explain who would have the political clout to protect the IEWSS. Butenko said that he and Bogomolov did know Andropov, but it was not as if they could just call and ask something of him. He said it was more important that "through the 'Andropov cadre,' it was possible to influence Brezhnev" – that is, through the people who had worked for Andropov in the Liaison Department. He mentioned Arbatov, Georgiy Shakhnazarov, and Aleksandr Bovin, the influential political commentator for *Izvestiya*. On the other hand, when pressed Butenko did admit that "if worse came to worse," he could use his connections, but that he rarely had to resort to this.

The Soviet political system was in many ways arcane and closed, and informal networks played a significant role. To what extent did Soviet authors know of tacit or explicit support in other quarters, and why did they start questioning the basic theoretical principles on which the system was based when they did? I have attempted to show that such debates as preceded the rise of Mikhail Gorbachev were really nothing new; it was the combination of political succession taking place amid a stagnant economy and social system that added a new element.

One cardinal question of Soviet studies was always that of continuity between Imperial and Soviet Russia. We may pose the same questions today between Soviet and post-communist Russia concerning any number of questions, not least how the tradition of informal political networks will influence future political development in the remains of the former Soviet Union.

Appendix

This Appendix includes biographical information on the most important participants of the ideological debates examined in this study. It should help the reader keep the participants straight, and may make clearer the web of personal connections in the Soviet political establishment. Full names have been provided when known.

To simplify the matter of citation, I have used the following abbreviations for the series of directories put out by the US Central Intelligence Agency. These directories contain a wealth of fairly reliable information.

Directory of Soviet Officials, National Organizations

Publishing agencies:
    1966 – US Dept. of State, Bureau of Intelligence and Research
    1973–78 – US CIA, Directorate of Intelligence
    1979–82 – US CIA, National Foreign Assessment Center
    1982–9 – US CIA, Directorate of Intelligence
Dates of issue:

February 1966	DSO–1
November 1973	DSO–2
December 1975	DSO–3
September 1978	DSO–4
November 1979	DSO–5
May 1981	DSO–6
August 1982	DSO–7
August 1983	DSO–8
November 1984	DSO-9
June 1986	DSO-10
June 1987	DSO–11
November 1989	DSO–12

Directory of Soviet Research Organizations

US CIA, Directorate of Intelligence, 1978 – DSRO

Another useful aid is the *Soviet Biographical Service* [SBS], by John Scherer, (n.p.) volumes 1 through 7, 1986–present.

Ambartsumov, Yevgeniy Arshakovich: Former deputy director of the Institute of the International Workers' Movement (which published the journal *Rabochiy Klass i Sovremenniy Mir*) (DSRO, 1978); head of a section in the Department of General Political and Economic Problems in the Institute of the Economics of the World Socialist System (IEWSS); now the head of that department, a deputy of the Russian Supreme Soviet and an ardent supporter of Boris Yel'tsin.

Arbatov, Georgiy: Another of the group of Liaison Department consultants under Andropov (Burlatskiy, 1990); headed the group after Burlatskiy's departure, 1965–7 (Kosolapov, *Domostroy*, no. 4, Feb. 5, 1991); left to become head of the newly created USA and Canada Institute in May 1967; with Bovin, reportedly a speechwriter for Brezhnev in the 1970s; had his memoirs criticized by Kosolapov in the spring of 1991 (*Domostroy*, no. 4, Feb. 5, 1991).

Bikkenin, Naily Bariyevich: Former head of the Journals section in the Central Committee Propaganda Department from January 1973 (DSO–3); deputy chief of the Propaganda Department from February 1986 until May 1987; left that position to become editor-in-chief of *Kommunist* (see no. 9, 1987).

Bogomolov, Oleg Timofeyevich: Director of the IEWSS since 1969 (DSO–5); before that served in the group of consultants in the CC Liaison Department under Andropov with Burlatskiy, Bovin, Shakhnazarov, and others (Burlatskiy, 1990: 254; see also Hough, 1980: 124).

Borisov, O. B., Borisov, O. V.: Pseudonyms for Oleg Borisovich Rakhmanin (SBS, January 1986).

Bovin, Aleksandr Yevgen'yevich: Member of editorial board of *Kommunist*, 1959–63; worked with Burlatskiy and others in CC Liaison Department; head of LD group of consultants from 1967 to 1972 (Hough, 1980: 124; see also DSO–2); in 1972 he became political observer for the Government newspaper *Izvestiya*, a position he still holds; Burlatskiy and others have noted his role as speechwriter for Brezhnev in the 1970s, with Arbatov.

Bugayev, Yevgeniy: Head of a section in the CC Propaganda Department, late 1950s (*Pravda*, June 2, 1958); later member of the editorial board of *Kommunist* (with Kosolapov) until his removal in late 1986.

Burlatskiy, Fëdor Mikhaylovich: Worked in CPSU theoretical journal *Kommunist* in late 1950s (Burlatskiy, 1990); joined Bovin, Bogomolov, Shakhnazarov, Arbatov and others under Andropov in Liaison Department in early 1960s; accompanied Nikita Khrushchev abroad and served as speechwriter; left the *apparat* after fall of Khrushchev, to work in *Pravda*, 1965–7; with Butenko was one of originators of term "developed socialism;" 1967–75 Deputy Director of Institute of Concrete Social Research; 1975–87 head of the Philosophy section, Institute for Social Science; from 1976 a deputy chairman of the Soviet Association of Political Science; rather idealistic, by own admission; most recently, political observer and then editor of *Literaturnaya Gazeta*, the newspaper of the USSR Writers Union; deposed as editor in September 1991 by the paper's collective for alleged inaction during the attempted coup in August (see *Nezavisimaya Gazeta*, Sept. 19, 1991, p. 7).

Butenko, Anatoliy Pavlovich: Served in Second World War; graduated Moscow State University 1951–52; worked in party theoretical journal *Kommunist* in the late 1950s (information from personal conversation) before going to IEWSS in 1964; headed department known variously as the Department of International Relations, the Department of Political and Ideological Problems, the Department of General Problems of Socialism; it is now called the Department of General Political and Ideological Problems; he no longer heads this department, and is instead Senior Scientific Researcher (something on order of department head emeritus) at the former IEWSS, the Institute of International Economic and Political Research (Russian acronym, IMEPI).

Chernyayev, Anatoliy: From 1971, a deputy chief of the International Department (DSO–2) with responsibility for England and the United States; frequently mentioned as a person of "progressive" views and protector of reform-minded intellectuals; most recently, advisor to Gorbachev (DSO–10).

Fedoseyev, Pëtr Nikolayevich: Noted Soviet philosopher; editor of *Kommunist* 1946–8; director of Institute of Marxism-Leninism in 1960s; later Vice President of the Academy of Sciences for the Social Sciences (from 1971, DSO–4). Often at odds with Kosolapov in the 1970s and 1980s, and with Suslov in the early 1950s.

Katushev, Konstantin Fëdorovich: From early 1968 to May 1977, head of the Liaison Department (Teague, 1980); then, demoted to become Soviet representative to Council for Mutual Economic Assistance (DSO–4); received further demotion and exile in 1982 as Ambassador to Cuba (DSO–8); staged something of a comeback under Gorbachev to become chairman of the State Committee for Foreign Economic Relations in November 1985.

Kosolapov, Richard Ivanovich: Graduated Moscow State University early 1960s; worked in IEWSS from September 1964 to May 1966 under Butenko, at which point he became a lecturer in the Propaganda Department (*Domostroy*, no. 4, Feb. 5, 1991); identified as a consultant in that department in October 1968 (DSO–2); worked in *Pravda*, 1974–6, developing ties to Mikhail Zimyanin, later a CC secretary for ideology and propaganda; became chief editor of *Kommunist* in May 1976; removed after 27th CPSU Party Congress; most recently taught in the Philosophy Department at Moscow State University, and was chief ideologue for the United Front of Laborers (Russian acronym OFT), an old-style orthodox movement whose head, A. A. Sergeyev, ran for vice-president of the Russian Federation in June 1991 as the running mate of Soviet Army General Albert Makashov.

Ligachëv, Yegor Kuz'mich: Brought to Moscow from Omsk in December 1983; conservative; clashed with Yel'tsin at CC plenum in October 1987; as "second secretary" in 1988, defended class interests as the basis of Soviet foreign policy; became head of Agriculture Commission in October of that year; finally removed from leadership at 28th CPSU Congress in mid-1990.

Medvedev, Vadim Andreyevich: First an instructor (1971; DSO–2) then deputy chief of the Propaganda Department (also from 1971; DSO–3); left in April 1978 to become rector of the Academy of Social Sciences after its reorganization and merger with the Higher Party School and Higher Party Correspondence School (DSO–5); in August 1983 returned to the *apparat* to head the Science and Educational Institutions Department, thus becoming responsible for scientific institutions in the Academy of Sciences (DSO–9); became CC secretary and head of the Liaison Department March 1986 (DSO–10); from September 1988, headed Ideological Commission after CC reorganization (DSO–12); removed as secretary and Ideological Commission chief at the 28th CPSU Congress, after criticism for his mishandling of ideological leadership.

Novopashin, Yuriy Stepanovich: Graduated Moscow State University philosophy department; worked at IEWSS early 1960s; spent 1969–74 in Prague at *World Marxist Review*; returned to IEWSS to head sector of Theoretical Problems of World Socialist System; served as Institute's party secretary from 1977 to 1980; in 1986 became deputy director of the Institute of Slavonic and Balkan Studies.

Rakhmanin, Oleg Borisovich: From May 1968, first deputy of the Liaison Department (Teague, 1980); primarily a China specialist; wrote most frequently in the journal *Voprosy Istorii KPSS* (Questions of History of the CPSU) under the pseudonyms O. B. or O. V. Borisov, and in *Pravda* as O. Vladimirov, (SBS, 1986); removed from Liaison Department in 1986.

Rusakov, Konstantin Viktorovich: Chief of the Liaison Department from March 1968 to June 1972; like Rakhmanin, also a China specialist; aide to Leonid Brezhnev on socialist countries (DSO–2); resumed position as Liaison Department chief in March 1977 and made CC secretary in May 1977 (DSO–4); removed in March 1986 after 27th Party Congress.

Shakhnazarov, Georgiy Khozreyevich: Member of group of consultants with Burlatskiy, Bovin, Arbatov, Bogomolov under Andropov in LD in early 1960s (Burlatskiy, 1990: 251); worked as responsible editor at *World Marxist Review* in late 1960s to early 1970s (see WMR, no. 10, 1971); identified as a deputy chief of the Liaison Department (one of three) in July 1972 (DSO–4); from 1974, chairman of Soviet Association for Political Science; liberal, frequently wrote on domestic Soviet issues; since March 1988, has served as advisor to Mikhail Gorbachev (DSO–12).

Shevardnadze, Eduard Amvroseyevich: Former head of Georgian Ministry of Internal Affairs; then First Secretary, Georgian CP; Politburo candidate member from November 1978 (DSO–9); full member and Foreign Minister from July 1985 (DSO–10); resigned from Politburo after 28th Party Congress; resigned as Foreign Minister, warning of ascendancy of conservatives in December 1990.

Smirnov, Georgiy Lukich: Appointed first deputy chief of Propaganda Department in July 1974 (DSO–5); in September 1983 made Director of Institute of Philosophy (DSO–9); identified as aide to Gorbachev in December 1985 (DSO–10); moved to Institute of Marxism-Leninism in February 1987 (DSO–11); member of CC Ideological Commission, November 1988 (DSO–12).

Sobolev, Aleksandr Ivanovich: Responsible worker, then head of consultants group in Propaganda Department, 1944–52; 1952–5, a member of the editorial board of *Pravda*; December 1955 to mid-1958, deputy editor of *Kommunist*; from 1958 to 1967, a responsible editor of *Problems of Peace and Socialism* (*World Marxist Review*); 1967–71, head, department of the History of the International Workers Movement, Institute of Marxism-Leninism; from 1971 to death in 1981, chief editor of *Rabochiy Klass i Sovremenniy Mir* (*The Working Class and the Modern World*), journal of the Institute of the International Workers Movement.

Stepanyan, Tsolak Aleksandrovich: Prominent philosopher since the mid-1950s, developing official line on contradictions in debates in Khrushchev period; from 1978, head of the Department of Scientific Communism of the Institute of Philosophy (DSO–5).

Suslov, Mikhail Andreyevich: Secretary of the CC CPSU from 1947; 1947–8, head of Propaganda Department; 1949–50, editor of *Pravda* (most likely maintained position as head of Propaganda Department as well); 1952–3, 1955–82, member of CPSU Presidium/Politburo; through 1940s and 1950s, was secretary with responsibility for relations with foreign communist parties; maintained some oversight in capacity as chief ideologist under Brezhnev.

Tolkunov, Lev Nikolayevich: Consultant, then deputy chief, Liaison Department, 1957–65; editor-in-chief, *Izvestiya*, 1965–76, and 1983–4.

Trapeznikov, Sergey Pavlovich: Head of the CC Science and Educational Institutions Department from 1965 to 1983; known for harsh, neo-Stalinist views.

Yakovlev, Aleksandr Nikolayevich: From April 1966 (DSO–2) to mid-1973, first deputy chief, Propaganda Department; removed for attacks on Russian nationalists in *Literaturnaya Gazeta* (May 1972) and made Ambassador to Canada, 1973 to mid-1983; Director of Institute of World Economy and International Relations, 1983–5; head of Propaganda Department, 1985–6 (DSO–10); secretary, CC CPSU, 1986–90 (DSO–10); advisor to Soviet President from 1990;

known as the "father of perestroika'; warned of possible conservative coup days before attempted putsch in August 1991.

Zimyanin, Mikhail Vasil'yevich: Former ambassador to Vietnam and Czechoslovakia; editor-in-chief of *Pravda* from 1967–75; secretary for ideology and propaganda, CC CPSU, 1976–86; labelled as "secretary for ideology" under Andropov by Kosolapov (*Domostroy*, no. 4, Feb. 5, 1991) and by Burlatskiy (1990: 356).

Notes

Introduction

1 See the statement by Oleg Bogomolov in 1988 that his institute had sent a letter of protest to the Soviet leadership shortly after the invasion. *Literaturnaya Gazeta*, March 16, 1988, as reported in US Foreign Broadcast Information Service, *Soviet Union Daily Report*, FBIS–SOV–88–050, March 14, 1988.
2 These concepts of ideology, negative and positive, are utilized in the very informative study on ideology by Larrain, 1980.

1 Ideology and the ideologists

1 A point made by Kenneth Minogue, "On Identifying Ideology," in *Ideology and Politics*, Maurice Cranston and Peter Mair, eds., (Alphen an den Rijn: Sijthoff, 1980), pp. 27–41.
2 Beginning with Alfred G. Meyer's article in the January 1966 issue, thirteen articles were published in this informal debate, ending with the July 1969 issue.
3 I use Warsaw Pact documents instead of Council for Mutual Economic Assistance (CMEA) documents for this purpose for two reasons. In the first place, the Pact was an effective lever of pressure on recalcitrant allies and the guarantor of socialism in Eastern Europe. In addition, using Pact documents rather than CMEA means that the non-European members of the socialist bloc – Cuba, Vietnam and Mongolia – do not influence the outcome of the statements.
4 Biographical information on the major personalities involved in this study is provided in the Appendix.
5 This institute was renamed the Institute of International Economic and Political Studies (with a Russian acronym of IMEPI) in the spring of 1990, but will be referred to throughout this study under its original name.
6 In private conversations with a Central Committee official, he stated that prior to the reorganization of the party apparatus in 1988, the Central Committee received, free of charge, the scholarly output of every Soviet institute. One effect of Gorbachev's reforms was that the Central Committee was forced to pay for any research done by Academy of Sciences institutes,

which would seem to have severely lessened the quality and amount of independent input into the policy-making process.

7 This department was absorbed in October 1988 into the International Department, significantly lessening its stature within the party *apparat*. It is known in the West by several names and acronyms; the most accurate seems to be "Otdel po svyazam s kommunisticheskimi i rabochimi partiyami sotsialisticheskikh stran" – "Department for liaison with communist and workers' parties of the socialist countries." The appropriate English abbreviation, therefore, would be DLCWPSC. For purposes of brevity, however, in this study I shall refer to the Liaison Department, or LD.

There seems to be some mystery surrounding the CC department which for years was most intimately involved in asserting Soviet control over Eastern Europe. I have not been able to find reference in a Soviet publication to the LD before its dissolution into the International Department in October 1988 (see *Izvestiya TsK KPSS*, no. 1, 1989: p. 86). The CIA (see the *Directory of Soviet Officials*, various issues) in fact lists this department under the long name given above.

Hahn (1984: 20, n. 31) has discovered a reference to the Liaison Department in the 1959 *Spravochnik partiynogo rabotnika*, which he claims is the only time its full name appeared in the Soviet press. Apparently the second was on the occasion of its dissolution.

When asked what to call this department in Russian, Soviets more often than not replied, "we just call it the *otdel* (department)" (personal conversations with Nodari Simoniya and Georgiy Mirskiy, both of the Institute of the World Economy and International Relations (IMEMO), in September 1988 and March 1990, respectively). Yuriy Novopashin reiterated this, but as someone who had more contact with the LD, confirmed the official title given above (personal conversation, July 1991, Moscow).

8 For biographical information on Rakhmanin and his pseudonyms, see J. L. Scherer, *Soviet Biographical Service*, 11, 1 (January 1986), pp. 24–5.

2 The ideological basis

1 Lenin was commenting on Bukharin's characterization of capitalism as an "antagonistic, contradictory system." Next to the word "contradictory," Lenin placed the notation of "arch-inaccurate," and the quote above.

2 *Bolshevik* was the title of the CPSU theoretical journal between 1924 and 1952, when it was renamed *Kommunist*.

3 Hahn (1982: 152) notes that Sobolev was listed as the "leader of a group of lecturers" in the April 19, 1952 *Pravda*, which would suggest a higher post than responsible worker. There were twelve ranks listed in the Central Committee hierarchy in US CIA *Directories of Soviet Officials* (see especially 1978). In descending order, they were: department chief; first deputy department chief; deputy department chief; consultants' group leader; sector chief; deputy sector chief; consultant; inspector; instructor; lecturers' group leader; lecturer; and responsible worker. In addition, there were also advisors to members of the Politburo and Secretariat.

4 The 1955 document would seem to fit the general pattern of how such documents were written; the host country would begin the process by circulating a draft which was then amended by visiting countries. The 1956 document, however, should have been initiated by the Soviets as the host of the Tito–Khrushchev meetings. See the discussion in Chapter 3, p. 58.

5 Butenko claimed that Andropov had called him first to invite him to work in the Liaison Department, and he referred them to Burlatskiy (personal conversation, Moscow, April 1991).

6 Personal conversations with Anatoliy Butenko and Yuriy Novopashin, Moscow, April and June, 1991.

3 Contradictions and internationalism in the 1970s: the Eurocommunist challenge

1 In July 1991, the Central Committee's Administrator of Affairs, Nikolay Kruchin, refuted the allegations of former Czechoslovak party secretary Jan Bil'ak that the East European communist parties each year sent $500,000 in cash to the CPSU, who in turn distributed it to less well-off parties. See *Nezavisimaya Gazeta*, July 2, 1991, 2.

Then in November 1991, the Communist Party of Great Britain admitted receiving large sums of money directly from the CPSU over a twenty-year period, from 1959 to 1979. In addition to receiving cash for themselves (sometimes as much as £100,000), CPGB leaders were also asked to pass it on to the communist parties operating illegally in other countries. We can only assume the East Europeans performed similar services (see *The New York Times*, Nov. 15, 1991, A6).

2 Interview with a consultant in the CPSU Central Committee who had worked in the Liaison Department for almost 25 years, Moscow, April 1991.

3 This includes eight communiqués of the meetings themselves and four declarations of policy; declarations devoted to special international topics such as the Middle East or Vietnam were not considered.

4 Internationalism may be either *proletarian* or *socialist* (in some cases, the hybrid term "proletarian socialist internationalism" was used). The former primarily referred to relations between non-ruling communist parties, whereas the latter was more often used to describe relations between socialist states. For our purposes, socialist internationalism is taken to be synonymous with proletarian.

5 There is some indication that despite his hard line toward the Prague Spring, Katushev may have been something of a "closet reformer." He was removed in May of 1977 (Teague, 1980: 20) and, like other Soviets who fell foul of the conservative establishment, was eventually sent to effective exile as an ambassador. (Aleksandr Yakovlev was removed as First Deputy Chief of the Propaganda Department in mid-1973 and made Ambassador to Canada, for example.) Anatoliy Butenko suggested it was "no accident" that Katushev had remained in charge of foreign economic ties throughout the Gorbachev years (personal communication, Moscow, April 1991).

6 Much of the following discussion relies on Leonhard, 1979, chapters 11–13.

7 Bovin went to *Izvestiya* in 1972 (a CIA biography suggests he was "transferred by Suslov"). According to publishing information in the back of the book, it was "selected for publication" (*sdano v nabor*) in December 1974. Even then it was not signed to the press (*podpisano k pechati*; that is, passed the censorship of the CC Propaganda Department) until September 1975, a full nine months later. Given the time lag between the writing of a manuscript and its publication, it is therefore conceivable that Bovin may have written this piece while still in the Central Committee.

What is more, in a personal communication in June 1991, Butenko asserted that the book had been written in the mid-1960s but that Kosolapov, who by now worked in the Central Committee Propaganda Department, used his position to delay its publication in order to publish his own pamphlet on the topic separately. (Kosolapov (*Domostroy*, no. 4, Feb. 5, 1991) has written that he had finished his pamphlet, *Socialism and International Relations* in 1966.) I think it more likely that Kosolapov would have delayed the book so that it would not hurt his Central Committee career. Kosolapov would obviously wish to avoid being associated with views such as those expressed in this book.

4 Socialist internationalism, 1980–1989: demise of a concept

1 See, for example, the following conferences: *Zakonomernosti sblizheniya sotsialisticheskikh stran* (Regularities of the drawing together of the socialist countries), Yu. S. Novopashin, ed., Moscow: IEWSS, 1979; *Voprosy vliyaniya real'-nogo sotsializma na mirovoy revolyutsionnyy protsess* (Questions of the influence of real socialism on the world revolutionary process), Yu. S. Novopashin, ed., Moscow: IEWSS, 1982; and *Sovremennyye problemy i puti razvitiya sotsialisticheskoy demokratii* (Contemporary problems and paths of development of socialist democracy), Ye. Ambartsumov, ed., Moscow: IEWSS, 1983. Novopashin was notably more active than most others in fulfilling the Institute's plan of scientific work in this period, although Butenko certainly contributed his share as well.

2 Novopashin claimed in July 1991 that he had never noticed this similarity, and that he had written his article well before its publishing date of September–October, and that only afterwards did he learn of Rakhmanin's article (personal communication, Moscow, July 1991).

3 In a sign that Gorbachev was to make good on his promise to take greater account of the views of his allies, the decision was made to hold yearly PCC meetings.

4 Rakhmanin declined to be interviewed for this study.

5 See, for example, the articles by CPCz Presidium members Vasil Bil'ak (*Kommunist*, no. 2, 1986) and Josef Lenárt (*Kommunist*, no. 11, 1986).

6 Personal communication from Central Committee official, Moscow, May 1991.

7 One intriguing piece of information about Ostroumov is that a "G. S. Ostroumov," most likely the same Georgiy S., was listed as a member of the editorial board for the book *Socialism and International Relations* (1975), along

with Butenko, Kosolapov, and Vadim Pechenev, later an advisor to Chernenko. It would be interesting to know what role Ostroumov played in this book, and his position at the time. In 1990, he moved from the International Department to Gorbachev's Chancellery. See Scherer, Soviet Biographical Service, vol. 6.

8 See, for example, statements by Yevgeniy Ambartsumov, Nikolay Shishlin, and article by Viktor Sheynis and Yuriy Levada (all 1989).

9 Another former member of the Liaison Department consultants group under Burlatskiy (1990: 256).

5 Socialism redefined

1 The article was also published in the Russian language version, *Problemy Mira i Sotsializma* (*Problems of Peace and Socialism*).

2 Ernst Kux characterizes this article as a response to Butenko's "Yeshchë raz." This is unlikely, however; Kosolapov's article was published in *Literaturnaya Gazeta* on February 1, but according to the publishing information in *Voprosy Filosofii*, no. 2, 1984, Butenko's piece was not published until February 13 (although undoubtedly prepared beforehand). See Kux, 1984.

3 Kosolapov agreed with this assessment, saying: "In our practice, all pretenders to the first 'parallel,' they have to do something on the order of a defense of a diploma work. And here, at this conference, that's what Gorbachev did. He came out with a seeking (*iskatel'nyi*) work, searching for a 'degree' ... That was a very representative party *aktiv*, scientific society, *intelligentsia* [at the conference]. It was a very prestigious conference; there hadn't been one for a very long time. Much of the success of his career was tied to his speech at that conference" (personal communication, Moscow, July 1991).

4 Kosolapov affirmed this as well in an interview. "I understood that for him, 'living creativity of the masses,' in the social sphere, was connected to the development of spontaneous processes of economy, in essence connected to private initiative" (Moscow, July 1991). Butenko, by contrast, was quite pleased with the speech, saying later "when we read his speech, we saw these were all ideas we agreed with" (personal communication, Moscow, June 1991).

5 In an interview, Kosolapov recalled that the *Pravda* version of Gorbachev's speech was a condensed version. In other words, it was not the case that additions were made to the speech after the conference for publication in the booklet, but that changes were made to the *Pravda* version (personal communication, Moscow, July 1991). For a discussion of the differences between the two versions, see Remington, 1988: 21–3.

6 See Kosolapov, 1991, for his claim that he only met with Brezhnev rarely in his capacity as editor of *Kommunist*; the one episode he mentions is at the beginning of his tenure there, when a new design for the front cover needed Brezhnev's approval. In an interview, he stated that Suslov simply didn't pay much attention to the journal (personal communication, Moscow, July 1991).

7 It should be apparent by this time that there was certainly no love lost between these two, and an element of personal animosity seems to have crept into the debate.

8 This letter is actually very interesting for the insights it provides into the aesopian techniques used by Soviet authors in the 1970s. Butenko, for instance, stated that one of developed socialism's most important criteria was a high standard of living for workers. He then proceeds to point out that "for anyone who remembers those years … it was clear that, despite official declarations, Soviet society of that time did not correspond to the objective criteria of the construction of developed socialism." In other words, he laid out the criteria, expecting his readers to make the connection that *reality* did not match the normative statements of what *should* be.

Fëdor Burlatskiy, the originator of the term "developed socialism" (see Burlatskiy, 1966), later made a similar assertion that the term was meant to illustrate what the Soviet Union should be striving for, not what it had built (see Burlatskiy, 1990: 333). The Brezhnev leadership, however, more or less appropriated the term and claimed the Soviet Union had reached that stage. In other words, a leader had selected a term on the ideological menu, and re-interpreted it (consciously or not) to serve another purpose.

9 The preface to the article states that the discussion took place in April 1987, which was obviously a misprint given the number of references to events in 1988.

6 Ideological debates and Eastern Europe

1 The interviews with Anatoliy Butenko, Richard Kosolapov, and Yuri Novopashin mentioned in this section were done in Moscow in April, June, and July of 1991.

2 Literally: "… *potomu chto u menya byla spina nemnozhko prochneye, u menya tovarishchi yest' v TsK*" (personal communication, Moscow, June 1991).

Bibliography

Ambartsumov, Yevgeniy (1984) "Analiz V. I. Leninym prichin krizisa 1921 g. i putey vykhoda iz nego" ("Lenin's Analysis of the 1921 Crisis and the Means of Overcoming It"). *Voprosy Istorii*, 4 (April), 15–29.

(1989) Interviewed by Ezio Mauro in *La Repubblica* (Rome), August 13–14, as reported in US Foreign Broadcast Information Service (FBIS), *Daily Report: Soviet Union* (hereafter FBIS–SOV), FBIS–SOV–89–157, August 16, 27–9.

Ambartsumov, Yevgeniy, and A. Dobieszewskii, eds. (1984) *Polityka i socijalizm* (*Politics and Socialism*). PWN: Warsaw, 1982, reviewed by L. Shevtsova in *Voprosy Filosofii*, 3 (March), 155–8.

Andropov, Yuriy (1982) "Leninizm – Neischerpayemyy istochnik revolyut-sionnoy energii i tvorchestva mass" ("Leninism – The Inexhaustible Source of Revolutionary Energy and the Creativity of the Masses"). *Pravda*, April 23, 1, 2.

(1983) "Ucheniye Karla Marksa i nekotoriye voprosy sotsialisticheskogo stroitel'stva v SSSR" ("The Teaching of Karl Marx and Certain Questions of Socialist Construction in the USSR"). *Voprosy Filosofii*, 4 (April), 3–16.

Angelov, S. and A. P. Butenko, eds. (1979) *Sotsialisticheskiy Internatsionalizm: Teoriya i praktika mezhdunarodnykh otnosheniy novogo tipa.* (*Socialist Internationalism: Theory and Practice of International Relations of a New Type*). Moscow: Politizdat.

Aspaturian, Vernon, (1980) "Conceptualizing Eurocommunism," in Aspaturian, 3–23.

Aspaturian, Vernon, Jiri Valenta, and David Burns (1980) *Eurocommunism between East and West*. Bloomington, Indiana: Indiana University Press.

Axen, Hermann (1978) "The Great October and Proletarian Internationalism Today," in *Einheit* (East Berlin), no. 32 (October/November), 32, as reported in US Joint Publications Research Service (hereafter JPRS), no. 70417, January 5, 14–27.

Baldwin, David (1985) *Economic Statecraft*. Princeton, Princeton University Press.

Bejda, Vasil (1986) "The Line of Accelerating National Development and the Ideological Work of the Party," *Tribuna* (Prague), July 2, as reported in US Joint Publications Research Service, *East Europe Report* (JPRS–EER), JPRS–EER–86–118, August 5, 55–65.

Bell, Daniel (1965) "Ideology and Soviet Politics," *Slavic Review*, 24, 4 (December), 591–603.

Berlinguer, Enrico (1976) "Vystupleniye tovarishcha Enriko Berlinguera" ("Speech of Comrade Enrico Berlinguer"). *Pravda*, February 28, 8, 9.

Bil'ak, Vasil (1977) "Socialist Internationalism – Principle of International Activity of the Communist Party of Czechoslovakia," *Nova Mysl* (Prague), 9 (August), as reported in JPRS, no. 70355, December 20, 18–21.

Bisztyga, Jan (1989) "News Conference," Warsaw Domestic Service, in Polish, August 22, as reported in US Foreign Broadcast Information Service (FBIS), *Daily Report: Eastern Europe* (hereafter FBIS-EEU), FBIS-EEU-89-162, August 22, 39–40.

Bogomolov, Oleg (1985) "Soglasovaniye ekonomicheskikh interesov i politiki pri sotsializma" ("The Concordance of Economic Interests and Policy under Socialism"). *Kommunist*, 10 (July), 82–93.

(1988) *Literaturnaya Gazeta*, March 16, as reported in FBIS-SOV-88-050, March 14, 19.

(1989) Interview with Aleksey Novikov, in *Komsomol'skaya Pravda* (Moscow), October 3, as reported in FBIS-SOV-89-205, October 25, 94–98.

(1990) "Ne mogu snyat' s sebya viny" ("I Cannot Absolve Myself of Guilt"). *Ogonëk*, no. 35 (August), 2, 3.

Borisov, O. B. (1980) (pseudonym for Oleg Rakhmanin) "Ucheniye V. I. Lenina – nauchnaya osnova razvitiya real'nogo sotsializma" ("The Teaching of V. I. Lenin is the Scientific Basis of the Development of Real Socialism"). *Voprosy Istorii KPSS*, 8 (August), 3–16.

(1981) (pseudonym for Oleg Rakhmanin) "KPSS o razvitii mirovogo sotsializma i ukreplenii yedinstva bratskikh partiy" ("The CPSU on the Development of World Socialism and the Strengthening of the Unity of the Fraternal Parties"). *Voprosy Istorii KPSS*, 9 (September), 15–29.

Borisov, O. V. (1984) (pseudonym for Oleg Rakhmanin) "Soyuz novogo tipa" ("Union of a New Type"). *Voprosy Istorii KPSS*, 4 (April), 34–49.

Bovin, Aleksandr (1965) *Internatsionalizm i nasha epokha* (*Internationalism and our Epoch*). Moscow: Znaniye.

(1975) "Protivorechiya v razvitii mirovoy sistemy sotsializma i puti ikh razresheniya" ("Contradictions in the Development of the World System of Socialism and Means of their Resolution") in Butenko, 249–75.

Brahm, Heinz (1989) "Stagnation, Perestrojka, Krise" ("Stagnation, Perestroika, Crisis"). *Berichte des Bundesinstituts für ostwissenschaftliche und internationale Studien* (Köln), 68, (English summary).

Brezhnev, Leonid (1968) "Rech' tovarishcha L. I. Brezhneva" ("Speech of Comrade L. I. Brezhnev"). *Pravda*, November 13, 1, 2.

(1971) *24th Congress of the CPSU. Report of the Central Committee of the Communist Party of the Soviet Union*. Moscow: Novosti.

(1976a) "Rech' glavy delegatsii KPSS tovarishcha L. I. Brezhneva" ("Speech of the Head of the CPSU Delegation Comrade L. I. Brezhnev"). *Pravda*, June 30, 1, 2.

(1976b) *Report of the CPSU Central Committee and the Immediate Tasks of the Party in Home and Foreign Policy*. Moscow: Novosti.

(1978) "Vystupleniye tovarishcha L. I. Brezhneva na Plenume TsK KPSS" ("Speech of Comrade L. I. Brezhnev at the Plenum of the CC CPSU"). *Pravda*, November 28, 1, 2.

(1981) *Report of the Central Committee of the CPSU to the XXVI Congress of the Communist Party of the Soviet Union and the Immediate Tasks of the Party in Home and Foreign Policy*. Moscow: Novosti.

Brutents, Karen (1989) Interview with P. Lukyanchenko in *Argumenty i Fakty*, 30 (July 29–August 4), as reported in FBIS-SOV-89-152, August 9, 7–9.

Brzezinski, Zbigniew (1967) *The Soviet Bloc: Unity and Conflict*. Revised edition. Cambridge, Massachusetts: Harvard University Press.

Brzezinski, Zbigniew and Samuel Huntington (1965) *Political Power: USA/USSR*. New York: Viking Press.

Bugayev, Ye. (1964) "Strannaya pozitsiya" ("A Strange Position"). *Kommunist* 14 (September), 119–26.

Bunce, Valerie (1985) "The Empire Strikes Back: The Evolution of the Eastern Bloc from a Soviet Asset to a Soviet Liability." *International Organization*, 39, 1 (Winter), 1–46.

Burlatskiy, Fëdor (1966) "O stroitel'stve razvitogo sotsialisticheskogo obsh-chestva" ("On the Construction of a Developed Socialist Society"). *Pravda*, December 12, 4.

(1990) *Vozhdi i sovetniki* (*Leaders and Advisors*). Moscow: Politizdat.

Butenko, Anatoliy (1979a) "Proletarskiy internatsionalizm kak kategoriya marksizma; vozniknoveniye i osnovnyye cherty sotsialisticheskogo inter-natsionalizma" ("Proletarian Internationalism as a Category of Marxism; the Origin and Basic Features of Socialist Internationalism"), in Angelov and Butenko.

(1982a) "Socialism: Forms and Deformations." *New Times*, no. 6 (February), 5–7.

(1982b) "Protivorechiya razvitiya sotsializma kak obshchestvennogo stroya" ("Contradictions of the Development of Socialism as a Social Structure"). *Voprosy Filosofii*, 10 (October), 16–29.

(1984) "Yeshchë raz o protivorechiyakh sotsializma" ("Once More on the Contradictions of Socialism"). *Voprosy Filosofii*, 2 (February), 124–9.

(1987b) "Teoreticheskiye problemy sovershenstvovaniya novogo stroya: o sotsial'no-ekonomicheskoy prirode sotsializma" ("Theoretical Problems of the Perfection of the new System: On the Socio-economic Nature of Socialism"). *Voprosy Filosofii*, 2 (February), 17–29.

(1987c) "Po povodu pis'ma R. I. Kosolapova" ("Concerning the Letter of R. I. Kosolapov"). *Voprosy Filosofii*, 12 (December), 146–50.

Butenko, Anatoliy, et al., eds. (1975) *Sotsializm i mezhdunarodnyye otnosheniya* (*Socialism and International Relations*). Moscow: Nauka.

Butenko, Anatoliy, and Yuriy Novopashin (1979b) "O zakonomernosti pos-tepennogo sblizheniya sotsialisticheskikh stran" ("On the General Law of the Gradual Drawing Together of Socialist Countries"), in Novopashin, 1979c.

Butenko, Anatoliy, and L. Yu. Vodopyanova (1987a) "The Dialectics of Produc-tive Forces and Production Relations in Socialist Society." *Filosofskiye*

Nauki, 1 (January), as reported in US Joint Publications Research Service, *Soviet Union: Political Affairs* (hereafter JPRS-UPA), UPA-87-003, 41–9.

Bystřina, Ivan (1958) "Ob osobennostyakh vosniknoveniya i razvitiya narod-noy demokratii v Chekhoslovakii" ("On the Peculiarities of the Origin and Development of People's Democracy in Czechoslovakia"). *Voprosy Filosofii*, 4 (September–October), 26–40.

(1961) *Narodnaya demokratiya v Chekhoslovakii* (*People's Democracy in Czecho-slovakia*). Irina Kryukova, trans. Moscow: Izdatel'stvo yuridicheskoy literatury.

Carillo, Santiago (1978) *Eurocommunism and the State*. Westport, Connecticut: Lawrence and Hill.

Carr, Edward Hallett (1982) *Twilight of the Comintern*. New York: Pantheon.

Ceausescu, Nicolae (1976) "Rech' glavy delegatsii RKP tovarishcha N. Chau-chesku" ("Speech of the RCP Delegation Head Comrade N. Ceausescu"). *Pravda*, July 1, 4.

(1986) "Ceausescu Speech to Pact Foreign Ministers," *Scinteia*, in Romanian, Oct. 16, as reported in FBIS-EEU-86-203, October 21, AA1-AA6.

Chernenko, Konstantin (1982) "Avangardnaya rol' partii kommunistov. Vazh-noye usloviye eë vozrastaniya" ("The Vanguard Role of the Party of Communists. An Important Condition of its Growth"). *Kommunist*, 6 (April), 25–43.

Cohen, Stephen F. (1980) *Bukharin and the Bolshevik Revolution*. New York: Oxford University Press.

(1986) *Rethinking the Soviet Experience*. New York: Oxford University Press.

"Contrary" (1977) "Contrary to the Interests of Peace and Socialism in Europe." *New Times*, 26 (June), 9–13.

Cranston, Maurice and Peter Mair, eds. (1980) *Ideology and Politics*. Alphen an den Rijn: Sijthoff.

D'Agostino, Anthony (1988) *Soviet Succession Struggles: Kremlinology and the Russian Question from Lenin to Gorbachev*. Boston: Allen and Unwin.

d'Encausse, Hélène Carrère (1987) *Big Brother: The Soviet Union and Soviet Europe*. George Holoch, trans. New York: Holmes and Meier.

Dahm, Helmut (1985) "Die Ideologie als Chiffre der Politik. Das Sozialökono-mische und das geistigkulturelle Krisenbewusstsein in die Sowjetunion und seine politische Verfälschung" ("Ideology as a Code of Politics. Socio-Economic and Intellectual-Cultural Crisis Awareness in the Soviet Union and its Political Adulteration"). *Berichte des Bundesinstituts für ostwissenschaftliche und internationale Studien* (Köln), 25, (English summary).

Daniels, Robert V. (1987) *A Documentary History of Communism*. Revised edition. Hanover, New Hampshire: University Press of New England.

Dawisha, Karen (1984) *The Kremlin and the Prague Spring*. Berkeley, CA: Univer-sity of California Press.

(1986) "Gorbachev and Eastern Europe: A New Challenge for the West?" *World Policy Journal*, Spring.

(1990) *Eastern Europe, Gorbachev and Reform*. Second edition. New York: Cambridge University Press.

Dawisha, Karen, and Jonathan Valdez (1987) "Socialist Internationalism in Eastern Europe." *Problems of Communism*, 37, 2 (March–April), 1–14.

"Deklaratsiya" (1955) "Deklaratsiya Pravitel'stv Soyuza Sovetskikh Sotsialisti-cheskikh Respublik i Federativnoy Narodnoy Respubliki Yugoslavii" ("Declaration of the Governments of the Union of Soviet Socialist Republics and the Federative People's Republic of Yugoslavia"). *Pravda*, June 3, 1, 2.

(1957) "Deklaratsiya Konferentsii predstaviteley kommunisticheskikh i rab-ochikh partiy sotsialisticheskikh stran" ("Declaration of the Conference of Representatives of Communist and Workers Parties of the Socialist Countries"). *Pravda*, November 22, 1–2.

(1978) "Deklaratsiya gosudarstv-uchastnikov Varshavskogo Dogovora. Prinyata na soveshchaniya Politicheskogo konsul'tativnogo komiteta gos-udarstv-uchastnikov Varshavskogo Dogovora" ("Declaration of the State-Participants of the Warsaw Treaty. Adopted at the Meeting of the Political Consultative Committee of the State-Participants of the Warsaw Treaty"). *Pravda*, November 24, 1–3.

(1987) "Deklaratsiya o sovetsko-pol'skom sotrudnichestve v oblasti ideolo-gii, nauki i kul'tury" ("Declaration on Soviet-Polish Cooperation in the Fields of Ideology, Science and Culture"). *Pravda*, April 22, 1, 4.

Dimitrov, Georgi (1948a) "5-y s"yezd Bolgarskoy rabochey partii (kommunis-tov). Doklad G. M. Dimitrova" ("5th Congress of the Bulgarian Workers Party (Communists). Speech of G. M. Dimitrov"). *Pravda*, December 21, 3–4.

(1948b) "Zaklyuchitel'noye slovo G. M. Dimitrova na 5-m s"ezde Bolgarskoy rabochey partii" ("Concluding Address of G. M. Dimitrov at the 5th Congress of the Bulgarian Workers Party"). *Pravda*, December 27, 4.

"Diskussiya" (1984) "Diskussiya po aktual'noy probleme. Obzor otklikov" ("Discussion on a Topical Problem. A Survey of Responses"). *Voprosy Filosofii*, no. 2 (February), 116–23.

"Druzheskaya vstrecha" (1971) "Druzheskaya vstrecha rukovodyashchikh deyateley bratskikh stran" ("Friendly Meeting of the Leading Figures of the Fraternal Countries"). *Pravda*, August 3, 1.

"Druzheskaya vstrecha" (1972) "Druzheskaya vstrecha rukovoditeley kom-munisticheskikh i rabochikh partiy" ("Friendly Meeting of the Leaders of the Communist and Workers Parties"). *Pravda*, August 1, 1.

"Druzheskaya vstrecha" (1989) ("Friendly Meeting"). *Pravda*, October 8, 1.

Dudel', S. (1983) "Razvitiye li eto marksistsko-leninskogo ucheniya o proti-vorechii?" ("Is This a Development of the Marxist-Leninist Teaching on Contradiction?"). *Kommunist*, 7 (May), 111–15.

Dzirkals, Lilita, Thane Gustafson, and A. Ross Johnson (1982) *The Media and Intra-Elite Communication in the USSR.* (Rand Report R-2869) Santa Monica, California: The Rand Corporation.

Edelman, Murray (1988) *Constructing the Political Spectacle.* Chicago: University of Chicago Press.

Falin, Valentin (1989) "Falin Views Impact of Bucharest Parley." Interview by S. Polzikov in *Sovestkaya Rossiya* (Moscow), July 12, p. 5, as reported in FBIS-SOV-89-136, 6–8.

Farberov, N. P. (1949) "Novyye momenty v razvitii narodnoy demokratii" ("New Moments in the Development of People's Democracy"). *Sovetskoye Gosudarstvo i Pravo*, 1 (January), 40–54.

Fedoseyev, Pëtr (1948) "Marksistskaya teoriya klassov i klassovoy borby" ("The Marxist Theory of Classes and Class Struggle"). *Bolshevik*, 14 (July), 63–80.

——— (1981b) "The Dialectics of Social Life." *World Marxist Review*, 24, 9 (September), 24–9.

——— (1981a) "Zrelyy sotsializm i obshchestvennyye nauki" ("Mature Socialism and the Social Sciences"). *Kommunist*, 11 (November), 42–54.

——— (1983) "K. Marks i sovremennost'" ("K. Marx and the Present"). *Voprosy Filosofii*, 4 (April), 17–39.

——— (1957) I. Pomelov, and V. Cheprakov "O proyekte programmi Soyuza kommunistov Yugoslavii" ("On the Draft of the Program of the League of Communists of Yugoslavia"). *Kommunist*, 6 (April), 16–39.

Figurnov, P. K. (1950) "Perekhodnyy period ot kapitalizma k sotsializmu v yevropeyskikh stranakh narodnoy demokratii" ("The Transitional Period from Capitalism to Socialism in the European Countries of People's Democracy"). *Voprosy Filosofii*, 1 (January), 77–98.

"The Foreign Policy" (1990) "The Foreign Policy and Diplomatic Activity of the USSR (April 1985–October 1989)." *International Affairs*, January, 5–111.

Garthoff, Raymond L. (1985) *Détente and Confrontation*. Washington, DC: The Brookings Institution.

Geertz, Clifford (1973) *The Interpretation of Cultures*. New York: Basic Books.

Gorbachev, Mikhail (1984) *Zhivoye tvorchestvo naroda* (The Living Creativity of the People). Moscow: Politizdat.

——— (1985a) "Kursom yedinstva i splochënnosti" ("On a Course of Unity and Solidarity"). *Pravda*, February 21, 2.

——— (1985b) "Rech' M. S. Gorbachëva" ("Speech of M. S. Gorbachev"). *Pravda* (Moscow). March 12, 3.

——— (1985c) "Vystupleniye tovarishcha M. S. Gorbachëva" ("Statement of Comrade M. S. Gorbachev"). *Pravda*, April 27, 2.

——— (1986) "Political Report of the CPSU Central Committee to the 27th Congress," in *The Challenges of Our Time: Disarmament and Social Progress. Highlights, 27th Congress, CPSU*. New York: International Publishers.

——— (1987a) "Miting Chekhoslovatsko-Sovetskoy druzhby. Rech' tovarishcha Gorbacheva M. S." ("Meeting of Czechoslovak–Soviet Friendship. Speech of Comrade Gorbachev M. S."). *Pravda*, April 11, 1, 2.

——— (1987b) "Rech' tovarishcha Gorbacheva M. S." ("Speech of Comrade Gorbachev M. S."). *Pravda*, April 22, 1, 2.

——— (1987c) "Gorbachev Speech to GOSR Meeting," Moscow Television Service, in Russian, November 2, as reported in FBIS-SOV-87-212, November 3, 38–61.

——— (1988a) "O nekotorykh mezhdunarodnykh aspektakh ideologii perestroyki. Iz rechi na Plenume TsK KPSS 18 fevralya 1988 g." ("On Certain International Aspects of the Ideology of Perestroika. From a Speech at the Plenum of the CC of the CPSU February 18, 1988.") *Vestnik MID SSSR*, 5 (March 15), 1–4.

(1988b) "Gorbachev Delivers Report," Moscow Television Service, in Russian, June 28, as reported in FBIS-SOV-88-125, June 29, 1–35.

(1988c) "Vstrecha v Seyme PNR. Vystupleniye M. S. Gorbacheva" ("Meeting in the Sejm of the PPR. Speech of M. S. Gorbachev"). *Pravda*, July 12, 2.

(1988d) "Vystupleniye M. S. Gorbachëva v Organizatsii Ob"edinënnykh Natsiy. 7 dekabrya 1988 g." ("Speech of M. S. Gorbachev at the Organization of the United Nations. December 7, 1988"), in *Spavochnik partiynogo rabotnika*, vyp. 29, Moscow: Politizdat, 273–90.

(1989a) "Rech' M. S. Gorbachëva na vstreche s trudyashchimisya v g. Kieve" ("Speech of M. S. Gorbachev at the Meeting with Workers in Kiev"). *Pravda*, February 24, 1–3.

(1989b) "Speech to Council of Europe," Moscow Television Service, in Russian, July 6, as reported in FBIS-SOV-89-129, July 7, 29–34.

(1989c) "Sotsialisticheskaya ideya i revolyutsionnaya perestroyka" ("The Socialist Idea and Revolutionary Restructuring"). *Kommunist*, 18 (December), 3–20.

"Government, strikers reach agreement" (1980) "Government, strikers reach agreement. Shipyard meeting, 30 August," Gdansk Domestic Service in Polish, August 30, as reported in FBIS-EEU-80-171, Sept. 2, G1-G10.

Grósz, Károly (1989a) "Grosz 'Hard-Line' CEMA Stance Viewed," Budapest Television Service in Hungarian, March 24, 1989, as reported in FBIS-SOV-89-057, March 27, 29–30.

(1989b) "Grosz Says USSR Supportive on Reforms," Moscow Television Service in Russian, March 25, 1989, as reported in FBIS-SOV-89-057, March 27, 30.

Hager, Kurt (1986) "A Turning Point of Historic Significance," *Einheit* (East Berlin), April–May, as reported in JPRS-EER-86-092, June 23, 33–43.

Hardt, John P. (1984) "Soviet Energy Policy in Eastern Europe," in Terry, 1984a, 189–220.

Hassner, Pierre (1984) "Soviet Policy in Western Europe," in Terry 1984a, 285–314.

Herspring, Dale (1980) "The Warsaw Pact at 25." *Problems of Communism*, 29, 5 (September–October), 1–15.

Hill, Ronald (1980) *Soviet Politics, Political Science and Reform*. White Plains, New York: M. E. Sharpe.

Hoffmann, Erik and Frederic Fleron, eds. (1980) *The Conduct of Soviet Foreign Policy*. Second edition. New York: Aldine.

Holmes, Leslie (1988) *Politics in the Communist World*. Oxford: Oxford University Press.

Hough, Jerry (1980) *Soviet Leadership in Transition*. Washington, DC: Brookings.

(1985) "Debates About the Postwar World," in *The Impact of World War II on the Soviet Union*. Susan J. Linz, ed., Totowa, New Jersey: Rowman & Allenheld, 253–81.

Hough, Jerry (1979) and Merle Fainsod. *How the Soviet Union is Governed*. Cambridge, Massachusetts: Harvard University Press.

"HSWP CC Communiqué" (1989) "HSWP CC Communiqué on the Burial of Imre Nagy," Hungarian Telegraph Agency (MTI) (Budapest), in English, May 31, as reported in FBIS-EEU-89-104, June 1, 41–42.

Hutchings, Robert (1983) *Soviet–East European Relations*. Madison, Wisconsin: University of Wisconsin Press.

"Iz istorii sozdaniya programm," (1991) "Iz istorii sozdaniya programm Kommunisticheskoy partii Sovetkskogo Soyuza" ("From the History of the Creation of the Programs of the Communist Party of the Soviet Union"). *Izvestiya TsK KPSS*, 3 (March), 120–33.

Jaruzelski, Wojciech (1985) "Vystupleniye tovarishcha V. Yaruzel'skogo" ("Statement of Comrade W. Jaruzelski"). *Pravda*, April 27, 2.

(1987) "Rech' tovarishcha V. Yaruzel'skogo" ("Speech of Comrade W. Jaruzelski"). *Pravda*, April 22, 2.

Jones, Christopher (1981) *Soviet Influence in Eastern Europe*. New York: Praeger.

Joravsky, David (1966) "Soviet Ideology." *Soviet Studies*, 18, 1 (July), 2–19.

"K novomy obliku" (1989) "K novomu obliku sotsializma" ("On the New Face of Socialism"). *Kommunist*, 13 (September), 3–24.

"K sovremennoy kontseptsii" (1989) "K sovremennoy kontseptsii sotsializma" ("On the Modern Conception of Socialism"). *Pravda*, July 14, 16, and 17.

Karambovich, I. M. (1989) *K istorii voprosa o protivorechiyakh pri sotsialimza. (On the history of the question of contradictions in socialism)*. Drogobych, USSR, dissertation abstract.

Kase, Francis (1968) *People's Democracy: A Contribution to the Study of the Communist Theory of State and Revolution*. Leyden, Neth.: Sithjoff.

Katushev, Konstantin (1973a) "The Main Direction: Tendency and Objective Necessity for Closer Unity of Socialist Countries." *World Marxist Review*, 8 (August), 3–14.

(1973b) "Ukrepleniye yedinstva sotsialisticheskikh stran – zakonomernost' razvitiya mirovogo sotsializma" ("The Strengthening of the Unity of the Socialist Countries is a Regularity of the Development of World Socialism"). *Kommunist*, 16 (November), 17–31.

Keller, Bill (1989) "Gorbachev, in Finland, Disavows Any Right of Regional Intervention." *New York Times*, October 26, A1, A12.

Kelley, Donald (1988) *The Politics of Developed Socialism*. Westport, Connecticut: Greenwood Press.

Khrushchev, Nikita (1956) "Otchëtnyi doklad Tsentral'nogo Komiteta Kommunisticheskoy Partii Sovetskogo Soyuza XX S"ezdu partii. Doklad pervogo sekretarya TsK KPSS tovarishcha N. S. Khrushchëva" ("Report of the Central Committee of the Communist Party of the Soviet Union to the 20th Congress of the Party. Speech of Comrade N. S. Khrushchev"). *Pravda*, February, 1–11.

"Kommyunike" (1969) "Kommyunike soveshchaniya Politicheskogo konsul'-tativnogo komiteta gosudarstv-uchastnikov Varshavskogo Dogovora" ("Communiqué of the Meeting of the Political Consultative Committee of the State-Participants of the Warsaw Treaty"). *Pravda*, March 18, 1.

(1974) "Kommyunike soveshchaniya Politicheskogo konsul'tativnogo komiteta gosudarstv-uchastnikov Varshavskogo Dogovora" ("Communiqué of the Meeting of the Political Consultative Committee of the State-Participants of the Warsaw Treaty"). *Pravda*, April 19, 1–2.

(1976) "Kommyunike soveshchaniya Politicheskogo konsul'tativnogo komiteta gosudarstv-uchastnikov Varshavskogo Dogovora" ("Communiqué of the Meeting of the Political Consultative Committee of the State-Participants of the Warsaw Treaty"). *Pravda*, November 27, 1.

(1978) "Kommyunike soveshchaniya Politicheskogo konsul'tativnogo komiteta gosudarstv-uchastnikov Varshavskogo Dogovora" ("Communiqué of the Meeting of the Political Consultative Committee of the State-Participants of the Warsaw Treaty"). *Pravda*, November 24, 1, 3.

(1980) "Kommyunike soveshchaniya Politicheskogo konsul'tativnogo komiteta gosudarstv-uchastnikov Varshavskogo Dogovora" ("Communiqué of the Meeting of the Political Consultative Committee of the State-Participants of the Warsaw Treaty"). *Pravda*, May 16, 1, 3.

(1983) "Kommyunike soveshchaniya Politicheskogo konsul'tativnogo komiteta gosudarstv-uchastnikov Varshavskogo Dogovora" ("Communiqué of the Meeting of the Political Consultative Committee of the State-Participants of the Warsaw Treaty"). *Pravda*, January 6, 1, 2.

(1985) "Kommyunike o vstreche vysshikh partiynykh i gosudarstvennykh deyateley stran-uchastnits Varshavskogo Dogovora" ("Communiqué on the Meeting of the Highest Party and Government Figures of the State-Participants of the Warsaw Treaty"). *Pravda*, April 27, 1.

(1986) "Kommyunike soveshchaniya Politicheskogo konsul'tativnogo komiteta gosudarstv-uchastnikov Varshavskogo Dogovora" ("Communiqué of the Meeting of the Political Consultative Committee of the State-Participants of the Warsaw Treaty"). *Pravda*, June 12, 1, 2.

(1987) "Kommyunike soveshchaniya Politicheskogo konsul'tativnogo komiteta gosudarstv-uchastnikov Varshavskogo Dogovora" ("Communiqué of the Meeting of the Political Consultative Committee of the State-Participants of the Warsaw Treaty"). *Pravda*, May 30, 1, 2.

(1988) "Kommyunike soveshchaniya Politicheskogo konsul'tativnogo komiteta gosudarstv-uchastnikov Varshavskogo Dogovora" ("Communiqué of the Meeting of the Political Consultative Committee of the State-Participants of the Warsaw Treaty"). *Pravda*, July 17, 1, 2.

(1989) "Kommyunike soveshchaniya Politicheskogo konsul'tativnogo komiteta gosudarstv-uchastnikov Varshavskogo Dogovora" ("Communiqué of the Meeting of the Political Consultative Committee of the State-Participants of the Warsaw Treaty"). *Pravda*, July 9, 1, 2.

Kosolapov, Richard (1973) "Soviet Society: Analysis of its Structure." *World Marxist Review*, 16, 5 (May), 32–9.

(1974), "The Approach to the Study of Developed Socialism," *World Marxist Review*, 17, 9 (September), 63–72.

(1981) "Atakuyushiy klass" ("The Attacking Class"). *Pravda*, July 31, 1981, 2, 3.

(1983) "Sotsializm: organicheskaya tselostnost' sotsial'noy sistemy" ("Socialism: Organic Unity of a Social System"). *Pravda*, March 4, 2, 3.

(1984a) "Siloy razuma i chuvstva ..." ("By Strength of Reason and Feeling ...") "Topical interview," by Yuriy Zarechkin, *Literaturnaya Gazeta* (Moscow), February 1, 1, 2.

(1984b) "Sotsializm i protivorechiya" ("Socialism and Contradictions"). *Pravda*, July 20, 2, 3.

(1985) "Aktual'nyye voprosy kontseptsii razvitogo sotsializma" ("Topical Problems of the Conception of Developed Socialism"). *Sotsiologicheskiye Issledovaniya*, 2 (April-May-June), 14–21.

(1987) "Pis'mo v redaktsiyu" ("Letter to the Editor"). *Voprosy Filosofii*, 12 (December), 142–6.

(1989) "Posledniy rabochiy god Lenina" ("The Last Working Year of Lenin"). *Politicheskoye obrazovaniye*, 17 (November).

(1991) "Kavaler Kaban'ey Nogi" ("Cavalier of the Wild-Boar Leg"). *Domostroy* (Moscow), 4 (February 5).

Kotok, V. F. (1951) "K voprosu ob osnovnykh funktsiyakh narodno-demokraticheskogo gosudarstva" ("On the Question of the Basic Functions of the People's-Democratic State"). *Sovetskoye Gosudarstvo i Pravo*, 11 (November), 44–52.

(1952) "O klassovoy strukture narodno-demokraticheskoy Chekhoslovakii" ("On the Class Structure of People's-Democratic Czechoslovakia"). *Sovetskoye Gosudarstvo i Pravo*, 5 (May), 39–51.

Kovalëv, S. (1968) "Suverenitet i internatsional'nyye obyazannosti sotsialisticheskikh stran" ("Sovereignty and the International Obligations of Socialist Countries"). *Pravda*, September 26, 4.

Kozharov, Asen. (1976) *Monizm i plyuralizm v ideologii i politike* (Monism and Pluralism in Ideology and Politics). Moscow: Progress.

(1977) "On Ideological and Political Pluralism." *World Marxist Review*, 20, 1 (January), 114–123.

Kramer, Mark (1989) "Beyond the Brezhnev Doctrine: A New Era in Soviet–East European Relations?" *International Security*, 14, 3 (Winter 1989/90), 25–67.

Kudrna, Frantisek (1977) "In Berlin a Year Ago," *Tribuna* (Prague), 27 (July 6) as reported in JPRS, no. 69599, August 12, 11–17.

Kux, Ernst (1984) "Contradictions in Soviet Socialism." *Problems of Communism*, November-December, 1–27.

Kuzmen'ko, B. (1984) "Obshchestvoznaniye: Nekotoryye aspekty diskussiy, kritiki i samokritiki. Zametki na polyakh" ("Social Research: Certain Aspects of Discussion, Criticism and Self-Criticism. Notes in the Margins.") *Kommunist*, 11 (July), 111–17.

Lapshin, A. O., and Yu. S. Novopashin (1984) "Na vazhnom napravlenii" ("In an Important Direction"). *Voprosy Filosofii*, 11 (November), 154–158.

Larrain, Jorge (1979) *The Concept of Ideology*. Athens, Georgia: University of Georgia Press.

"Laws" (1971) "Laws Governing Development of Socialist World System." *World Marxist Review* 10 (October), 3–43.

Lenin, Vladimir (1931) "Zamechaniya na knigu N. I. Bukharina" ("Remarks on the Book of N. I. Bukharin"), in *Leninskiy sbornik* (*Leninist Collection*). V. V. Adoratskiy, ed. Moscow: Institute of Marxism-Leninism, second edition, 11, pp. 347–403.

(1967) "The Proletarian Revolution and the Renegade Kautsky," in *Selected Works*, New York: International Publishers, 39–127.

(1975) "State and Revolution," in V. I. Lenin, *Collected Works in Three Volumes*, Moscow: Progress, 238–327.

Leonhard, Wolfgang (1979) *Eurocommunism: Challenge for East and West*. Mark Vecchio, trans. New York: Holt, Rinehart and Winston.

Leont'yev, A. (1947) "Ekonomicheskiye osnovy novoy demokratii" ("Economic Foundations of New Democracy"). *Planovoye Khozyaystvo*, 4 (July-August), 63–78.

Levada, Yuriy (1989) "A Reactive Recoil: Rethinking the Prague Spring," *Moscow News*, August 27–September 3, as reported in FBIS-SOV-89-181, September 20, 27–8.

Ligachev, Yegor (1988a) "Down to Business Without Delay," *Pravda*, August 6, as reported in FBIS-SOV-88-152, August 8, 36–40.

(1988b) "Television Carries Comments," Moscow Television Service, in Russian, August 5, as reported in FBIS-SOV-88-152, August 8, 40–43.

Light, Margot (1988) *The Soviet Theory of International Relations*. New York: St. Martin's Press.

Lynch, Allen (1989) *The Soviet Study of International Relations*. Cambridge: Cambridge University Press.

(1990) "The Continuing Importance of Ideology in Soviet Foreign Policy." *The Harriman Institute Forum*, 3, 7 (July). New York: Harriman Institute.

MacGregor, James (1978) "The 1976 European Communist Parties Conference." *Studies in Comparative Communism*, 11, 4 (Winter), 339–360.

Mankovskiy, B. S. (1949) "Klassovaya sushchnost' narodno-demokraticheskogo gosudarstva" ("Class Essence of the People's-Democratic State"). *Sovetskoye Gosudarstvo i Pravo*, 6 (June), 7–17.

Marer, Paul (1984) "The Political Economy of Soviet Relations with Eastern Europe," in Terry, 1984a, 155–88.

"Marksistsko-leninskaya filosofiya" (1984) "Marksistsko-leninskaya filosofiya – ideyno-teoreticheskaya osnova sovershentsvovaniye razvitogo sotsializma" ("Marxism-Leninism – the Ideo-theoretical Basis of the Perfection of Developed Socialism"). *Voprosy Filosofii*, 10 (October), 3–19.

Martynov, A. (1986) "Vazhnyy etap v zhizni kommunistov GDR" ("Important Stage in the Life of GDR Communists"). *Kommunist*, 12 (August), 94–103.

McCagg, William (1978) *Stalin Embattled, 1943–1948*. Detroit, Michigan: Wayne State University Press.

Medvedev, Vadim (1984) "Klyuchevaya problema dialektiki razvitogo sotsializma" ("The Key Problem of the Dialectic of Developed Socialism"). *Voprosy Filosofii*, 8 (August), 3–10.

(1988a) "Velikiy Oktyabr' i sovremennyy mir" ("Great October and the Modern World"). *Kommunist*, 2 (January), 3–18.

(1988b) "K poznaniyu sotsializma. Otvety na voprosy zhurnala 'Kommunist'" ("Toward Cognition of Socialism. Answers to Questions from the Journal 'Kommunist'"). *Kommunist*, 17 (November), 3–18.

Meyer, Alfred (1966) "The Functions of Ideology in the Soviet Political System." *Soviet Studies*, 17, 3 (January).

Migranyan, Andranik (1989) "An Epitaph to the Brezhnev Doctrine: The USSR and Other Socialist Countries in the Context of East–West Relations," *Moscow News*, August 27–September 3, as reported in FBIS-SOV-89-181, September 20, 20–2.

Mills, C. Wright (1962) *The Marxists*. New York: Dell.

Mirov, Ya. (1947) "Kompartii yevropy v bor'be za mir, demokratiyu i nezavisi-most'" ("The Communist Parties of Europe in the Struggle for Peace, Democracy and Independence"). *Bolshevik*, 21 (December).

Mitchell, R. Judson (1982) *Ideology of a Superpower*. Stanford, CA: Hoover Institution Press.

Molotov, Vyacheslav (1946) "Vybornaya rech'" ("Election Speech"). *Sovetskoye Gosudarstvo i Pravo*, 2 (February), 11–16.

Moore, Barrington (1950) *Soviet Politics – The Dilemma of Power*. Cambridge, Massachusetts: Harvard University Press.

Nazorov, V. D. (1975) "Problemy mezhdunarodnykh otnosheniy novogo tipa v sovetskoy nauke" ("Problems of International Relations of a New Type in Soviet Science") in Butenko, 39–84.

Nicolaevsky, Boris I. (1965) *Power and the Soviet Elite*. New York: Praeger.

Novopashin, Yuriy (1975) "Struktura mirovoy sotsialistichekoy sistemy," ("Structure of the World Socialist System"), in Butenko, 151–80.

(1979a) *Mirovaya sistema sotsializma i mify burzhuaznykh ideologov* (*The World System of Socialism and the Myths of Bourgeois Ideologists*). Novoye v zhizni, nauki, tekhnike: Seriya "Istoriya" (New in Life, Science, Technology: "History" Series). Moscow: Znaniye, no. 9.

(1979b) "Printsipy mezhdunarodnykh otnosheniy novogo tipa" ("Principles of International Relations of a New Type"), Chapter 3, sections 1 and 3, in Angelov, 98–110, 120–34.

(1983) "K voprosu o razrabotke teorii razvitiya mirovoy sistemy sotsializma i mezhdunarodnykh otnosheniy novogo tipa." ("On the Question of the Working Out of a Theory of the Development of the World System of Socialism and of International Relations of a New Type"). *Nauchnyy Kommunizm*, 5 (September–October).

(1985) "Politicheskiye otnosheniya stran sotsializma" ("Political Relations of the Countries of Socialism"). *Rabochiy Klass i Sovremennyy Mir*. 5 (September–October), 55–65.

(1989) "Past 'Strong-arm' Policies Toward Allies Assailed." Interview by A. Novikov in *Komsomolskaya Pravda* (Moscow), December 6, 2–3, as reported in FBIS-SOV-89-234, 4–7.

ed. (1979c) *Zakonomernost' sblizheniya sotsialisticheskikh stran. Materialy mezh-dunarodnogo simpoziuma, 23–26 oktyabrya, 1978* (*The General Law of the Drawing Together of Socialist Countries. Materials of an International Sympo-sium, October 23–26, 1978*). Moscow: IEWSS.

"O ser"ëznykh nedostatkakh" (1954) "O ser"ëznykh nedostatkakh i oshibkakh v rabote Gosudarstvennogo izdatel'stva yuridicheskoy literatury" ("On Serious Shortcomings and Mistakes in the Work of the State Publisher of Juridical Literature") in *O sovetskoy i partiynoy pechati: sbornik dokumentov* (*On the Soviet and Party Press: A Collection of Documents*). Moscow: Pravda, 625–6.

"Ob Otnosheniyakh" (1956a) "Ob otnosheniyakh mezhdu Soyuzom Kommu-nistov Yugoslavii i Kommunisticheskoy Partiyey Sovetskogo Soyuza" ("On Relations Between the League of Communists of Yugoslavia and the Communist Party of the Soviet Union"). *Pravda*, June 20, 2.

"Ob Otnosheniyakh" (1956b) "Ob Otnosheniyakh Mezdhu Sotsialisticheskimi Stranami" ("On Relations Between Socialist States"). *Pravda*, October 31, 1.

"Obrashcheniye" (1969) "Obrashcheniye gosudarstv-uchastnikov Varshavskogo Dogovora ko vsem yevropeyskim stranam" ("Appeal of the Warsaw Pact State-Participants to all European Countries"). *Pravda*, March 18, 1.

"Ot redaktsionnoy kollegii" (1984) ("From the Editorial Board"). *Voprosy Istorii*, 12 (December), 97–102.

"Otkrytiye" (1948) "Otkrytiye 5-go s"yezda Bolgarskoy rabochey partii (kommunistov)" ("Opening of the 5th Congress of the Bulgarian Workers Party (Communists)"). *Pravda*, December 20, 4.

Pajetta, Gian Carlo (1980) "The Nature of Our Internationalism," in *L'Unita* (Rome), March 29, as reported in JPRS, no. 75523, April 18, 70–2.

Pavlov, T. D. (1957) "K voprosu o kharaktere bolgarskoy narodno-demokraticheskoy revolyutsii" ("On the Question of the Character of the Bulgarian People's-Democratic Revolution"). *Voprosy Filosofii*, 6 (November-December), 44–57.

Petroff, Serge (1988) *Red Eminence: Mikhail Suslov*. Clifton, New Jersey: Kingston Press.

Plissonier, Gaston (1976) "Vystupleniye tovarishcha Gastona Plisson'ye" ("Speech of Comrade Gaston Plissonier"). *Pravda*, February 29, 8.

"Polish–Romanian Documents" (1989) "Polish–Romanian Documents: Reply from the PZPR Central Committee Politburo to the Stance of the RCP Central Committee and to Nicolae Ceausescu, President of the Socialist Republic of Romania, Concerning an Assessment of the Current Situation in Poland, Including the Appointment of the PPR Government," *Gazeta Wyborcza*, September 29–October 1, as reported in FBIS-EEU-89-190, 39–41.

"Politicheskaya deklaratsiya" (1983) "Politicheskaya deklaratsiya gosudarstv-uchastnikov Varshavskogo Dogovora" ("Political Declaration of the State-participants of the Warsaw Treaty"). *Pravda*, January 7, 1, 2.

Ponomarëv, Boris N. (1957) "Boyevaya programma mirovogo kommunisticheskogo dvizheniya" ("Militant Program of the World Communist Movement"). *V Pomoshch' Politicheskomu Samoobrazovaniyu*, 12 (December), 3–19.

"Posle vystupleniya 'Kommunista'" (1984) ("After a Declaration of 'Kommunist'"). *Kommunist*, 17 (December), 127.

"Posledstviya" (1988) "Posledstviya gonki vooruzheniy dlya okruzhayushchey sredy i drugiye aspekty ekogolicheskoy bezopasnosti" ("Consequences of the Arms Race for the Environment and Other Aspects of Ecological Security.") *Pravda*, July 17, 2.

Primakov, Yevgeniy (1987) "Kapitalizm vo vzaimnosvyaznom mire" ("Capitalism in an Interdependent World"). *Kommunist*, 13 (September), 101–110.

"Problemy" (1988) "Problemy razrabotki kontseptsii sovremennogo sotsializma" ("Problems of Working Out a Conception of Contemporary Socialism"). *Voprosy Filosofii*, 11 (November).

"Program" (1986a) "The Program of the CPSU – A New Edition," in *Challenges of Our Time: Disarmament and Social Progress. Highlights, 27th Congress, CPSU*. New York: International Publishers.

(1986b) "Program of the Polish United Workers Party," *Trybuna Ludu*, February 10, as reported in FBIS-EEU-86-044, March 5, G6-61.

"Protivorechiya" (1989) "Protivorechiya i dvizhushchiye sily sotsialisticheskogo obshchestva" ("Contradictions and the Motive Forces of Socialist Society"). *Kommunist*, 4 (March), 47–55.

Ra'anan, Gavriel (1983) *International Policy Formation in the USSR: Factional "Debates" During the Zhdanovshchina*. Hamden, Connecticut: Scarecrow.

Radio Free Europe Research (1986a) *Background Report*, 183, December 16.

(1986b) *Situation Report: Bulgaria*, 12, December 30.

(1989a) *Background Report*, 123, July 7.

(1989c) *Background Report*, 130, July 27.

(1989b) *Background Report*, 202, November 10.

Remington, Robin Allison (1971) *The Warsaw Pact*. Cambridge, Massachusetts: MIT Press.

Remington, Thomas F. (1988) *The Truth of Authority: Ideology and Communication in the Soviet Union*. Pittsburgh, Pennsylvania: University of Pittsburgh Press.

"Rol' protivorechiy" (1985) "Rol' protivorechiy v razvitii obshchestva" ("The Role of Contradictions in the Development of Society"). *Voprosy Filosofii* [*Nauchnaya zhizn'* (Scientific life) section], 6 (June), 150–2.

Rosecranz, Richard (1986) *The Rise of the Trading State*. New York: Basic Books.

Rubbi, Antonio (1977) "The New Internationalism." *World Marxist Review*, 20, 1 (January), 123–129.

Savinov, K. I. (1983) "The CPSU and the World Communist Movement: The CPSU and Brother Parties of Socialist States in the Struggle to Strengthen International Relations of a New Type," *Voprosy Istorii KPSS*, 9 (September), as reported in JPRS, no. 84984, December 20.

Schapiro, Leonard (1980) "The Concept of Ideology as Evolved by Marx and Adapted by Lenin," in *Ideology and Politics*, Maurice Cranston and Peter Mair, eds. (Alphen an den Rijn: Sijthoff).

Scherer, John. *Soviet Biographical Service*. [n.p.] Various issues.

Schneider, Eberhard (1988) "Soviet Foreign-Policy Think Tanks." *Washington Quarterly*, Spring, 145–55.

Schurmann, F. (1968) *Ideology and Organization in Communist China*. Berkeley, California: University of California Press.

Seliger, Martin (1976) *Ideology and Politics*. New York: Free Press.

Semënov, Vadim (1982a, 1982b) "Problema protivorechiy v usloviyakh sotsializma" ("The Problem of Contradictions in the Conditions of Socialism"). *Voprosy Filosofii*, 7 and 9 (July, September), 17–32 and 3–21.

(1984) "K teoreticheskomy uglubleniyu i konkretizatsii analiza problemy protivorechiy v usloviyakh razvitogo sotsializma" ("On the Theoretical Deepening and Concretization of the Analysis of the Problem of Contradictions in the Conditions of Developed Socialism"). *Voprosy Filosofii*, 2 (February), 130–40.

Shakhnazarov, Georgiy (1974) *Socialist Democracy. Aspects of Theory*. Moscow: Progress.

(1985) "The CPSU Programme and the Future of Mankind." *New Times*, 47 (November), 3–5.

(1989) "Vostok-zapad. K voprosu o deideologizatsii mezhgosudarstvennykh otnosheniy" ("East–West. On the De-ideologization of Intergovernmental Relations"). *Kommunist*, 4.

Shevardnadze, Eduard (1988) "Shevardnadze Speaks on Foreign Policy," *Pravda*, July 26, as reported in FBIS-SOV-88-143, July 26, 29–31.

(1990) "Otchëty chlenov i kandidatov v chleny Politbyuro, sekretarey TsK KPSS. E. A. Shevardnadze" ("Reports of Members and Candidate Members of the Politburo, Secretaries of the CC CPSU. E. A. Shevardnadze"). *Pravda*, July 4, 2.

Sheynis, Viktor (1989) "August Harvest," *Izvestiya*, October 14, as reported FBIS-SOV-89-200, October 18, 97–102.

Shishlin, Nikolay (1989) Interview in *Liberation* (Paris), September 22, as reported in FBIS-SOV-89-188, September 29.

Shulman, Marshall (1985) *Stalin's Foreign Policy Reappraised*. Boulder, Colorado: Westview Encore Edition.

Skilling, H. Gordon (1961) "People's Democracy and the Socialist Revolution: A Case Study in Communist Scholarship." *Soviet Studies*, parts 1 and 2, vol. 12, nos. 3, 4, 241–262, 420–435.

Sobolev, Aleksandr Ivanovich (1951) "Narodnaya demokratiya kak forma politicheskoy organizatsiya obshchestva" ("People's Democracy as a Form of the Political Organization of Society"). *Bolshevik*, 19 (October), 25–38.

(1956) "Vsemirno-istoricheskoye znacheniye sotsialisticheskogo lagerya" ("The World-historical Significance of the Socialist Camp"). *Kommunist*, 3 (February), 15–32.

(1958) *Marksizm-Leninizm o formakh perekhoda ot kapitalizma k sotsializmu. (Marxism-Leninism on the Forms of Transition from Capitalism to Socialism).* Moscow: Politizdat.

(1981) "Aleksandr Ivanovich Sobolev." Obituary in *Rabochiy Klass i Sovremennyy Mir* 6 (November–December), 185.

"Sotsialisticheskiy obshchestvennyy klimat" (1984) ("The Socialist Social Climate"). *Kommunist*, 11 (July), 10–19.

"Sotsialisticheskiye mezhdunarodnyye otnosheniya" (1983) ("Socialist International Relations") Proceedings of a conference held in March 1983, as reported in *Nauchnyy Kommunizm*, 5 (September-October).

"Sovershenstvovaniye razvitogo sotsializma" (1984) "Sovershenstvovaniye razvitogo sotsializma i ideologicheskaya rabota partii v svete resheniy iyunskogo (1983 g.) plenuma TsK KPSS" ("The Perfection of Developed Socialism and Ideological Work of the Party in Light of the Decisions of the June (1983) Plenum of the CC CPSU"). *Pravda*, December 11, 2–3.

"Sovershenstvovaniye razvitogo sotsializma" (1985) "Sovershenstvovaniye razvitogo sotsializma i ideologicheskaya rabota partii v svete resheniy iyunskogo (1983 g.) plenuma TsK KPSS. Materialy Vsesoyuznoy nauchno-prakticheskoy konferentsii. Moskva, 10–11 dekabrya, 1984" ("The Perfection of Developed Socialism and Ideological Work of the Party in Light of the Decisions of the June (1983) Plenum of the CC CPSU. Materials of the All-Union Scientific-Practical Conference. Moscow, Dec. 10–11, 1984"). B. I. Stukalin, ed. Moscow: Politizdat.

Sovetsko-Bolgarskiye otnosheniya i svyazi: Dokumenty i materialy (*Soviet–Bulgarian Relations and Ties: Documents and Materials*). (1981) 2: September 1944–December 1958. Moscow: Nauka.

"Soviet–Finnish Declaration" (1989) "Soviet–Finnish Declaration – The New Thinking in Action," *Pravda*, October 27, as reported in FBIS-SOV-89-207, October 27, 41–42.

Spriano, Paolo (1977) "Freedom and Socialism," *L'Unita* (Rome), January 26, as reported in JPRS, no. 68646, February 17, 49–52.

Stalin, Joseph (1940) *Dialectical and Historical Materialism*. New York: International Publishers.

(1946) "Vybornaya rech'" ("Election Speech"). *Sovetskoye Gosudarstvo i Pravo* 2 (February), 1–10.

(1947) "Zapis' besedy tov. I. V. Stalina s deyatelem respublikanskoy partii SShA Garol'dom Stassenom, 9 aprelya 1947 goda" ("Transcript of a Conversation of Comrade I. V. Stalin with the Representative of the Republican Party of the USA Harold Stassen, April 9, 1947"). *Pravda*, May 8, 1–2.

(1954) "The International Situation and the Defence of the USSR," in J. V. Stalin, *Works*, 10. Moscow: Foreign Languages Publishing House, 3–62.

Stepanyan, Tsolak A. (1955) "Protivorechiya v razvitii sotsialisticheskogo obshchestva i puti ikh preodoleniya" ("Contradictions in the Development of Socialist Society and the Means of Overcoming Them"). *Voprosy Filosofii*, 2 (March-April), 69–86.

(1983) "On the Question of the Unity and Contradictoriness of the Development of Socialist Society," *Sotsiologicheskiye Issledovaniya*, 3 (July-August-September), as reported in JPRS, no. 84582, October 21, 18–28.

Stojanovic, Svetozar (1988) *Perestroika: From Marxism and Bolshevism to Gorbachev*. Buffalo, New York: Prometheus.

Stoyanov, Georgi (1989) "Some Topical Questions of Mutual Relations among Socialist Countries," *Rabotnichesko Delo* (Sofia), October 11, 1989, as reported in FBIS-EEU-89-197, October 13, 11–12.

Suslov, Mikhail (1956) "Doklad tovarishcha M. A. Suslova na torzhestvennom zasedanii Moskovskogo Soveta 6 noyabrya 1956 goda." ("Speech of Comrade M. A. Suslov at the Gala Session of the Moscow Soviet, November 6, 1956"). *Pravda*, November 7, 1–3.

(1967) *Velikiy Oktyabr' i mirovoy revolyutsionnyy protsess*. Moscow: Politizdat.

(1976) "Peredovyye rubezhi progressa" ("The Leading Frontiers of Progress"). *Pravda*, March 18, 2.

(1977) "Svet idey Oktyabrya" ("Light of the Ideas of October"). *Pravda*, November 11, 1, 4.

(1981) "Vysokoye prizvaniye i otvetstvennost'" ("A High Calling and Responsibility"). *Kommunist*, 11 (November), 4–11.

Szulc, Tad (1975) "Lisbon and Washington: Behind the Portuguese Revolution." *Foreign Policy*, 21 (Winter 1975–6), 3–63.

Szürös, Mátyás (1984) "The Reciprocal Effect of the National and International

Interests in the Development of Socialism in Hungary," *Tarsadalmi Szemle*, 1 (January) as reported in FBIS-EEU-84-018, January 26, F5–F9.

(1986a) "Promoting Unity." *World Marxist Review*, 5 (May), 31–9.

(1986b) "Szuros Analyzes Role of Small Countries in World Affairs," *Valosag*, in Hungarian, 7, as reported in JPRS-EER-86-162, 68–76.

Taras, Ray (1984) *Ideology in a Socialist State*. Cambridge: Cambridge University Press.

Teague, Elizabeth (1980) "The Foreign Departments of the Central Committee of the CPSU." *Radio Liberty Research Bulletin Supplement*, October 27.

(1988) *Solidarity and the Soviet Worker*. London: Croom Helm.

Terry, Sarah Meiklejohn, ed. (1984a) *Soviet Policy in Eastern Europe*. New Haven, Connecticut: Yale University Press.

(1984b) "Theories of Socialist Development in Soviet–East European Relations," in Terry, 1984a, 221–253.

Thompson, Terry (1989) *Ideology and Policy: The Political Uses of Doctrine in the Soviet Union*. Boulder, Colorado: Westview.

Tolkunov, L. (1961) "Noviy etap v razvitii mirovoy sistemy sotsializma" ("A New Stage in the Development of the World System of Socialism"). *Kommunist*, 3 (February), 14–27.

Traynin, I. P. (1947) "Demokratiya osobogo tipa" ("Democracy of a Special Type"). *Sovetskoye Gosudarstvo i Pravo*, 1 and 3 (January, March), 1–15, 1–14.

Ulam, Adam (1974) *Expansion and Coexistence*. New York: Holt, Rinehart and Winston. 2nd edition.

United States. Central Intelligence Agency. *Directory of Soviet Officials*. Washington, DC: US Government Printing Office, various editions.

United States. Foreign Broadcast Information Service. FBIS Memorandum (1987) United States. Foreign Broadcast Information Service. *Biographies of Leading Soviet Political Figures*. Washington, DC: US Government Printing Office.

"V obstanovke" (1989) "V obstanovke druzhby i serdechnosti" ("In an Atmosphere of Friendship and Cordiality"). *Pravda*, July 9, 2.

"V serdechnoy obstanovke" (1985) ("In a Cordial Atmosphere"). *Pravda*, October 24, 1.

"V Tsentral'nom Komitete KPSS" (1979) ("In the Central Committee of the CPSU"). *Pravda*, May 6, 1, 2.

Valenta, Jiri (1978) "Eurocommunism and Eastern Europe." *Problems of Communism*, 27, 2 (March–April), 41–54.

(1980) "Eurocommunism and the USSR," in Aspaturian.

Varga, Yevgeniy (1947) "Demokratiya novogo tipa" ("Democracy of a New Type"). *Mirovoye Khozyaystvo i Mirovaya Politika*, 3 (March), 1–14.

(1949) "Protiv reformistskogo napravleniya v rabotakh po imperializmu" ("Against the Reformist Trend in Works on Imperialism"). *Voprosy Ekonomiki*, 3 (March), 79–88.

Vass, Henrik (1978) "Socialist Internationalism – the Basic Principle for the Inter-State Relations of the Socialist Countries." *Propagandista* (Budapest), 1 (January), as reported in JPRS, no. 70758, March 9, 1–8.

Vladimirov, O. (1985) (pseudonym for Oleg Rakhmanin) "Vedushchiy faktor mirovogo revolyutsionnogo protsessa" ("The Leading Factor of the World Revolutionary Process"). *Pravda*, June 21, 3–4.

Volgyes, Ivan (1986) *Politics in Eastern Europe*. Chicago: Dorsey Press.

"Vstrecha" (1970) "Vstrecha rukovoditeley bratskikh stran" ("Meeting of Leaders of the Fraternal Countries"). *Pravda*, December 5, 1.

"Vstrecha" (1980) "Vstrecha rukovodyashchikh deyateley gosudarstv-uchast-nikov Varshavskogo Dogovora" ("Meeting of the Leading Figures of the State-Participants of the Warsaw Pact"). *Pravda*, December 6, 1.

White, Stephen (1991) *Gorbachev and After*. Cambridge: Cambridge University Press.

White, Stephen and Alex Pravda, eds. (1988). *Ideology and Soviet Politics*. London: MacMillan.

Willenz, Eric (1980) "Eurocommunist Perceptions of Eastern Europe: Ally or Adversary?" in Aspaturian, 254–70.

Yakimovich, Ya.V. (1975) "Osnovnyye printsipy vzaimnootnosheniy sotsialisti-cheskikh stran" ("Basic Principles of the Mutual Relations of Socialist Countries"), in Butenko, 249–75.

Yakovlev, Aleksandr (1988) "V interesakh strany i kazhdogo naroda" ("In the Interests of the Country and of Every People"). *Pravda*, August 13, 2.

Yotov, Yordan (1978) "On Proletarian Internationalism," Bulgarian Telegraph Agency (BTA), in English, April 15, as reported in JPRS, no. 71064, May 5, 34–8.

"Yugoslav–Soviet Declaration (Full Text)." (1988) Yugoslav National Tele-graph Agency (TANJUG), in English, March 18, as reported in FBIS-EEU-88-053, March 18, 46–49.

"Za mir" (1976) "Za mir, bezopasnost', sotrudnichestvo i sotsial'nyy progress v Yevrope" ("For Peace, Security, Cooperation and Social Progress in Europe"). *Pravda*, July 1, 1–3.

"Za novyye" (1976) "Za novyye rubezhi v mezhdunarodnoy razryadke, za ukrepleniye bezopasnosti i razvitiya sotrudnichestva v Yevrope" ("For New Advances in International Détente, for the Strengthening of Security and the Development of Cooperation in Europe"). *Pravda*, November 27, 1–2.

"Za ustraneniye" (1985) "Za ustraneniye yadernoy ugrozy i povorot k luchshemu v yevropeyskikh i mirovykh delakh" ("For Elimination of the Nuclear Threat and a Turn for the Better in European and World Affairs"). *Pravda*, October 24, 1–2.

"Zadachi" (1969) "Zadachi bor'by protiv imperializma na sovremonnom etape i yedinstvo deystviy kommunisticheskikh i rabochikh partiy, vsekh anti-imperialisticheskikh sil" ("Tasks of the Struggle against Imperialism in the Modern Era and Unity of Actions of the Communist and Workers' Parties, of all Anti-imperialist Forces"). *Pravda*, June 18, 1, 2, 3, 4.

Zarodov, Konstantin (1975) "Leninskaya strategiya i taktika revolyutsionnoy borby" ("The Leninist Strategy and Tactics of Revolutionary Struggle"). *Pravda*, August 6, 2, 3.

Zaslavskaya, Tat'yana. (1983) [Untitled]. *Materialy Samizdata* Edition 35/83, AS no. 5042, August 26.

"Zasedaniye" (1970) "Zasedaniye Politicheskogo konsul'tativnogo komiteta gosudarstv-uchastnikov Varshavskogo Dogovora" ("Session of the Political Consultative Committee of the Warsaw Pact"). *Pravda*, August 22, 1.

"Zayavleniye" (1970) "Zayavleniye po voprosam ukrepleniya bezopasnosti i razvitiya mirnogo sotrudnichestva v Yevrope" ("Declaration on Questions of the Strengthening of Security and the Development of Peaceful Cooperation in Europe"). *Pravda*, December 4, 1970, 1.

(1989a) "Zayavleniye rukovoditeley Bolgarii, Vengrii, GDR, Pol'shi i Sovetskogo soyuza" ("Declaration of the Leaders of Bulgaria, Hungary, the GDR, Poland and the Soviet Union"). *Pravda*, December 5, 2.

(1989b) "Zayavleniye Sovetskogo pravitel'stva" ("Declaration of the Soviet Government"). *Pravda*, December 5, 2.

Zhivkov, Todor (1976) "Rech' glavy delegatsii BKP tovarishcha T. Zhivkova" ("Speech of the BCP Delegation Head Comrade Todor Zhivkov"). *Pravda*, June 30, 3.

Zimmerman, William (1984) "Soviet Relations with Yugoslavia and Romania," in Terry, 1984a, 125–54.

Index

For EU product safety concerns, contact us at Calle de José Abascal, 56–1°, 28003 Madrid, Spain or eugpsr@cambridge.org